Pediatric Disorders
of
Regulation
in
Affect and Behavior

A Therapist's Guide to
Assessment and Treatment

Pediatric Disorders
of
Regulation
in
Affect and Behavior

A Therapist's Guide to Assessment and Treatment

Georgia DeGangi, PhD

*Integrated Therapy Services for
Children and Families Inc.
Kensington, Maryland*

Academic Press

San Diego   London   Boston   New York   Sydney   Tokyo   Toronto

Photographs by Karen Prince

Academic Press
A Harcourt Science and Technology Company
525 B Street, Suite 1900, San Diego, California 92101-4495, USA
http://www.academicpress.com

Academic Press
Harcourt Place, 32 Jamestown Road, London NW1 7BY, UK
http://www.academicpress.com

Library of Congress Catalog Card Number: 00-101592

International Standard Book Number: 0-12-208770-4

PRINTED IN THE UNITED STATES OF AMERICA
01   02   03   04   05   06   MM   9   8   7   6   5   4   3

CONTENTS

CHAPTER **2** **Assessment of Regulatory Problems in Children**

CHAPTER **3** **The Therapeutic Process: Working through the Parents**

CHAPTER **4** **Treatment of Irritability and Other Mood-Regulation Problems**

CHAPTER **5**   **Treatment of Sleep and Separation Problems**

CHAPTER **6**   **Treatment of Feeding Disorders in Children**

CHAPTER **7**   **Treatment of Attentional Problems**

Georgia DeGangi has written a very full account of the problems commonly occurring in infancy and early childhood. She describes the research that supports the thesis that there is a link between these early problems and the development of difficulties in later life. In addition, Dr. DeGangi sets us all the example of her own detailed clinical observations, theoretical and research knowledge, and thorough assessments. In this characteristically rigorous way she shows how important it is to first carefully assess not only the individual child but also how the child's environment (i.e., his family, day care, and preschool) impacts on, and is impacted by, the child's difficulties. She uses rich clinical case examples to draw us into the family's, the child's, and the clinician's experiences, always reminding us about the complexities in the process of understanding the multi-determined effects on development in infancy and early childhood and of deciding about how best to help the child and family.

Her position is clear. It is crucial to intervene as early as possible in order to minimize the detrimental effects of compromised development and contingent relational difficulties. Specialists working with this age group are always acutely aware of the related but sometimes competing needs to address the child's developmental problems and also to preserve, enhance, or rehabilitate the relationship between child and parent. Out of a sense of urgency and the fear that precious time will be lost, intervenors frequently focus on the child's problems and lose sight of the fact that the relationship between child and parent has fallen victim to the child's problems and/or that the relationship itself has a significant part to play in either the emergence, or the persistence, of the child's developmental struggle.

Dr. DeGangi provides us with a strong argument for intervening without further compromising the child's and parents' relationships. She shows how this can be done through a careful assessment and formulation of the presenting problem.

In this way consideration is given to not only constitutional factors but also to family relational factors. Out of this careful exploration she designs interventions that take all the relevant factors into consideration. The child and family receive a carefully seasoned broth that nourishes both the child's development and his/her relationships with parents and other family members.

What is remarkable and unusual about Dr. DeGangi's work is that she pays as much attention to internalized relational factors as she does the developmental and behavioral aspects of the clinical task. At last we have a developmentalist who incorporates the relational unconscious into her work. This is demonstrated in the unique way she uses the clinician's cognitive, emotional, and physiological responses in the clinical situation as a guide to understanding the motivations and experiences of the parents and children she is working with. We become very aware of how difficult this work is, and we have to recognize how much time has to be allocated to undertaking such interventions. It takes time to do a thorough assessment, and to build up the trust and a working alliance with the parents. And although in some cases we are able to help effect positive changes in only a few weeks, we know that in many cases it takes just as much time as the particular family and child require to reach a satisfactory conclusion.

Increasingly, there is pressure from politicians, institutional administrators, and program funders to find quick and easy interventions, to rush to apply formulaic solutions, and to dispense with the expertise of specialist skills. Georgia De-Gangi's book is a salutary reminder about the complexity and fragility of the vulnerable infant and young child and their family. She has revealed that families who come to us with these problems have to put a great deal more than their children in our hands. They have to put their own early experiences; their lifelong accommodations to early failures, losses and/or trauma; their familiar and safe but problematic interactional patterns; and their hope for something different in our hands. These hands have to be experienced hands.

I read Dr. DeGangi's book with recognition and relief. It is timely. I am relieved to know such a book is available for all professionals who work with this age group. Dare we hope that policymakers, institutional administrators, and program funders will also read it? Unquestionably, this book should be mandatory reading for all those who are either directly or indirectly responsible for infant and child developmental and mental health services.

Elisabeth Muir
Child Psychotherapist
June 1999

ACKNOWLEDGMENTS

Many people have helped me in the writing of this book. First and foremost, I would like to thank Evelyn Stefansson Nef who, provided financial support for this project, and the Reginald S. Lourie Center for Infants and Young Children in Rockville, Maryland, which made this book possible. I also wish to thank the Cecil and Ida Green Foundation, which provided financial support for my research in assessing and treating infants and children with regulatory disorders.

Three superb mentors have helped me over the years to discover new ways of working with and understanding young children. Stanley Greenspan helped me to integrate sensorimotor, emotional, and developmental frameworks into a holistic model of working with young children. Stephen Porges collaborated with me in researching disorders of self-regulation in children and taught me the importance of linking theories and research with clinical approaches. Both Drs. Greenspan and Porges helped me to understand the profound effect that constitutional problems have on the child's developmental course and the parent–child relationship. I am indebted to Polly Craft, who offered me the gift of discovering the special meaning that each child and parent have for one another. I was so fortunate to work with her in learning parent–infant psychotherapy. The work that is represented in this book is heavily influenced by the wonderful experiences I have had with these mentors.

I had the good fortune of working at the Reginald S. Lourie Center for Infants and Children in Rockville for many years. The wonderful opportunities they provided as both clinician and researcher allowed me to blossom as a professional and to blend my knowledge of occupational therapy with clinical and developmental psychology. It was at the Lourie Center that I learned the importance of fostering emotional health and development through the parent–child relationship and the value of early intervention and prevention in treating multiproblem families. I am very grateful to Ruth Sickel, Betty Ann Kaplan, Andrea Santman Wiener, Diane Hopkins, Polly Craft, and Cecilia Breinbauer, who collaborated with me on my Fussy Baby team at the Lourie Center. Their camaraderie of spirit and intellectual curiosity spurred the work that is presented in this book. Currently, I am fortunate to be part of a team of sterling professionals at ITS for Children and Families, Inc., in Kensington, Maryland, with whom I continue to collaborate on finding better ways to serve children and their families.

I greatly appreciate the invaluable advice that Polly Craft and Cecilia Breinbauer offered in reading versions of this book. I am also very grateful to Elisabeth Muir, who so graciously agreed to write the foreword. Many thanks to Karen Prince for the beautifully photographed pictures in this book and to the children and families who so graciously agreed to be photographed.

The case vignettes and examples described herein are based on real clinical examples. The names and pertinent identifying information on children and their families have been disguised to protect their identities. In most of the cases, the parents granted permission for their case vignette to be used. When it was not possible to obtain permission, case examples were written as a composite of several cases to further protect families' identities. I wish to thank all the families I have worked with over the years. They have taught me so much. Without them this book would not have been possible.

Last, but not least, I wish to thank my loving husband, Robert Dickey, who endured many hours listening to me as I formulated ideas for this book. I am extremely grateful for his unconditional support and encouragement for my professional endeavors.

Self-Regulation in Infants and Children

Parents and professionals have puzzled over the importance of early regulatory problems in babies. Most normal infants show irregularities in negotiating sleep cycles, digestion, and self-calming, which usually resolve around six months of age. However, some infants show persistent problems in sleep, self-consoling, feeding, and mood regulation (i.e., fussiness, irritability). As the infant grows into toddler and early childhood and problems become more evident, difficulties with attention, sensory processing, intolerance for change, a hyperalert state of arousal, and severe separation anxiety often occur. Infants experiencing these symptoms have been termed regulatory disordered (Greenspan, 1989, 1992; Zero to Three, 1994). Since infants and children with these behaviors are commonly observed in clinical practice, it is important to understand the symptoms underlying the regulatory disorder and how early problems with self-regulation may impact later development.

The chapter presents an overview of regulatory processes in infancy and describes the symptoms that constitute a regulatory disorder. The outcomes of preschool children who had regulatory disorders during infancy are described, along with how early symptoms may lead to these outcomes. Finally, the different types of regulatory disorders that have been proposed by the Diagnostic Classification: 0–3 are described. Case examples are presented to depict the symptomatology of the different subtypes.

NORMAL DEVELOPMENT OF REGULATORY PROCESSES IN INFANCY

The early regulation of arousal and physiological state is critical for successful adaptation to the environment. The development of homeostasis is important in the modulation of physiological states, including sleep–wake cycles and hunger and satiety. It is needed for mastery of sensory functions and for learning self-calming and emotional responsivity. It is also important for regulation of attentional capacities (Als *et al.*, 1982; Brazelton *et al.*, 1974; Field, 1981; Tronick, 1989). The foundations of self-regulation lie in the infant's capacity to develop homeostasis in the first few months of life when the infant learns to take interest in the world while simultaneously regulating arousal and responses to sensory stimulation (Greenspan, 1992; Lachmann & Beebe, 1997). As the infant matures, self-regulation depends on the capacity to read and give gestural and vocal signals, to internalize everyday routines, and to respond contingently to expectations from others (Kopp, 1987, 1989; Tronick, 1989). Although there are individual differences, the infant must learn to adapt to changing family and parental expectations to master self-regulation.

Self-regulatory mechanisms develop and refine over the first 2 years of life. Some of the important milestones include the formation of affective relationships and attachments, purposeful communication, use of self and others to control internal states, an understanding of causal relationships, and development of self-initiated organized behaviors. It is generally recognized that self-regulatory mechanisms are complex and develop as a result of physiological maturation, caregiver responsivity, and the infant's adaptation to environmental demands (Lyons-Ruth & Zeanah, 1993; Rothbart & Derryberry, 1981).

In the early stages of development, the caregiver soothes the young infant when distressed and facilitates state organization (Als, 1982). Greenspan (1992) describes the infant's first task as learning to regulate himself or herself and taking interest in the world. The capacity for engagement and attachment has to do with the ability to modulate and process sensory experiences. It also involves the ability to coordinate simple motor actions. To facilitate sensorimotor modulation, parents normally provide sensory input through play and caretaking experiences such as dressing and bathing. Touch and movement, together with auditory and visual stimulation, are integrated into multiple parent–infant experiences throughout the infant's first 18 months of life. The baby learns how to self-soothe early in life by sucking, holding onto hands or feet, or by looking at sights or listening to pleasant sounds.

Greenspan (1998) describes the next stage occurring between 8 and 18 months as one of intentionality, reciprocal interactions, and organized affects. Kopp (1987) further elaborates that during this time the infant learns to modify actions in relation to events and object characteristics. According to Kopp, it is not until 9 months of age that the infant shows intentionality or an awareness of situational meanings. For example, the baby learns to distinguish between when daddy is putting on his coat to go to work or to take them for a stroller ride based on other

A baby self-soothes through sight and touch in her father's arms.

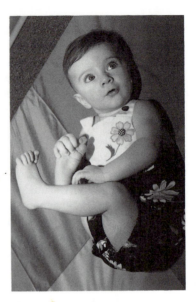

A baby self-soothes
by grasping her feet.

verbal and contextual cues. It is at this age that the baby is also able to initiate, maintain, and inhibit physical actions. There is an emergence of problem solving, intentionality, and awareness that actions lead to a goal. The growing awareness of self as a separate identity contributes to the infant's capacity to differentiate his responses from the actions of others.

The emergence of self-control is the next phase beginning at 18 months. The child of this age can create mental images that can be manipulated through his or her pretend play and functional use of language. Because of these skills, the infant is able to internalize routines and requests made by others. Kopp describes the toddler as learning to delay his or her actions and to comply with social expectations without needing external cues. The development of representational thought and recall memory is central to this stage. Verbal mediation of thoughts and actions helps the child organize self-regulatory behavior (Kopp *et al.*, 1983). As the child begins to differentiate emotions and his or her sense of self from others, expressions of negative affects and aggression are apt to occur. The caregiver attaches affective meanings to situations and provides social expectations and values related to specific emotional responses, which helps the infant to label and understand emotions (Kopp, 1987). The development of action schemes (e.g., vocalizations, self-distractions, or other motor responses), cognitive organization (e.g., representational thinking, self-monitoring), motivation, and external support from caregivers appear to be key elements in attainment of emotion regulation (Kopp, 1989).

WHAT IS A REGULATORY DISORDER?

Although some constitutionally based traits are transient in nature and resolve once the child develops internal self-organizational mechanisms (Thelen, 1989), others are not. For example, infants frequently display sleep disturbances and/or colic that resolve spontaneously by 5 or 6 months of age. If, however, early signs of irritability do not resolve by 6 months, the fussiness experienced by the infant persists and is coupled with other symptoms, such as poor self-calming, intolerance for change, and a hyperalert state of arousal. Using Greenspan's clinical constructs, these infants recently have become recognized as regulatory disordered (Zero to Three, 1994). The diagnostic criteria for regulatory disorders are provided in the *Diagnostic Classification of Mental Health and Developmental Disorders of Infancy and Early Childhood* (Zero to Three, 1994). A regulatory disorder is one in which problems exist in both behavioral regulation and sensorimotor organization. Typically, the regulatory-disordered infant displays problems in sleep, self-consoling, feeding, attention and arousal, mood regulation, or transitions. Often these infants are hyper- or hyposensitive to sensory stimuli, including auditory, tactile, visual, and vestibular stimulation (DeGangi & Greenspan, 1988).

In our research on infants with regulatory disorders (RDs), we found that none of the infants in either the regulatory-disordered or control groups had obvious or serious medical or developmental problems. However, we found that there were some differences on the perinatal and medical histories of infants with regulatory disorders. The presence of frequent headaches during pregnancy and use of forceps in delivery occurred in higher frequencies in the regulatory-disordered sample. Headaches during the pregnancy may reflect stress or anxiety in the mother. Medical diagnoses of eating problems—including reflux, elimination problems, colic, and frequent colds—were present as well in the regulatory-disordered sample. Ear infections were not more prevalent in the RD sample.

Because the diagnostic category of regulatory disorder is a rather new one, there are relatively few studies. In addition to further studies that document the symptoms of infants and children with regulatory disorders and the long-term outcomes of children experiencing these problems, prevalence studies are needed.

OUTCOMES OF REGULATORY-DISORDERED INFANTS

The clinical significance of poor regulation of arousal and state is demonstrated by the high incidence of children with sleep disturbances who have behavioral disturbances, attention deficit disorder with hyperactivity, and depression (Mattison *et al.*, 1987). Infants with problems associated with regulating sensorimotor systems (i.e., hypersensitivity to stimulation) tend to develop emotional difficulties in the school-aged years (Fish & Dixon, 1978; Walker & Emory, 1983). Similar consistencies have been reported between negative temperamental characteristics assessed during infancy (e.g., distractibility, difficult temperament) and poor behavioral control, dependency, and aggressive behaviors in the preschool years (Forsyth & Canny, 1991; Himmelfarb *et al.*, 1985; Oberklaid *et al.*, 1993; Rai *et al.*, 1993; Sroufe *et al.*, 1983), reactive depression in late adolescence (Chess *et al.*, 1983), and later learning disabilities and psychopathology (Rutter, 1977). In a 15-year longitudinal study, infants with difficult temperaments were more likely to have psychiatric symptoms in adolescence, although demanding children whose families received mental health interventions were less likely to develop these problems (Teerikangas *et al.*, 1998). Children with difficult temperament in high-conflict families are at greater risk for developing aggression in the preschool years than children with an easy temperament from similar families (Tschann *et al.*, 1996). In addition, children with psychiatric disorders were more likely to have temperamental difficulties and their parents showed a higher level of psychopathology than those without disorders, which supports the relationship between parent and child as well as temperament on child psychopathology (Kashani *et al.*, 1991).

In reviewing the literature on temperament, it may seem that children with regulatory disorders are simply those who experience a difficult temperament. The constructs of poor self-regulation and difficult temperament clearly overlap; however, a child may have a regulatory disorder but not have a difficult temperament and vice versa. Our research suggests that many children with difficult temperament also have a regulatory disorder. It is also important to distinguish children who have sensory integration dysfunction from those with regulatory disorders. Although many children with regulatory disorders also have poor sensory processing and motor planning problems, not all children with sensory integrative dysfunction have a regulatory disorder. It is important for clinicians to examine the symptoms that underlie a regulatory disorder in making a differential diagnosis. The criteria for children with moderate to severe regulatory disorders are ones that experience at least three of the following symptoms: poor self-calming with high irritability, sleep problems, feeding problems, inattention, mood regulation problems, and sensory processing problems. These symptoms are described in more detail later in the chapter.

As can be seen by this review of the literature, children with early features of regulatory disorders are at high risk for developing long-term emotional and developmental problems. Since these studies focused on children with difficult temperament, we conducted a longitudinal study to investigate the long-term significance of fussy babies who were diagnosed as regulatory disordered at 8 to 11 months of age. These infants exhibited sleep disturbances, hypersensitivities to sensory stimulation, irritability and poor self-calming, and mood and state deregulation (DeGangi *et al.*, 1993). When we looked at group differences, we found that children initially identified as regulatory disordered differed significantly from their normal peers in perceptual, language, and general cognitive skills at 4 years of age. Although the regulatory-disordered sample did not differ from their normal counterparts in developmental parameters during infancy, at 4 years of age, five of the nine regulatory-disordered infants had either motor or overall developmental delays. There was a high incidence of vestibular-based sensory integrative deficits (e.g., poor bilateral coordination and postural control), tactile defensiveness, motor planning problems, hyperactivity, and emotional/behavioral difficulties in the sample as well. These preliminary findings implied that regulatory-disordered infants were at high risk for later perceptual, language, sensory integrative, and behavioral difficulties in the preschool years. Further follow-up studies on 39 infants with mild to moderate regulatory disorders have shown that at age 3 years they differ from their normal peers in sensory integration, mood regulation, attention, motor control, sleep, and behavioral control (DeGangi *et al.*, 1996).

In a more recent study examining diagnostic outcome, we compared the performance of infants ranging in age from 7 to 30 months who were normally developing ($n = 38$), and 32 infants with regulatory disorders (10 mild and 22 with moderate to severe regulatory disorders) (DeGangi *et al.*, in press). Two child psychiatrists unfamiliar with the subjects' diagnostic classification during infancy reviewed the 3-year data and videotapes of parent–child interactions. Diagnoses were made by them using the DSM-IV and Diagnostic Classification: 0–3. Children who were initially in the normal sample were highly likely to be normal at age 3 years (97.5%). One of the 38 subjects in this group (2.5%) was rated as having a regulatory disorder using the Diagnostic Classification: 0–3.

Six of the 10 infants and toddlers with mild regulatory disorders were found to be normal at 3 years. The remaining 40% had regulatory disorders in addition to a DSM-IV diagnosis. These diagnoses included developmental coordination disorder (10%), expressive/receptive language disorder (20%), sleep disorder (20%), or a parent–child relational problem (10%) (e.g., score in clinical range on the Child Behavior Checklist and exhibit significant emotional problems). In addition, half of the 40% with diagnoses were found to have sensory integrative problems. None of these diagnoses except regulatory disorder reached the level of significance in discriminating children in the mild RD group from the normative sample.

The group that was most at risk for later developmental problems were the infants and toddlers who had moderate to severe regulatory disorders. These were infants who had three or more symptoms (i.e., sleep problems, irritability, sensory hypersensitivities). All but one subject had a DSM-IV diagnosis (95.5%), and 86% had two or more diagnoses. The most predominant diagnoses included regulatory disorder (50%), developmental coordination disorder (40.9%), cognitive delay (40.9%), parent–child relational problems (40.9%), and expressive/receptive language disorder (36%). In addition, 59% were rated as having sensory integrative problems. We also found that children who were more apt to develop parent–child relational problems at 3 years had feeding problems during infancy.

EARLY SYMPTOMS AND THEIR RELATIONSHIP TO LATER DIAGNOSTIC OUTCOMES

In this next section, the early symptoms of children with moderate regulatory disorders will be described as they relate to later diagnostic problems. The data presented in this section are based on our study of 155 normal infants and 77 infants who had regulatory disorders from 7 to 30 months. Parents completed a comprehensive checklist of symptoms related to regulatory functioning. Findings on the checklist were confirmed through an intake interview and clinical observations. The long version of the Infant–Toddler Symptom Checklist (ITSC) used in this study is described in detail in Chapter 2 (Assessment of Regulatory Problems in Children). The ITSC is a parent report measure for infants ranging in age from 7 to 30 months and focuses on the infant's responses in the following domains: (1) self-regulation, (2) attention, (3) sleep, (4) feeding, (5) dressing, bathing, and touch, (6) movement, (7) listening, language and sound, (8) looking and sight, and (9) attachment/emotional functioning.

In our studies of regulatory-disordered infants, we found certain symptoms between 7 and 30 months of age that were likely to lead to later developmental and behavioral problems. However, we found that the symptoms tend to evolve and may have different meanings at different ages. In the first year of life, the symptoms that are likely to be meaningful included irritability, inconsolability, demandingness, poor self-calming, and sleep problems. The infants also showed sensory hypersensitivities to touch and light, a high need for movement, fear of novelty, problems giving clear gestural and vocal signals, and severe separation anxiety. These symptoms are related to the capacity to develop basic homeostasis (e.g., self-calming, regulation of arousal states, and physiological regulation) and early sensory processing.

Many of these symptoms persisted in the second year of life; however, other symptoms emerged. Attentional problems were seen in some infants who were distractible and overstimulated by busy environments. Sensory problems were manifested by a dislike for restraint (e.g., car seats, being dressed), a dislike for new food textures, distress with loud sounds, and a fear of movement. In addition, interactive problems were demonstrated by a lack of reciprocal interactions, difficulties with limit setting, and a need for total control of the environment, while problems giving clear gestural signals emerged. Persistent problems with basic homeostasis occurred in conjunction with difficulties with gestural communication (e.g., signal reading and giving), affective expression, attentional capacities, reciprocal play, and negotiating autonomy and control. These symptoms may

TABLE 1.1   Prevalence of Overall Problems in Regulatory-Disordered (RD) Sample Versus Normal Sample (N)

	Age range (in months)									
	7–9		10–12		13–18		19–24		25–30	
Domain	RD	N	RD	N	RD	N	RD	N	RD	N
Self-regulation	89%	3%	85%	7%	94%	16%	92%	13%	67%	6%
Sleep	37%	3%	54%	7%	35%	3%	15%	3%	20%	3%
Feeding	0%	0%	31%	0%	0%	0%	38%	3%	0%	0%
Attention	0%	0%	0%	0%	24%	3%	31%	13%	40%	3%
Movement	16%	0%	14%	0%	41%	12%	54%	3%	33%	3%
Listening	0%	0%	46%	3%	47%	6%	62%	6%	0%	0%
Visual	11%	0%	46%	17%	41%	0%	23%	6%	20%	0%
Tactile	52%	0%	69%	7%	82%	12%	85%	10%	60%	23%
Emotional	26%	0%	69%	7%	82%	16%	38%	3%	27%	3%
Mean percent	25%	0.6%	46%	5%	50%	7%	49%	7%	30%	5%

be the early warning signs of later attentional, emotional, and behavioral problems.

Although it would be expected that symptoms of poor self-regulation would be greatest in the first year of life, the data suggest that infants between 10 and 24 months experience the most symptoms when a regulatory disorder is present under 30 months of age. The mean percentage of symptoms displayed in Table 1.1 demonstrates this point. It is important to note that the changing distributions of symptoms observed reflect the developmental challenges presented to the child over time. For example, as more cognitive demands are placed upon the child, more attentional difficulties begin to emerge in the second year of life. Likewise, feeding problems at 13 to 24 months become exacerbated when food textures are introduced.

The findings from this study support the notion that children with regulatory disorders have underlying deficits in self-regulation, attention and arousal, sensory processing, and emotion regulation. However, different symptoms occur at different ages based on the developmental level of the child. Understanding how these symptoms change over time is important in developing a working definition of what constitutes a regulatory disorder. In the next section, a developmental profile is constructed for each category of behavior measured by the Symptom Checklist. Only the more prevalent behaviors are described.

IMPACT OF EARLY SYMPTOMS ON LATER DEVELOPMENTAL OUTCOME

There were a number of symptoms that differentiated the performance of normal and regulatory-disordered infants (DeGangi & Breinbauer, 1997). Although some normal infants display these symptoms at times in their development, it is the number and intensity of symptoms that differentiates the typically developing child from one with regulatory disorders. For infants and toddlers with regulatory disorders, we found developmental differences across ages for different symptoms. These will be described next.

Self-Regulation

The process of self-regulation involves the capacity to modulate mood, self-calm, delay gratification, and tolerate transitions in activity. Most babies can self-calm by bringing a hand to the mouth to suck, touching their hands together, rocking, and looking or listening to preferred visual or auditory stimuli. These behaviors are often unavailable to infants with regulatory disorders. Once upset, such infants require extreme efforts to calm down. The caregiver may spend from

A mother comforts her crying baby through her loving touch.

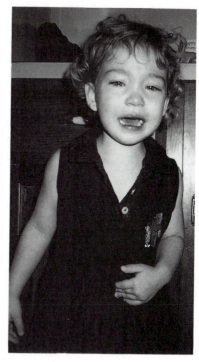

An irritable child
cries inconsolably.

2 to 4 hours a day attempting to calm his or her infant. With older infants, severe temper tantrums are often present.

The most pervasive trait of infants with regulatory disorders is that of fussiness. Between 23 and 54% of the infants in the regulatory-disordered sample had problems with irritability. Their caregivers described them as escalating quickly from a pleasant mood to an intense cry (27 to 57%) and to have difficulty with self-calming (20 to 46%).

Maternal perception of difficultness may be confirmed through the use of temperament scales (e.g., Bates's Infant Characteristics Questionnaire, fussy-difficult subscale) (Bates, 1984). When the parents do not view their child as difficult despite clinical evidence of mood deregulation, further investigation is needed to determine if such problems as parental inexperience, denial, maternal depression, or other problems exist. In many cases, the fussiness and irritability are very disruptive to the family and result in a high degree of family stress.

In our study examining the symptomatology of infants and toddlers with regulatory disorders (DeGangi & Breinbauer, 1997), we found that a high percentage of these infants had irritability, inconsolability, demandingness, and poor self-calming in the first year of life. Although it is expected that symptoms of poor self-regulation would be greatest in the first year of life, we found that infants between 10 and 24 months experienced more symptoms when a regulatory disorder was present under 30 months of age. Problems with irritability, crying, and self-calming persisted through 24 months. As these behaviors diminished at 25 to 30 months, problems tolerating change emerged. We also found that a pervasive trait of children with regulatory disorders from 7 to 30 months was demandingness. There was a relative decrease in self-regulatory problems at 25 to 30 months to 67% of the sample, which may have reflected a developing capacity to resolve distress without help from others, to comply with requests, to delay gratification, and to anticipate social routines. The development of internal control and related cognitive abilities may help the child with regulatory disorders to be better able to tolerate changes and modulate distress. These abilities have been described by Kopp (1987, 1989) as important to the development of emotion regulation. Difficulties with this most basic task seems to have a negative impact on the development of cognition, language, skilled movement, behavioral and emotional control, and sensorimotor modulation at 3 years. The self-regulatory profile of children with regulatory disorders is presented in Figure 1.1.

Sleep Problems

Persistent sleep disorders have been found to result in biochemical changes in stress hormones and biological rhythms, and states of arousal (Weissbluth, 1989). Fussy and irritable behaviors may occur during the day because the infant is overtired and unable to fall and stay asleep. Children with sleep deficits often exhibit a high state of arousal and are unable to inhibit their alert state to allow sleep. Sometimes the child is not able to fall into a deep REM sleep and wakes frequently throughout the night. When a sleep disturbance is present, the infant has difficulty regulating sleep–wake cycles and has difficulty falling and staying asleep.

Between 15 and 38% of the children with regulatory disorders under 2 years wake frequently in the night. Between 32 and 47% of 7- to 18-month olds need extensive help to fall asleep at night (e.g., over an hour of preparatory activities). Sleep problems were more prevalent among mild regulatory-disordered infants. The problems typically affecting these infants included frequent waking in the night and difficulties falling asleep. Our research also shows that many children with sleep problems often have hypersensitivities to touch, a strong craving for movement, and high separation anxiety. In our study examining the symptomatology of regulatory-disordered infants (DeGangi & Breinbauer, 1997), we found that sleep problems tended to improve with maturity, with no significant differences between regulatory-disordered infants and the normative group after 25 months of age. This may be why infants who showed a sleep disorder early in life were more likely to resolve their problems if their regulatory disorder was mild and they did not experience other developmental challenges.

FIGURE 1.1

Self-regulatory profile of children with regulatory disorders.

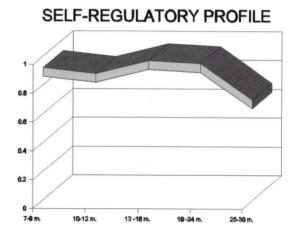

SELF-REGULATORY PROFILE

	7–9 m	10–12 m	13–18 m	19–24 m	25–30 m
Irritability	xxxxx	xxxxx	xxxxx		
Cries easily	xxxxx	xxxxx	xxxxx		
Poor self-calm	xxxxx	xxxxx	xxxxx	xxxxx	
Unable to wait	xxxxx	xxxxx		xxxxx	
Demandingness	xxxxx	xxxxx	xxxxx	xxxxx	xxxxx
Need preparation for change				xxxxx	
Distress with transition					xxxxx

Our data suggest that different problems are associated with sleep disturbances at different ages, which supports the notion that sleep problems are related to both biological and social regulation, and the ability to form a secure attachment to the caregiver (Anders, 1994). At 7 to 9 months, sleep problems were often associated with a high need for vestibular stimulation. Caregivers often reported that the only way to help their baby fall asleep was to bounce or rock them for long periods of time. At 10 to 12 months, separation anxiety seemed to compound the sleep disturbance. Caregivers often reported that their infant was clingy and could only fall asleep in their arms. Distress upon awakening in the night may have been accompanied by anxiety that the child was alone in their own crib rather than being in their parent's arms. By 13 to 18 months, we found that many children with sleep problems showed a high need for movement stimulation. Often parents reported how their child's excessive need for movement seemed to increase their

FIGURE 1.2

Sleep profile of regulatory-
disordered infants.

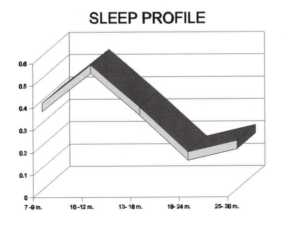

SLEEP PROFILE

	7–9 m	10–12 m	13–18 m	19–24 m	25–30 m
Wakes frequently	xxxxx	xxxxx	xxxxx	xxxxx	
Difficulty falling asleep	xxxxx	xxxxx	xxxxx		

arousal, making it more difficult for the child to fall asleep at night. Distress at sounds in the environment was often present at 13 to 18 months. Many parents reported how they needed to screen environmental sounds by using white noise (i.e., oscillating fans, white noise audiotapes) to help their children sleep. In addition, severe separation anxiety often persisted at this age, exacerbating the sleep problem. By 19 to 24 months, falling asleep was less an issue; however, waking in the night remained. Many of these children craved movement and appeared restless throughout the night. Figure 1.2 presents the sleep profile for children with regulatory disorders.

Feeding

The feeding problems exhibited by infants with regulatory disorders usually include difficulty establishing a regular feeding schedule, distress around feeding with regurgitation, refusal to eat, and other feeding problems not related to specific allergies or food intolerance. Resistance to eating a variety of food textures often emerges after 9 months. Some infants spit out lumpy food textures or refuse to eat anything but a few preferred foods, usually consisting of firm, crunchy textures or pureed foods. This problem may relate to tactile hypersensitivities that cause the child to prefer certain food textures. Occasionally, growth retardation or failure to thrive may be diagnosed secondary to the feeding disturbance. Craving certain foods is seen in 18 to 46% of 13 to 24 month olds. In addition, reflux is a problem sometimes experienced by children with regulatory disorders.

Feeding problems of children in our study included reflux, oral tactile sensitivities related to a tendency to reject certain food textures, and craving of certain foods. Interestingly, the only diagnosis at 3 years that was related to early feeding problems was social–emotional problems. In one of our preliminary follow-up studies (DeGangi *et al.*, 1996), we found that maternal depression and less attachment as measured by the Parenting Stress Index (Abidin, 1986) were related to feeding and communication problems. The fact that we are finding long-term emotional problems in children who initially had feeding disorders points to the importance of addressing parent–child interactive components in treatment when the feeding problem is first identified.

Attention

Problems with attention have been underestimated in infants and young children because of the difficulties encountered in measuring attention in infancy. Our data suggest that between 13 and 30 months there is a steady increase in the number of symptoms associated with attentional problems. These range from being overstimulated by busy environments, to distractibility and problems shifting or engaging attention. Parents often describe their baby with regulatory problems as being intense, wide-eyed, or "hyper." Frequently the child will go from one toy to another, often not playing with any toy long enough to develop a toy preference.

Using the Test of Attention in Infants (DeGangi, 1995), we found that 55 to 64% of infants with regulatory disorders show problems sustaining their attention during novel visual, auditory, tactile, or multisensory activities. Their caregivers often report that they view their children with regulatory disorders as being highly distracted by sights and sounds (13 to 31% for 13 to 30 month olds). Difficulties shifting attention to something new was found in 15 to 31% of 10 to 30 month olds. Attentional problems were more commonly reported after 18 months of age.

Attentional problems commonly observed in our sample included distractibility to sights and sounds, becoming overly excited by busy environments, and difficulties shifting attention to something new. We found that children experiencing these symptoms early in life were more apt to develop cognitive problems and motor delays at 3 years when the child had a regulatory disorder. It is possible that motor problems identified at 3 years were related to an underlying deficit in motor planning, a problem commonly seen in children who also experience attentional problems (Fisher *et al.*, 1991). Figure 1.3 presents the developmental profile for attentional problems in children with regulatory disorders.

FIGURE 1.3

Attentional profile for children
with regulatory disorders.

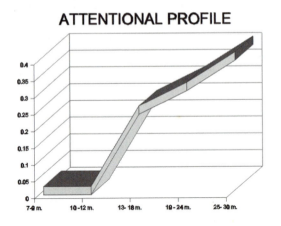

	7–9 m	10–12 m	13–18 m	19–24 m	25–30 m
Can't shift attention	xxxxx			xxxxx	
Excited by busy environments			xxxxx		xxxxx
Distracted				xxxxx	
Difficult to engage attention			xxxxx		

Sensory Processing

Many infants with regulatory problems respond by crying, withdrawal, or other negative behaviors when confronted with normal everyday sensory stimulation involving touch (i.e., being held by parent), movement (i.e., rough housing with parent), or sights and sounds (i.e., busy environment such as supermarket). The common sensorimotor challenges experienced by infants and toddlers with regulatory disorders are described below.

1. *Overreactivity to loud noises*: Infants with regulatory disorders at 13 to 18 months often become distressed by loud sounds such as the doorbell, a vacuum cleaner, or a siren (53%). Many normal children show this at 10 to 12 months (31%).

2. *Hypersensitivity to light and visual stimulation*: Thirty-one percent of 7 to 9 month olds with regulatory disorders are highly sensitive to light. Some are also overly excited when in busy environments such as shopping malls (20 to

44%). This latter problem is often seen in typically developing children at 10 to 12 months (30%).

Visual problems reported during infancy in the children with regulatory disorders were typically a sensitivity to light. Early problems in this area seemed to relate to a multitude of diagnoses, except cognitive problems for children in the moderate RD group. For children with pervasive developmental disorders (PDDs), visual problems seemed to contribute to the diagnosis of PDD at 3 years. This symptom in and of itself is not enough to result in poor developmental outcome; however, when it is coupled with other sensory and regulatory challenges, it may have an effect on the child's overall processing capacities.

3. *Tactile defensiveness or underreactivity to touch*: Tactile hypersensitivities may be exhibited in a number of ways in the young child with regulatory problems. The child may dislike wearing clothing (18% at 13 to 18 months), resist cuddling (14 to 41% in 10 to 30 month olds), hate having their face washed (38 to 59% in 7 to 18 months olds), or dislike being stroked on the body (41 to 100% based on results on the Test of Sensory Functions in Infants). A few children with regulatory disorders are undersensitive to touch and don't notice pain during such experiences as receiving a flu shot or falling down.

Tactile hypersensitivities were common among the children with regulatory problems (DeGangi & Breinbauer, 1997). Manifestations of tactile defensiveness tended to vary by age. From 7 to 12 months, tactile problems were shown by a dislike for being held and having the face washed and resisting dressing or being placed in certain body positions. These behaviors persisted into the second year of life along with other symptoms of tactile defensiveness. From 13 to 24 months, children with regulatory problems showed a dislike for wearing clothing or a preference for certain clothing, hating the car seat, and avoiding touching textures or getting the hands messy. These problems relate to the phenomenon of tactile defensiveness, an aversion to being touched by others and distress when touching textured objects (Fisher *et al.*, 1991). Tactile problems were common in children with both moderate regulatory disorders and PDD and related to a wide range of clinical diagnoses. Our data seem to suggest that underlying process deficits in any one or more senses (e.g., tactile, vestibular-proprioceptive) can have a profound effect on later developmental outcomes.

5. *Gravitational insecurity or underreactivity to movement*: The child with regulatory disorders may show an overreactivity to postural changes and a fear of body movement. We found that 55 to 95% of our sample had hypersensitivities to movement when tested with the Test of Sensory Functions in Infants (DeGangi & Greenspan, 1989). Fear of movement was reported in 20% of 25 to 30 month olds. Underreactivity to movement exhibited by a craving of

movement activity was found in 43 to 46% of 7- to 9- and 13- to 24-month-old children.

In our study examining symptomatology (DeGangi & Breinbauer, 1997), we found that responses to movement stimulation varied from fear of movement to craving of movement in the regulatory-disordered children, with many children showing a combination of the two. Oftentimes the child would crave linear movement such as swinging, rocking, or bouncing and preferred upright body postures, but showed fear when moved in planes that involved neck and trunk rotation or quick unexpected movement. In contrast, some children showed an underreactivity to movement (e.g., craving of movement activity, need to be in constant motion). Clumsiness and poor balance were also reported for toddlers at 19 to 24 months of age. Problems with the vestibular sense seemed related to later problems with self-regulation, motor and language delays, and social–emotional problems. It is interesting that, of the sensory processing problems tapped by the Symptom Checklist, hypersensitivities to movement or a craving for movement activities was more apt to relate to social–emotional problems than early tactile problems. This finding is puzzling and may be an artifact of the low sample size. One would expect that children who are tactually defensive are as much at risk for social–emotional problems as those who are insecure with movement or who crave movement experiences. Further research is needed before one may draw conclusions about the link between sensory dysfunction and social–emotional problems.

6. *Motor planning problems*: Difficulty sequencing and organizing purposeful movement was found in about 50% of our sample when tested using the Test of Sensory Functions in Infants. In addition, caregivers reported clumsiness and poor balance in 38% at 19 to 24 months. of age.

Figure 1.4 presents the sensory profile of children with regulatory problems.

Attachment/Emotional Functioning

Problems with social interactions that were reported in infants with regulatory problems included poor eye contact, somber affect, difficulties initiating and sustaining reciprocal interactions, difficulty reading the child's cues, aggressive behavior, difficulties responding to limits, a need to "run the show," severe separation anxiety, and a fearfulness of new people and situations (DeGangi & Breinbauer, 1997). A high need to control the environment was reported by caregivers, who stated that their children "ran the show" and did not respond to limits. Intolerance to change and new situations as well as difficulties adapting to the demands of others seemed to underlie these problems.

Our study examining symptomatology showed developmental differences in the manifestations of these problems. Parents of 7 to 9 month olds often reported

FIGURE 1.4

Sensory profile of children with regulatory disorders.

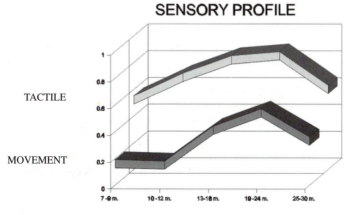

	7–9 m	10–12 m	13–18 m	19–24 m	25–30 m
TACTILE					
Hates face washing	xxxxx		xxxxx		
Resists cuddling		xxxxx	xxxxx		
Distress with dressing		xxxxx			
Dislikes new food textures				xxxxx	
Hates car seat				xxxxx	
Resists certain body positions	xxxxx	xxxxx	xxxxx	xxxxx	
MOVEMENT					
In constant motion	xxxxx				
Craves motion	xxxxx		xxxxx	xxxxx	xxxxx
Fear of movement					xxxxx
Clumsy				xxxxx	
LISTENING					
Distress with loud sounds			xxxxx		
Repeats words				xxxxx	
VISUAL					
Sensitive to light	xxxxx				

that they had difficulty reading their child's cues. This seemed related to problems that some children have in organizing clear gestural signals. At 19 to 24 months, some of the children with regulatory disorders had difficulty organizing reciprocal interactions. In a systematic study examining the play interactions of 94 children who were regulatory disordered and 154 controls ranging in age from 7 to 30 months, we found that infants with regulatory disorders showed more noncontingent responses, more aggression, less tactile exploration, and flat affect only when engaged in tactile play situations (DeGangi *et al.*, 1997). No differences were found in the infant behaviors during symbolic and vestibular play. It is possible that children with regulatory disorders become distressed by everyday sensory experiences, which affects their capacity to organize social interchanges.

These early problems with emotional and behavioral control seemed associated with a wide range of diagnoses for children with moderate regulatory disorders. The only diagnosis that was not associated with early emotional and behavioral problems was sensory integrative dysfunction for children in the moderate RD group. It seems that young children who have problems with behavioral control are likely to persist in such problems and develop other developmental problems, except for problems in sensory processing. It appears then that sensory integrative dysfunction is not something that is usually acquired over time, but may persist if it was initially present from birth. Figure 1.5 presents the emotion regulation profile for regulatory-disordered children.

TYPES OF REGULATORY PROBLEMS

Three main types of regulatory disorders have been described in the Diagnostic Classification: 0-3. Through systematic reporting of cases from various centers, the Zero to Three task force (1994) developed a database that served as the foundation for identifying recurring patterns in children with regulatory disorders. The three subtypes that they proposed are empirical and have not been validated. The attributes underlying each type are based on different behavioral and sensorimotor profiles. A brief description of each of these types of regulatory problems are presented. A brief case vignette is provided to illustrate the symptoms of each type of regulatory disorder.

1. *The Hypersensitive Type*: The child with hypersensitivities is overwhelmed by sensory stimulation and reacts in two ways: by becoming fearful and cautious in overwhelming situations, or by becoming negative and defiant. These behaviors are adaptations for the child and provide a means of fending off overwhelming stimuli.

    a. The *fearful and cautious type* has the following symptoms: dislikes changes in routines, is fearful of new people and situations, and has severe separation anxiety. This type of child becomes

FIGURE 1.5

Emotion regulation of children
with regulatory disorders.

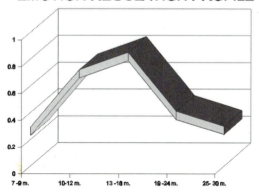

EMOTION REGULATION PROFILE

	7–9 m	10–12 m	13–18 m	19–24 m	25–30 m
Runs the show	xxxxx	xxxxx		xxxxx	xxxxx
Difficult to read cues of	xxxxx				
Severe separation anxiety			xxxxx	xxxxx	
No response to limits			xxxxx	xxxxx	
No reciprocal interactions interactions				xxxxx	
Destructive				xxxxx	
Fearful of new people, situations					xxxxx

easily upset and irritable and has difficulty self-calming. The sensory profile that may accompany these characteristics is an overreactivity to touch, movement, loud noises, and bright lights. Motor planning problems may also be evident.

b. The *negative and defiant* type also has difficulty tolerating change,
is highly irritable, and is controlling of the environment or "runs
the show." These children may be overreactive to touch and sound
with motor planning problems.

2. *The Underreactive Type:* Children who are underreactive are undersensitive
to sensory stimulation and have a tendency to become withdrawn, difficult to
engage, or self-absorbed. Children who are withdrawn and difficult to engage

may appear depressed and avoid eye contact. Infants with this pattern may engage in repetitive sensory activities. They may tend to be underreactive to movement, yet have either an over- or underreactivity to touch. When the child is self-absorbed, he or she may tend to tune into his or her own thoughts or play rather than being responsive to others in reciprocal interactions. They tend to play by themselves when others do not actively join into their play. Infants with this problem are likely to have irregularities in their sensory processing. Since withdrawn or self-absorbed behavior is frequently a hallmark of children with autistic-like symptoms or those who have pervasive developmental disorder, it is possible that children with more global developmental delays are more likely to show this pattern. These children need to be carefully diagnosed.

3. *Motorically disorganized type*: Children with this problem often have motor planning and organizational problems, resulting in the child being disorganized and impulsive. The infant may have a high activity level and may be aggressive as well. This type of child may show a pattern of craving sensory input. The child may be unable to wait for food, toy, or activity, and may be destructive.

These three proposed subtypes for regulatory disorders need to be validated in samples of regulatory-disordered infants to determine if they represent the symptomatology of regulatory-disordered infants. In our sample with infants who scored within normal limits on the Bayley Scales of Infant Development, Motor and Mental Scales (Bayley, 1993), we found the hypersensitive type to be more prevalent.

Case Example of Hypersensitive, Fearful and Cautious Type

Gabriella was a 5-year-old child who was socially withdrawn at school. She was a very bright child with a good vocabulary who was already writing sentences on the computer. She was teaching herself to read and loved looking at books. Gabriella enjoyed music and could pick out tunes on the piano as well as sing long audiotapes by heart. She was a sweet child who was very kind toward others. Gabriella was small for her age and, since she was very young, seemed to experience low muscle tone and poor motor coordination. As an infant, her parents noticed her to be floppy and to sit with a slouch. Although Gabriella seemed content to play alone for long periods of time, they were not concerned about her social skills until she went to preschool, when the teacher remarked about her behavior.

Gabriella was having difficulty with social interactions. She was reluctant to engage in group activities at school, needing considerable help to draw her out of a "trance" to pay attention to what the group was doing. She tended to engage in solitary play, sometimes humming to herself and appearing oblivious to others. If an adult spoke to her, she usually would not answer back. At school she was just beginning to participate in circle time, but oftentimes the teacher needed to repeat her name several times and get her attention by physically touching her. When interacting with other children, Gabriella tended to use scripts and rituals from TV shows or videos. On play dates, she tended to be very quiet, but she liked other children and would ask for play dates.

Gabriella did not engage in spontaneous pretend play, although she could organize simple symbolic actions such as hold and snuggle a doll if it had a "boo-boo" or put the baby doll to sleep. She liked to act out things that she had seen on TV or in a movie, a favorite being Dorothy from *The Wizard of Oz*. Her favorite play activities were puzzles, looking at books, or blowing bubbles.

Gabriella had a strong preference for things being done a certain way. For example, she often insisted that her parents walk about 10 feet ahead of her up the pathway to their front door. If they looked back at her, she would want to begin from the curb again. She was still drinking from a bottle and wanted it offered to her only by her mother with a certain tone of voice. Gabriella had other rituals that involved her mother, such as being carried a certain way into her bedroom at night and wishing her stuffed animals be lined up a certain way on the bed before she would go to sleep. When walking down the upstairs hall, she insisted on touching certain flowers on the wallpaper in a set way.

Gabriella also had troubles falling asleep, taking almost an hour to settle and waking multiple times in the night. Her mother would lie down with her to help her fall asleep. Gabriella would twirl her mother's hair over and over again for almost 20 minutes before she would finally drift off to sleep. While sleeping, Gabriella would thrash about in bed, waking once or twice in the night for a brief period. Her parents had tried a behavioral sleep program (e.g., the Ferber method) for 2 months, but Gabriella became very anxious about separating from her mother. She became extremely distressed at bedtime, clinging to her mother. Mrs. C. found that the only way she would tolerate the bedtime situation was to sleep with Gabriella; then she wouldn't have to go into her bedroom several times a night to calm her.

When I met Gabriella, I was impressed by her strong verbal capacities. She explored some of the toys in my playroom but remained cautious in her explorations, selecting only a few toys that interested her. Her cautiousness seemed related to two problems: motor planning problems in organizing new play activities and a reticence to interact with me and a novel environment. Occasionally she would play with me, but she remained hesitant, and often turned her back to me. Even when playing with her mother, she did not become animated and would turn her back on her as well. Gabriella often sought toys or activities that provided more sensory feedback (e.g., plastic tubes that could be pulled to make a funny noise). I was most successful in engaging her in play when I used materials that provided more sensory input (e.g., use of bright blue shaker to symbolize "fire" in the doll house, climbing on top of large foam blocks and sliding down).

Gabriella showed obvious pleasure in these kinds of activities. The movement and body contact seemed to provide her with more sensory support for social engagement.

Gabriella had some inconsistencies in tolerating sensory experiences. Although she avoided swings, she loved slides. She seemed to have mild sensitivities to touch that caused her to withdraw in group situations. She resisted hair washing and preferred wearing as little clothing as possible. Getting her dressed in the morning was a major production since Gabriella resisted wearing pants, leggings, or socks and shoes in the wintertime. Motor planning and coordination problems affected her ability to dress herself, ride a tricycle, and catch a ball with two hands.

Gabriella is an example of a child with motor planning problems who is hypersensitive to sensory stimulation. Her fearful and cautious behavior impacted her ability to explore the environment and interact with others. Significant problems with self-calming were present, coupled with problems modulating mood when distressed. In addition, Gabriella had many ritualistic and obsessive-like behaviors that seemed part of her disorder.

Case Example of Hypersensitive, Negative and Defiant Type

Myles was a 3-year-old child with severe problems related to sensory hypersensitivities and aggressive behavior. He was developing normally except for his expressive language, which fell at the 18-month level. He had considerable difficulty understanding directions from others and needed adults to speak slowly and in short utterances in order for him to understand. When Myles wanted something, he would point, then hit his parents to get attention. He could speak in short one- or two-word utterances but did not use his language to express his needs.

Symptoms that his parents noticed when Myles was a baby were the high irritability and problems self-calming. Myles craved movement stimulation, so the only things that seemed to calm him were swinging in an infant swing, riding in the stroller or car for long periods of time, and rough housing with Dad. Mrs. H. reported that Myles was happiest when she took him to a baby swim class or Gymboree to play on the slides and equipment. He did not engage in vocal play or try to make his wants understood through pointing or sounds. When he wanted something, he would resort to tantrums. Myles also had troubles settling down for sleep. It usually took his parents more than an hour to get him to fall asleep, but once settled Myles usually slept through the night.

Myles was a child who would become highly overstimulated when taken places. If his mother took him to the supermarket or a drugstore, he would run up and down the aisles, pulling things off shelves. After any type of outing, the family would return to the house and Myles would be overwhelmingly active, running up and down the stairs and yelling, throwing toys, or hitting his parents and older brother. Myles needed to be constantly occupied or structured in what he was doing; otherwise he would become destructive, breaking toys or tearing papers into shreds. He was constantly climbing onto furniture and getting into things that he shouldn't. Despite child-proofing the house, his parents found they were constantly exhausted watching Myles, wondering what disaster might befall them next. He would be found playing with a can of bug spray or holding a kitchen knife in his hand while running across the room. The only play activities that seemed to organize Myles were watching videos, playing with Legos and puzzles, or running outside and climbing on playground equipment. When engaged in movement activities, Myles would be happy, but he would quickly become overly excited, usually resulting him in shuddering throughout his body or biting his own hand. In addition to Myles's language problems and a high tendency to becoming overstimulated, he had tactile hypersensitivities. It was impossible to wash his face or brush his teeth. Diapering him was a nightmare and dressing him was a huge struggle, with him screaming the whole time. He was also very sensitive to sounds and would scream if mother tried to use any kitchen appliances, if his older brother played his trumpet or would laugh or make noise while playing, or when there were everyday noises such as the doorbell ringing or the vacuum running. Myles was a very picky eater, eating only Chicken McNuggets, crunchy cereal, or macaroni and cheese.

Mr. and Mrs. H. were at the end of their rope when they came in for an evaluation for Myles. They claimed that they couldn't set any limits on Myles because he would hit or bite them as soon as they said "No." Myles would scream and cry most of the day unless occupied with videos, outdoor play, or Legos. Mrs. H. was especially exhausted and Mr. H. dreaded coming home from work because of Myles's behavior. Mrs. H. felt that she was neglecting their older son. She found that she was constantly telling the older son to be quiet so that Myles would not be set off. No matter what they did, Myles was always going after them to hit or bite, or he was off destroying something in the house.

Myles is an example of a child who is experiencing sensory hypersensitivities, communication problems, and severe regulatory problems that causes him to disorganize and become impulsive, destructive, negative and defiant. Interventions are needed to address the underlying causes of his problem and to help him to better tolerate a range of sensory experiences while interacting with objects and people.

Case Example of Underreactive, Withdrawn and Self-Absorbed Type

Jared was a 7½-year-old who was gifted intellectually, with exceptional skills in reading and math. He did well in school but was having difficulties attending to questions during reading activities. He could not finish his homework without considerable help, and at home and school he was very distracted, particularly at mealtimes. When the teacher spoke to teach lessons, he often daydreamed. Although attentional problems were the main focus of the parents' concerns, they reported that as a young child Jared would often tune out when spoken to, seemed overwhelmed in busy settings like a shopping mall, and would be content to play alone for long periods of time.

Jared's favorite activities were drawing pictures of things like the solar system and playing computer games. He liked to play by himself and did not seem to have a desire to play with other children; yet he would speak warmly of other children and they seemed to like him. He liked to play tag with other children and enjoyed wrestling with his older brother. When Jared did not know what to do in social situations, he would usually resort to silly behavior. At times Jared would engage in long monologues that he recited from memory from movies that he had seen or books that he had read, or recall a past event in excessive detail. His parents found that they often had to go up to his face and speak loudly, repeating their request several times before they could get his attention.

Jared experienced tactile hypersensitivities. He resisted being touched and was never cuddly. When he approached other people to show affection, he would nuzzle against them or he would pinch them with the back of his fingers. He tended to be more comfortable with touch from familiar persons. Jared disliked bathing and washing his hair, complained that other people bumped into him, overreacted to physically painful experiences, and complained about tags in his clothing. Occasionally he engaged in repetitive licking of his lips or pulling at his shirt in a peculiar manner. Sometimes he would exclaim "Ouch" out of the blue, saying, "I hurt myself," and seemed uncomfortable with the contact of clothing against his body. Jared liked movement activities and sought out rocking and swinging activities. He liked to jump and skip, and often flapped his arms, smiling while he was doing these things.

When I played with Jared, I was struck by the toys that he was interested in. First, he selected a vibrating ball that he enjoyed holding and passing back and forth to me. He also enjoyed playing a game of hide-and-seek in a pile of foam blocks. When I asked Jared to draw a picture of a person, he decided to draw something that he liked to do all the time, an elaborate picture of a castle with a boy standing outside the castle. He developed a whole story about the castle that contained elements of a computer game that he was familiar with. His story evolved into one with ghosts and bats in the castle, and a king with a magic wand who could transform the ghosts into other animals. Jared became so absorbed in this activity that it was difficult to shift him away from it to do other drawings or activities. I attempted to ask him some questions about himself (e.g., likes and dislikes) and his family (e.g., what they like to do together), but it was difficult to engage him in a verbal interchange that was not linked to his drawing of the castle.

During the play interview, I noticed how Jared had difficulty scanning the environment for important visual cues. For example, he drew his castle with my pen, then after several minutes he suddenly noticed the basket of markers right in front of him that I had pointed out earlier. At the end of the session, he asked me where all the toys were and seemed not to notice the many shelves of toys that had been available to him.

Jared is an example of a child with regulatory problems who is underreactive, withdrawn, and self-absorbed. Despite his tactile hypersensitivities, he needed proprioceptive and movement stimulation to increase his arousal for social engagement. In addition, he had significant problems in exploring the environment effectively, particularly in using his vision. His rigid interactive style, fixation on particular thoughts, and problems reading social cues make Jared similar in many ways to children who suffer from Asperger's syndrome. Although it is likely that he had Asperger's syndrome, he certainly shows many features of children with the underreactive type of regulatory disorder.

Case Example of Hypersensitive, Motorically Disorganized Type

Juan was a 3-year-old child with significant motor delays and regulatory problems. His mother was concerned about his difficulties with sleep, self-calming, and auditory hypersensitivities. She also reported that he had delays in motor planning and control, and communication. He had been receiving early intervention services, including occupational and physical therapy and speech and language therapy, since he was 8 months old to help him develop better muscle tone, posture and balance, gross and fine motor skills, and communication skills.

Juan loved banging objects together, looking at books and interesting toys, playing in water and listening to music. He liked movement activities such as swinging and enjoyed having his arms and legs massaged. He enjoyed singing and action games like ring around the rosy, eensy-weensy spider, or peek-a-boo, brightening and smiling as he played these games with his parents. He had just begun to walk but tended to crawl as his main mode of ambulation. He was just beginning to explore the environment.

Despite these strengths, Juan had considerable difficulty organizing himself to remain calm for any length of time. He became easily irritable and overstimulated. Adult conversation (e.g., parents talking together) upset him. When not engaged in a sensory activity or singing game with his parents, Juan tended to be purposeless in his explorations. He quickly became frustrated, at which time he would begin to shake his head from side to side, bang his legs vigorously, and flap his hands. Teeth grinding occurred, particularly when exposed to tactile stimulation to the hands. When engaged in an interaction that was more novel (e.g., with a stranger), Juan would blink his eyes, seemingly to modulate the amount of visual stimulation that he was receiving. He also engaged in some behaviors that showed that he was seeking deep proprioceptive input (e.g., finding corners of the room, head butting into a person, tackling his brother).

His parents did a beautiful job of helping Juan self-calm, but his repertoire of soothing devices was limited to looking at videotapes, listening to music, roughhouse play, or being massaged. He responded better when the lights were dimmed or his parents spoke in a soft voice. He never mouthed objects and seemed distressed whenever objects were placed in his mouth by others. Once upset, Juan would often have a tantrum and needed his parents to divert him to something right away or the crying would last up to an hour.

Eating and sleeping were also challenging areas for Juan. He did not mouth objects, tended to drool, and ate a pureed diet. He was not yet self-feeding and seemed to have difficulty tolerating objects or textures in his mouth. Since feeding and sucking are major ways to self-soothe, helping Juan be less hypersensitive to touch in the mouth was considered an important aspect of his program. Juan needed help in falling and staying asleep. He woke twice in the night, after which he needed consoling. He was currently sleeping with his parents, relying on contact from their bodies and stroking his mother's face to console him for sleep. Putting Juan to sleep next to large body pillows under a weighted blanket helped to organize him at bedtime. Since he liked to stroke his mother's face, a soft doll with hair was introduced at bedtime.

It was important for Juan to learn ways to sooth himself that did not depend on his parents consoling him. The environment was set up with things such as a pup tent filled with pillows, vibrating toys, weighted blankets, and music boxes that he could seek out on his own. Encouraging him to explore his environment and find things that were organizing for him was important. For example, having large foam blocks available that he could push over encouraged exploration while providing him with sensory organization. When his parents engaged in floor time with him, they selected materials that provided organizing sensory input, then encouraged him to self-initiate exploration of the environment while they remained engaged in interacting with him. During this floor time, the objects that were most successful were the ones that provided opportunities for both tactile–proprioceptive (i.e., bin of dried beans with cups and utensils inside) and movement experiences (i.e, inner tube to bounce on). Because of Juan's sound sensitivities, it was useful to encourage play with toys that made noises that he could activate in play (i.e., pushcart that made music when pushed, musical ball toy).

Juan needed to learn how to broaden his range of play experiences and to tolerate novel sensory experiences. This would give him the opportunity to broaden his play repertoire and interest in the world and make being his caretaker easier. To begin this process, his parents put out a variety of toys that Juan enjoyed and then waited for him to indicate which one he wished to play with. At first, Juan selected only toys that he was most comfortable playing with, but the mere exposure to new things helped. It was also useful to combine a new toy with a medium that he enjoyed, such as water, thus increasing his tolerance for novelty. Juan also responded well to having new movement opportunities that he could do by himself (i.e., rocking himself in a small chair, moving on a waterbed or a large foam "cloud").

As Juan learned ways to self-calm, his parents tried talking to him from across the room so that he could learn to be soothed by their voices from a distance rather than relying solely on proximal modes of comforting (e.g., holding). Routines and structure were stressed so that Juan could learn to anticipate events. However, a goal was to help Juan learn to tolerate new things. New experiences were introduced by varying slightly familiar situations or activities or by pairing something familiar with a new stimulus.

Juan showed a clear attachment and warmth toward his parents in how he related to them (e.g., wishing to be held, reaching toward them, giving occasional glances in their direction). He was affectionate toward them, loving to be held, and he showed pleasure in the activities they did with him. He also understood that different persons had different meanings (e.g., play roughhouse games with dad, other games with brother or mother). Juan had strengths in forming relationships with familiar persons but was overly dependent on his parents to soothe him. Developing a special relationship with a few important people in his life (e.g., favorite family friend, therapist, babysitter) and learning how to sooth himself with a range of persons would help him. He also needed to learn how to seek out interactions with persons rather than rely on others to come to him and organize his play. For instance, his parents were prompted by me to play ring around the rosy with Juan. When I began this game with Juan's brother, he came over to play with us. Juan needed to see others doing interesting things, and then join in with them.

Juan had difficulty initiating intentional interactions through actions or vocalizations except for a few activities (i.e., banging objects, pushing a cause–effect toy). Motor planning issues seemed to compound his difficulties in organizing gestural and vocal signals. When sufficiently motivated, he could go up to his parents and indicate that he wanted to play by tugging on their hands. For the most part, Juan's communication skills were limited, thus requiring his parents to put forth considerable effort to be attuned to what he needed. Juan had the elements of intentional two-way communication but had problems in initiating new actions on his own without structure from others. He needed to develop a better capacity for engaging in spontaneous reciprocal interchanges in new and unfamiliar activities (e.g., taking turns back and forth in a range of activities). He also needed to develop more skills in communicating to others his needs and wishes. It appeared that his limitations in movement and language were a great source of frustration to him, and some of his crying may have related to this. He needed opportunities to express himself and to learn new activities that he could find rewarding. To begin this process, activities stressed learning how to take turns and to self-initiate what he wished to do. In this floor-time approach, his parents learned when to structure the activity and when to wait for Juan to show a response. In order for Juan to progress in his skills and to decrease the amount of distress he experienced, he needed to develop a sense of mastery and accomplishment that he could do things on his own.

Overall, Juan was a complex 3-year-old child who had needs in the areas of self-regulation, sensory processing, and communication. His problems fall within the realm of regulatory disorder, hypersensitive and motorically disorganized type. He showed a warm attachment to his parents but relied heavily on them as major sources for comfort and organization. He would become overwhelmed by novel information, particularly in new, unfamiliar environments. He showed some attentional capacities for certain sensory activities such as playing in dried beans or roughhouse games, but he needed to develop a broader repertoire of things that he could attend to and that promoted learning and sensory awareness. He could engage in simple reciprocal interactions with his parents around certain structured tasks (e.g., ring around the rosy, peek-a-boo), but he needed to be better able to self-initiate an interest in more activities and develop a sense of mastery for learning new things. He also needed to find better ways of consoling himself and resolving frustration than crying or depending solely on his parents' comforting. Developing relationships with others, learning how to communicate in close and far (e.g., across a room) spaces with his parents and learning to self-feed and sleep by himself were areas of need.

SUMMARY

Children with regulatory disorders seem to have underlying deficits in self-regulation, attention and arousal, sensory processing, and emotion regulation. Regulatory-disordered infants may be normal in their developmental skills in the first 2 years of life; however, their symptoms seem to evolve over time and eventually involve other process domains that build on problems with basic homeostasis and sensory regulation. Evaluation of symptoms and how they affect functional performance is important.

The importance of identifying infants with regulatory difficulties is crucial in light of our research. We found that infants initially diagnosed with moderate to severe regulatory disorders are at high risk for later perceptual, language, sensory integrative, and emotional/behavioral difficulties in the preschool years. Children with milder regulatory disorders, particularly if they have only a sleep disorder, appear to be less likely to develop later developmental and behavioral problems. Through early detection of regulatory disorders, it may be possible to prevent more serious, long-term perceptual, language, sensory integrative, attachment, and behavioral difficulties. Continued research is needed with larger samples to further explore the clinical significance of regulatory disorders.

ACKNOWLEDGMENTS

The research reported in this chapter was supported by a five-year Cooperative Agreement (#MCU-243-927, under Title 5, Social Security Act) with the Bureau of Maternal and Child Health (MCH) of the Health Resources and Services Administration.

REFERENCES

Abidin, R. R. (1986). *Parenting stress index.* Charlottesville, VA: Pediatric Psychology Press.

Als, H. (1982). Patterns of infant behavior: Analogues of later organizational difficulties? In F. H. Duffy & N. Geschwind (Eds.), *Dyslexia: A neuroscientific approach to clinical evaluation* (pp. 67–92). Boston: Little, Brown.

Als, H., Lester, B. M., Tronick, E. Z., & Brazelton, T. B. (1982). Towards a research instrument for the Assessment of Preterm Infants' Behavior (APIB). In H. Fitzgerald, B. M. Lester, & M. W. Yogman (Eds.), *Theory and research in behavioral pediatrics* (pp. 35–132). New York: Plenum.

Anders, T. F. (1994). Infant sleep, nighttime relationships, and attachment. *Psychiatry, 57,* 11–21.

Bates, J. E. (1984). *Infant Characteristics Questionnaire, Revised.* Bloomington: Indiana University Press.

Bayley, N. (1993). *Bayley Scales of Infant Development.* San Antonio, TX: Psychological Corporation.

Chess, S., Thomas, A., & Hassibi, M. (1983). Depression in childhood and adolescence: A prospective study of six cases. *Journal of Nervous and Mental Disease, 171,* 411–420.

DeGangi, G. A. (1995). *The test of attention in infants.* Dayton, OH: Southpaw Enterprises.

DeGangi, G. A., & Breinbauer, C. (1997). The symptomatology of infants and toddlers with regulatory disorders. *Journal of Developmental and Learning Disorders, 1*(1), 183–215.

DeGangi, G. A., & Greenspan, S. I. (1988). The development of sensory functioning in infants. *Physical and Occupational Therapy in Pediatrics, 8*(3), 21–33.

DeGangi, G. A., & Greenspan, S. I. (1989). *The test of sensory functions in infants.* Los Angeles: Western Psychological Services.

DeGangi, G. A., Porges, S. W., Sickel, R., & Greenspan, S. I. (1993). Four-year follow-up of a sample of regulatory disordered infants. *Infant Mental Health Journal, 14*(4), 330–343.

DeGangi, G. A., Sickel, R. Z., Wiener, A. S., & Kaplan, E. P. (1996). Fussy babies: To Treat or Not to Treat? *British Journal of Occupational Therapy, 59*(10), 457–464.

DeGangi, G. A., Sickel, R. Z., Kaplan, E. P., & Wiener, A. S. (1997). Mother–infant interactions in infants with disorders of self-regulation. *Physical and Occupational Therapy in Pediatrics, 17*(1), 17–44.

DeGangi, G. A., Breinbauer, C., Roosevelt, J., Greenspan, S., & Porges, S. (in press). Prediction of childhood problems at 36 months in children experiencing symptoms of regulation during infancy. *Infant Mental Health Journal.*

Field, T. (1981). Gaze behavior of normal and high-risk infants and during early interactions. *Journal of the American Academy of Child Psychiatry, 20,* 308–317.

Fish, B., & Dixon, W. J. (1978). Vestibular hyporeactivity in infants at risk for schizophrenia. *Archives of General Psychiatry, 35,* 963–971.

Fisher, A. G., Murray, C. A., & Bundy, A. C. (1991). *Sensory integration: Theory and practice.* Philadelphia: F. A. Davis.

Forsyth, B. W., & Canny, P. F. (1991). Perceptions of vulnerability 3½ years after problems of feeding and crying behavior in early infancy. *Pediatrics, 88*, 757–763.

Greenspan, S. I. (1989). *The development of the ego: Implications for personality theory, psychopathology, and the psychotherapeutic process*. Madison, CT: International Universities Press.

Greenspan, S. I. (1992). *Infancy and early childhood: The practice of clinical assessment and intervention with emotional and developmental challenges*. Madison, CT: International Universities Press.

Greenspan, S. I. (1998). *The child with special needs*. Reading, MA: Merloyd Laurence.

Himmelfarb, S., Hock, E., & Wenar, C. (1985). Infant temperament and noncompliant behavior at four years: A longitudinal study. *Genetic*, Social, and General Psychology Monographs, *111*, 7–21.

Kashani, J. H., Ezpeleta, L., Dandoy, A. C., Doi, S., & Reid, J. C. (1991). Psychiatric disorders in children and adolescents: The contribution of the child's temperament and the parents' psychopathology and attitudes. *Canadian Journal of Psychiatry, 36*(8), 569–573.

Kopp, C. B. (1987). The growth of self-regulation: Parents and children. In N. Eisenberg (Ed.), *Perspectives in developmental psychology*, (pp. 34–55). New York: Wiley.

Kopp, C. B. (1989). Regulation of distress and negative emotions: A developmental view. *Developmental Psychology, 25*, 343–354.

Kopp, C. B., Krakow, J. B., & Vaughn, B. (1983). Patterns of self-control in young handicapped children. *Minnesota Symposium on Child Development, 16*, 93–128.

Lachmann, F. M., & Beebe, B. (1997). The contribution of self- and mutual regulation to therapeutic action: A case illustration. In M. Moskowitz, C. Monk, C, Kaye, & S. Ellman (Eds.), *The neurobiological and developmental basis for psychotherapeutic intervention* (pp. 91–121). Northvale, NJ: Jason Aronson.

Lyons-Ruth, K., & Zeanah, C. H. (1993). The family context of infant mental health, I: Affective development in the primary caregiving relationship. In C. H. Zeanah (Ed.), *Handbook of infant mental health.* (pp. 14–37). New York: Guilford.

Mattison, R. E., Handford, H. A., & Vela-Bueno, A. (1987). Sleep disorders in children. *Psychiatric Medicine, 4*, 149–164.

Oberklaid, F., Sanson, A., Pedlow, R., & Prior, M. (1993). Predicting preschool behavior problems from temperament and other variables in infancy. *Pediatrics, 91*(1), 113–120.

Rai, S., Malik, S. C., & Sharma, D. (1993). Behavior problems among preschool children. *Indian Pediatrics, 30*(4), 475–478.

Rothbart M. K., & Derryberry, D. (1981). Development of individual differences in temperament. In M. E. Lamb and A. L. Brown (Eds.), *Advances in developmental psychology*, Vol. 1. Hillsdale, NJ: Erlbaum.

Rutter, M. (1977). Individual differences. In M. Rutter and L. Hersov, L. (Eds.), *Child psychiatry: modern approaches* (pp. 3–31). Oxford: Blackwell Scientific.

Sroufe, L. A., Fox, N. E., & Pancake, V. R. (1983). Attachment and dependency in developmental perspective. *Child Development, 54*, 1615–1627.

Teerikangas, O. M., Aronen, E. T., Martin, R. P., & Huttunen, M. O. (1998). Effects of infant temperament and early intervention on the psychiatric symptoms of adolescents. *Journal of the American Academy of Child and Adolescent Psychiatry, 37*(10), 1070–1076.

Thelen, E. (1989). Self-organization in developmental processes: Can systems approaches work? In M. Gunnar (Ed.), *The Minnesota symposium in child psychology*, Vol. 22: *Systems in development* (pp. 77–117). Hillsdale, NJ, Erlbaum.

Tronick, E. Z. (1989). Emotions and emotional communication in infants. *American Psychologist, 44*(2), 112–119.

Tschann, J. M., Kaiser, P., Chesney, M. A., Aldon, A., & Boyce, W. T. (1996). Resilience and vulnerability among preschool children: family functioning, temperament, and behavior problems. *Journal of the American Academy of Child and Adolescent Psychiatry, 35*(2), 184–192.

Walker, E., & Emory, E. (1983). Infants at risk for psychopathology: Offspring of schizophrenic parents. *Child Development, 54*, 1269–1285.

Weissbluth, M. (1989). Sleep-loss stress and temperamental difficultness: Psychobiological processes and practical considerations. In G. A. Kohnstamm, J. E. Bates, and M. K. Rothbart (Eds.), *Temperament in childhood* (pp. 357–376). New York: Wiley.

Zero to Three (1994). *Diagnostic classification of mental health and developmental disorders of infancy and early childhood*. Arlington, VA: National Center for Clinical Infant Programs.

Assessment of Regulatory
Problems in Children

It is important to accurately assess infants with regulatory problems during infancy because problems early in life related to poor self-regulation may result in later perceptual, language, sensory integration, and emotional problems in the preschool and school-aged years (DeGangi *et al.*, 1993, DeGangi *et al.*, in press). Problems in early regulatory functions are often reported as concerns by parents to pediatricians, educators, and health professionals, but these may be dismissed by professionals until more serious and long-term difficulties become apparent. In the past, assessment of constitutionally based traits related to poor self-regulation in infants and young children has included the exclusive use of temperament scales. Typically, temperament scales focus on characteristics such as fussiness, adaptability, persistence, predictability, sociability, impulsivity, and dependency (Bates, 1984; Windle & Lerner, 1986). What is often missing from temperament scales are clinical observations of functional behaviors that place the child at risk for behavioral, developmental, or learning difficulties. Specifically, questions related to the areas of self-regulation (e.g., self-calming), attention, modulation of sleep–wake states, feeding, responses to sensory stimulation, auditory processing and communication, and emotion regulation and attachment are often overlooked in temperament scales.

Since these behaviors are not tapped by traditional developmental tests, a child with deficits in these areas may not be identified until more serious problems develop in later years. An increase in the number of children with long-term developmental difficulties places a financial burden on educational systems; undiagnosed difficulties increase the stress on the developing child, and on his family, yet may be preventable or ameliorated with early intervention in many cases. Therefore, an expanded model of evaluation is needed that assesses the symptoms typical of regulatory disorders including self-regulation, sensory processing, attention, and emotion regulation. This chapter describes the assessment process and provides details about useful assessments for infants with such problems.

ASSESSMENT STRATEGIES FOR THE REGULATORY-DISORDERED INFANT

A comprehensive assessment model for evaluating the infant with regulatory disorders is needed that (1) evaluates the child's performance in sensorimotor, regulatory, and attentional processes that affect functional learning and behaviors; (2) incorporates behavioral observations of parents about how the infant's behaviors affect the way in which he or she functions within the family and home environment; and (3) examines parent characteristics (e.g., parental stress, interactional styles) and the parents' availability to be involved in the assessment and treatment process (DeGangi, 1991). The assessment process begins with a comprehensive intake interview with the caregivers, followed by systematic observation of the infant. The intake interview and the assessment tools that are used are described in detail in this chapter.

Professionals skilled in making qualitative assessments in the areas of attention, interaction skills, and sensory processing should be involved in the assessment process (e.g., occupational therapists, clinical psychologists, developmental specialists, and infant mental health specialists). Differential diagnosis should include an assessment of "goodness of fit" between parent and child in addition to the contribution of parent and child traits to the presenting problem. For example, if a child displays substantial difficulties during the assessment yet the parent has no concerns, further exploration of such parental characteristics as maternal depression, anxiety, inexperience, or denial should be made. Or a child may display subtle difficulties during an assessment, but no problems are reported by the parents. In this latter case, the child may have shown developmental irregularities simply because of not feeling well, but the symptoms observed may indicate the need for repeated follow-up in a few months to assure that the symptoms do not reflect an ongoing developmental or behavioral problem not recognized by the parent.

Findings from the assessments of sensory processing, attention, and play should be interpreted in conjunction with information derived from the Infant–Toddler Symptom Checklist described in this chapter. Comprehensive developmental motor, cognitive, neuromotor, and language assessments should be conducted as well in order to make accurate decisions regarding the infant's needs. The collection of data obtained from observing the infant during structured and nonstructured situations provides valuable information about the infant's overall functioning across situations.

The Intake Interview

The diagnostic process is initiated by a comprehensive intake interview conducted by a mental health professional to evaluate parental concerns and parental perception of the child. The interview is useful in determining the presence of primary or secondary parental emotional problems, marital conflicts, or other contributing factors that may affect the parent–child dyad. In some situations, an initial interview may not be the best way to begin the assessment process. For example, in working with families experiencing multiple social and environmental stresses, who experience mental illness, or who mistrust professionals, it is best to develop a trusting relationship first before exploring more intimate details of their daily life and family background. As the family becomes comfortable divulging information, professionals on the team may be able to learn about the child and family.

Listed below are some questions that might be asked in the interview. These were compiled based on questions that seemed especially useful with regulatory-disordered infants. They are meant only as a guide for interviewing. Questions should be asked in a sensitive way to elicit the parent's concerns, child and family strengths, and needs. Questions should be reworded depending on the child's problems, the family's cultural orientation, and how responsive the parent is to being interviewed. A good interviewer follows a parent's emotional cues and explores the meaning of the child to the parent. Because of the sensitive nature of the information imparted in the interview, it is a vehicle for building therapeutic alliance. It is recommended that the case manager or person most likely to be the primary intervenor conduct the interview.

A. *Referral*

    1. Tell me what brought you here (or why you were referred).

    2. Who referred you?

B. *Chief Complaint*

    3. When did you first notice the problem? When did it start?

    4. Has the problem changed since it first started? In what way has it changed?

    5. What was the problem like at its worst? What was it like for you at that time? (In addition to finding out how bad the infant's behaviors might have gotten, it is important to empathize with the parents' experience of the problem. Issues around parental depression and child abuse might come up with this question.)

    6. What have you tried that has worked? What hasn't worked? (This question is useful in understanding how adaptable the parents are responding to the infant's problems as well as how responsive the infant has been to interventions.)

C. *Current Functioning*

    7. Tell me about your child. What does he like to do when he is with you? What does he like to play with? (How the child spends his time provides useful information about how the child organizes himself.)

    8. What do you enjoy about your child? What do you like doing with him or her?

    9. Tell me about a typical day. Let's start with when you get up in the morning. (Elicit specific information about what the child eats, when he eats and where, a typical day's activities, nap and sleep schedules, where the child sleeps, how the child entertains himself when alone or with other children, etc. As part of this question, you are interested in finding out how structured the day is, and what kinds of activities occur throughout the day.)

10. Is your child different when you take him/her places—a friend's house, school, the shopping mall, etc.? How? (Some children become overstimulated outside the home, while other regulatory-disordered children are "home devils and street angels.")

D. *Developmental and Pregnancy History*

11. I'd like to know about how your pregnancy went. How did you feel (e.g., feelings of well-being, health, anxiety)? Did you experience anything that was stressful to you (e.g., move to new house, loss of loved one)?

12. Was this a planned or unplanned pregnancy? (If planned, determine if there are issues around infertility.)

13. What prenatal care did you receive?

14. What were labor and delivery like?

15. What was your baby like when he/she was first born? (These first impressions about the baby are important, such as, "He was wide-eyed, hyperalert, cried constantly.")

16. What was your reaction to your baby when he/she was first born?

17. Many mothers experience "baby blues." How about you? How bad did it get? (This question can be followed further to rule out postpartum depression.)

18. Inquire about developmental milestones appropriate for child's problem and age (e.g., sitting, walking, first words, first smile, use of gestures).

19. Did you nurse your baby? Tell me about his/her eating and growth. If feeding is a problem, ask the following:
    a. What would you like mealtime to be like?
    b. Did you or any other family members have problems with appetite, eating, or weight?
    c. How does it make you feel when your child doesn't eat?
    d. What have you tried to help your child eat? (Ask about force feeding, frequent meals, feeding in places other than high chair or in parent's arms.)

20. Most children test limits. How do you handle discipline? Tell me about a typical instance when your child misbehaves. How do you handle this? Do you and your spouse discipline your child the same way? How is your way of setting limits the same or different from how your parents set limits with you?

E. *Health History of Child*

21. Has your child been healthy? Are there any allergies?

22. Any ear infections? How often?

23. Has your child had a problem with spitting up, regurgitating or reflux?

24. What does your child eat during the day?

25. How often do you visit your pediatrician?

26. Is your child up to date on immunizations?

F. *Diagnosis*

27. Has a doctor ever given your child a diagnosis?

28. What do you think caused the problem?

29. Who does your child remind you of?

30. Is there anyone in the family who had problems like your child's?

31. What do you think will help with your child's problems?

G. *Family History*

These next questions have more to do with your family.

32. Who lives with you in your house?

33. Do you have family, friends, or other resources that you can depend on if your family has a crisis? Who lives nearby to help you?

(Ask both mother and father these next questions.)

34. Tell me about where you grew up. Where do you fall in your family (birth order)? How many brothers, sisters?

35. What was your childhood like (e.g., happy, difficult times)? Were there any particular stresses or losses that you experienced growing up?

36. How long have you and your spouse been married? When did you first begin or plan to have children?

37. What does your family enjoy doing together?

38. Are there any particular stresses in your family right now that I should be aware of (e.g., loss of job, separations)?

H. *Parental Expectations for Child*

39. Did you have any fantasies or expectations about your child before he or she was born?

40. Did you have experience with children before parenting this child?

41. What do you think your child will be like 5 or 10 years from now?

42. For whom did you name your child?

43. Whom does your child look like?

44. Does his/her personality remind you of anyone? How is he similar to/different from siblings?

I. *Final History*

There are some questions that I need to ask of everyone. These are only to help me understand more about you and your child.

45. How much coffee or caffeine did you drink per day during the pregnancy? What prescription drugs did you take? What about nonprescription drugs? (Here you may ask about specific drugs such as crack cocaine, heroin, marijuana.) How much alcohol did you drink each day/week?

46. Did you or your spouse experience any physical abuse growing up? Sexual abuse?

47. Did anyone in your family have school-related problems? Emotional or behavioral problems? Anyone with depression? Anyone commit or attempt suicide? Any other medical/genetic problems?

THE HOME VISIT

Many early intervention programs provide services within the home in order to more effectively serve families. In clinic-based models, a home visit should be conducted by a home health specialist, nurse, or other member of the assessment team to observe characteristics of the home environment. Resources available to the family, lifestyles, or cultural values that may impact the family's management of their difficult child should be determined. The child's behaviors as well as parent–child interactions are observed in the familiar setting of the home. The *Home Observation for Measurement of the Environment* (HOME) (Caldwell & Bradley, 1978) is a very useful scale developed for infants that provides an objective measure of the home environment and measures such things as the mother's responsiveness to her infant, her organization of the home environment, and appropriateness of play materials. A preschool version for 3 to 6 year olds is also available (Bradley *et al.*, 1977). Using the HOME and other interview techniques (Hirshberg, 1993), parental concerns can be ascertained. Parents often feel free to discuss personal issues that may impact their relationship to the child in the security of their home.

CLINICAL ASSESSMENT OF THE CHILD

A comprehensive diagnostic assessment is conducted to evaluate constitutional factors that may be contributing to the child's regulatory difficulties. Specific instruments are used to provide five different types of information related to the development of infants, toddlers, and young children with regulatory difficulties: (1) self-regulation and sensory processing and reactivity, (2) child temperament and behavior, (3) sustained attention, (4) parent–child interactions, and (5) developmental cognitive and communication skills. There are many parent report measures and instruments for direct clinical observation. Several parent questionnaires are administered to ascertain the parents' perspective of their child's problem. The reliability and validity of parent report measures have been criticized over the years because they often reflect maternal rather than child characteristics. However, parent report measures are extremely valuable because they tap the areas that most concern parents and the parents' perception of their child. Parents can also provide valuable information about their child's day-to-day behaviors. By combining parent report measures with reliable and valid observational techniques, one may gain a better understanding of the parent and child. Some of the most relevant tools used to assess the following five areas will be commented on in this chapter. The scales included in this chapter are include the following:

A. *Self-Regulation and Sensory Processing and Reactivity*
   1. *Parent report measures*
       a. The Infant–Toddler Symptom Checklist (7–30 months) (De-Gangi *et al.*, 1995) (see Appendix A).
       b. The Sensorimotor History Questionnaire for Preschoolers (3–4 years) (see Appendix C).
       c. Parent interview about typical behaviors (Clinical Observations in Tables 2.1–2.3).
   2. *Instruments for direct clinical observation of the child*
       a. Test of Sensory Functions in Infants (TSFI) (4–18 months) (De-Gangi & Greenspan, 1989).
       b. DeGangi–Berk Test of Sensory Integration (3 to 5 years) (Berk & DeGangi, 1983).
       c. The Sensory Integration and Praxis Tests (4–8 years) (Ayres, 1989).
       d. Clinical observations of sensory processing in Tables 2.1–2.3.
B. *Child Temperament and Behavior*
   1. Parent report measures:
       a. Parenting Stress Index (Abidin, 1986).
       b. The Infant/Child Characteristics Questionnaire (ICQ) (Bates, 1984).
       c. Child Behavior Checklist (2 to 5 years) (Achenbach, 1989).

C. *Sustained Attention*

   1. *Parent report measures*

      a. Parent interview about clinical observations of attention (Table 2.4).

      b. Infant–Toddler Symptom Checklist (attentional domain).

      c. Conners' Rating Scales Revised (3–17 years) (Conners, 1997).

   2. *Instruments for direct clinical observation of the child*

      a. Fagan Test of Infant Intelligence (3–7 months) (Fagan & Detterman, 1992).

      b. Test of Attention for Infants (TAI) (7–30 months) (DeGangi, 1995).

      c. Bayley Scales of Infant Development, Infant Behavior Record (IBR) (birth through 4 years) (qualitative observations) (Bayley, 1995).

D. *Parent–Child Interactions*

   1. *Parent report measures*

      a. Infant–Toddler Symptom Checklist (emotional domain).

E. *Instruments for Direct Clinical Observation*

   1. Nursing Child Assessment Satellite Training (NCAST) Teaching and Feeding Scales (Barnard, 1979).

   2. Parent–Child Early Relational Assessment (Clark, 1985).

   3. Functional Emotional Assessment Scale (7 months to 4 years) (Greenspan & DeGangi, in press).

   4. Transdisciplinary Play-Based Assessment (6 months to 6 years) (Linder, 1990).

F. *Developmental Cognitive and Communication Skills*

   1. Bayley Scales of Infant Development, Mental Scale (Bayley, 1995).

The next section provides details on these different instrument.

SELF-REGULATION AND SENSORY PROCESSING AND REACTIVITY

Parent Report Measures

1. The parents' presenting concerns are assessed through the use of a comprehensive symptom checklist, the Infant–Toddler Symptom Checklist (DeGangi *et al.*, 1995). This checklist for infants from 7 through 30 months contains questions related to sleep, self-calming, feeding, sensory responses (e.g.,

touch, movement), communication and language, and emotional responses. The checklist is structured in such a way that it is possible to determine, beyond sensory processing problems, the extent of the child's regulatory problem and how different behavioral patterns occur over the course of development.

There are six versions of the checklist, one for each age range (7–9, 10–12, 13–18, 19–24, and 25–30 months) and a short version for general screening purposes. The checklists were derived from a set of 58 items from which each age-specific version of the checklist was derived. The complete checklist appears in Appendix A and has been modified for use with children from birth to 30 months of age. The age-specific versions and short version can be obtained from Therapy Skill Builders (Tucson, Arizona). The checklist may be self-administered or used in the context of an interview, particularly for parents who may be unable to complete a questionnaire without assistance because of illiteracy or cultural differences. The areas tapped by the checklist include the following:

a. Self-Regulation: fussy–difficult behaviors, including crying and tantrumming, poor self-calming, inability to delay gratification, difficulties with transitions between activities, and need for other regulation (e.g., constant adult supervision).

b. Attention: distractibility, difficulty initiating and shifting attention.

c. Sleep: difficulty staying and falling asleep.

d. Eating or feeding: gagging or vomiting that may be related to reflux or other oral–motor problems, food preferences, and behavioral problems during feeding.

e. Dressing, bathing, touch: tactile hypersensitivities related to dressing and bathing, aversion to exploring through the sense of touch, and intolerance to being confined (e.g., in a car seat).

f. Movement: high activity level and craving for movement, motor planning and balance problems, and insecurity in movement in space.

g. Listening, language and sound: hypersensitivities to sound, auditory distractibility, auditory processing problems, and expressive and receptive language problems.

h. Looking and sight: sensitivities to light, and visual distractibility.

i. Attachment/emotional functioning: gaze aversion, mood deregulation, flat affect, immaturity in play and interactions, separation problems, difficulty accepting limits, and other behavioral problems.

All of the questions can be answered with a "yes, most times," "past," or "never or sometimes." In order to make clinical judgments regarding a child's functioning on each domain and overall regulatory functioning, 0 points are assigned to "never or sometimes," 2 points to "yes, most times," and 1 to "past." Item 1-i is the only item scored differently (e.g., 0 points are assigned to 15-30 minutes; 1 point to 1–2 hours/day, and 2 points for 3 hours plus/day). The points are tallied for the total checklist. In order to determine if a child is at risk for a regulatory disorder, the total checklist score is compared to the cutoff score derived for each version of the checklist (e.g., each age range). A score falling at or above the cutoff score is considered at risk.

A criterion-group validation model was used to investigate the validity of the Symptom List. Optimal cutting scores were located to determine the best points of group discrimination for each category (Berk, 1976). Infants scoring at or above a cutoff score in any category are considered "at risk" and should be referred for further testing. False-normal and false-delayed error rates were calculated in the decision validity study. The cutting scores for each subtest were chosen to minimize the false-normal error rate, judged to be the more serious of the two types of error from the perspective of screening and diagnostic decision making. The false-delayed and false-normal error rates were very low, ranging from 0 to 14% for the various age ranges. In addition, it was found that 78% of infants initially identified as having problems with the Symptom Checklist were diagnosed as having developmental or behavioral problems at 3 years using standardized measures such as the Child Behavior Checklist (Achenbach, 1989), thus showing good predictive validity.

Instruments for Direct Clinical Observation of the Child

1. The *Test of Sensory Functions in Infants* (TSFI) (DeGangi and Greenspan, 1989) is a 24-item test developed to measure sensory processing and reactivity in infants from 4 to 18 months of age. It was designed specifically to be administered by occupational and physical therapists, pediatric psychologists, and infant educators with training and background in interpretation of test results in the domain of sensory integration. Other early intervention professionals may administer the TSFI, but they should consult with a therapist skilled in sensory integration when interpreting findings. The TSFI focuses on evaluation of the following:

   a. Responses to tactile deep-pressure. Deep touch is applied using a firm stroking pattern to the forearms and hands, soles of feet, abdomen, and around the lips. Cuddling at the shoulder is observed as well. Responses are coded for adverse reaction to touch (e.g., crying or total inability to tolerate contact), mildly defensive reaction (e.g., partial pulling away from contact), and normal toleration of touch (e.g., accepts contact and may express pleasure).

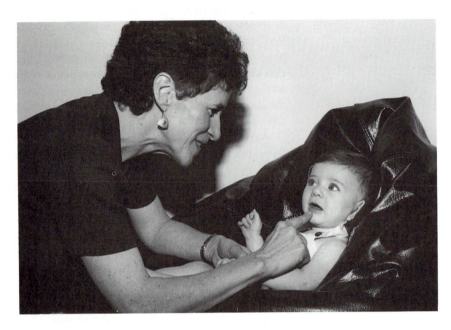

Infant's response to tactile deep pressure around mouth.

Infant demonstrating organized motor and tactile response on items from adaptive–motor and visual–tactile integration subtests.

b. Visual–tactile integration is examined by the infant's ability to visually recognize and tolerate contact from a tactile stimulus applied to parts of the body (e.g., masking tape on back of hand). These items are coded for defensive reactions, hyporeactive responses (e.g., fails to notice stimulus on body part), or normal responses to touch.

c. Adaptive motor skills are observed during administration of the visual–tactile integration items. Responses are observed in the infant's ability to plan and act on the toy or object in an organized way. Responses are coded for no motor response, disorganized response (e.g., arms flail and unable to react directly to object), partial response (e.g., partially removes object), and fully organized response (e.g., successfully removes object).

d. Ocular motor control is measured by two items: (1) the ability to laterally direct the eyes to a bright red yarn ball moving in the periphery toward the central visual field, and (2) the ability to smoothly track a visual target (e.g., finger puppet) in all planes.

e. Reactivity to vestibular stimulation is measured by the infant's toleration of bodily movement in space in different planes (e.g., vertical, circular spin, and inverted). Responses are coded for adverse reactions (e.g., crying or severe fear expressed), mildly defensive (e.g., mildly fearful expression on face), and normal toleration of movement (e.g., expresses pleasure or neutral response).

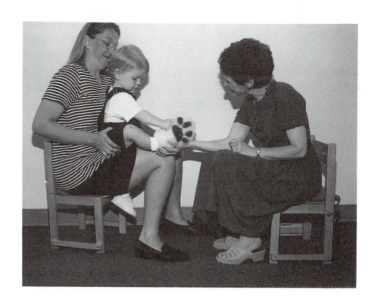

Infant demonstrating organized motor and tactile response on items from adaptive–motor and visual–tactile integration subtests.

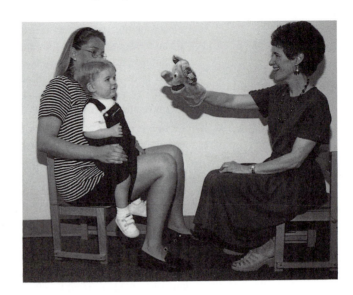

Infant demonstrating
visual tracking on
ocular–motor subtest
item.

The test can be administered in less than 20 minutes. Subtest and total test scores are interpreted for each of the age ranges tested. The instrument has been validated on a sample of 288 normals, 27 developmentally delayed, and 27 difficult temperament infants from 4 to 18 months of age. Psychometric studies of the instrument reveal that: (1) the items and subtests validly measure the domain of sensory functioning in infants, (2) the total test scores can be used reliably and validly for screening decisions, particularly for 7- to 18-month-old infants, and (3) the five subtests can be used reliably and validly for guiding clinical decisions for infants with delays or difficult temperament at 10 to 18 months of age (DeGangi *et al.*, 1988). Interobserver reliability ranged from .88 to .99 for the subtests, and the total test and test–retest reliability was .81. In addition, decision consistency reliability ranged from 81 to 96% for total test scores. Western Psychological Services (12031 Wilshire Boulevard, Los Angeles, California 90025) publishes the test.

2. The Sensorimotor History Questionnaire for Preschoolers (SHQP) (DeGangi & Balzer-Martin, 1999) may be used as a prescreening tool for 3- and 4-year-old children at risk for problems with sensory integration and self-regulation. The SHQP appears in Appendix C. It is a 51-item questionnaire that includes five subscales that prescreen for problems in self-regulation (e.g., attention and activity level), sensory processing of touch and movement, motor planning, and emotional maturity, and behavioral control. In addition, some clinical observations of attention, social interaction, and sensory reac-

tivity accompany the Miller Assessment for Preschoolers (Miller, 1982), although these have not been standardized. The Touch Inventory for Preschoolers (TIP) (Royeen, 1987) measures tactile defensiveness. It is a rating scale with 46 questions to be completed by the parents. The questionnaire has been validated on a sample of preschoolers and is useful in identifying children who have sensitivities to touch.

3. The *DeGangi–Berk Test of Sensory Integration* (Berk & DeGangi, 1983) may be used to test children for sensory integrative dysfunction once they reach the preschool years. This criterion-referenced test was designed either to measure overall sensory integration in 3- to 5-year-old children with delays in sensory, motor, and perceptual skills or to evaluate children suspected of being at risk for learning problems. Its focus is primarily on the vestibular-based functions and includes subtests measuring postural control, bilateral motor integration, and reflex integration. The TSI should be administered in conjunction with measures of functional motor performance such as the Peabody Developmental Motor Scales.

4. Once children reach the age of 5, more definitive testing of sensory integrative functions can be conducted. *The Sensory Integration and Praxis Tests* (Ayres, 1989) were designed to identify sensory integrative disorders involving form and space perception, praxis, vestibular-bilateral integration, and tactile discrimination. The tests are intended primarily for 4 to 8 year olds with learning disabilities. They are particularly useful in delineating areas of treatment for children with sensory integrative disorders (Fisher *et al.*, 1991).

5. In addition to administering the tests mentioned above, clinical observations of sensory processing may be made by using the listings in Tables 2.1–2.3. These may be directly observed, or the parent may be interviewed about typical behaviors. Observations of how the child plays with tactile materials and on moving equipment (e.g., slides, swings) are useful in drawing conclusions about the child's sensory processing abilities.

CHILD TEMPERAMENT: PARENT REPORT MEASURES

1. The *Parenting Stress Scale* (Abidin, 1986) is useful as a measure of child characteristics (e.g., adaptability and demandingness) and dimensions of parent stress (e.g., depression and sense of competence). It is a well-standardized assessment that measures both child characteristics and the dimensions of parent stress. The 47 items within the Child Domain measure adaptability, acceptability, demandingness, mood, distractibility/hyperactivity, and reinforcement to parents. The 54 items in the Parent Domain measure depression, attachment, restrictions of role, sense of competence, social isolation, relationship with spouse, and parent health. The instrument is self-administered by the parent and can be completed within 10 to 15 minutes. For parents who are unable to read, the scale may be completed with an examiner. The PSI

TABLE 2.1 Clinical Observations of Somatosensory Dysfunction

Tactile hypersensitivities:

1. Dislikes being touched or cuddled by others; pulls away from being held, arches, grimaces, or cries or whines
2. Distressed when people are near, even when they are not touching (e.g., standing nearby, sitting in a circle)
3. Avoids touching certain textures; hates getting hands messy (e.g., fingerpaints, paste, sand)
4. Likes firm touch best (e.g., seeks firm hugs from others)
5. Prefers touch from familiar people
6. Dislikes having face or hair washed; especially dislikes having a haircut
7. Prefers long sleeves and pants even in warm weather, or prefers as little clothing as possible, even when it's cool
8. Touches everything in sight
9. Bumps hard into other people or objects
10. Withdraws from being near others, particularly groups
11. May hit, kick, or bite others and is aggressive in play
12. Has a strong preference for certain food textures (e.g., only firm and crunchy, or only soft)
13. Dislikes being dressed or undressed
14. Resists being placed in certain positions (e.g., stomach, back)

Tactile hyposensitivities:

1. Seems unaware of touch unless it is very intense
2. Does not react to pain (e.g., shots, scrapes)
3. Bites or hits self
4. Likes to hang by arms or feet off of furniture or people
5. Unaware of messiness around mouth or nose

Poor tactile discrimination (for children over 2 years)

1. Difficulty with fine motor tasks (e.g., holding pencil, buttoning)
2. Always looks at hands when they are manipulating objects
3. Uses mouth to explore objects

Manual reported reliabilities ranging from .62 to .70 for the Child Domain and from .55 to .80 for the Parent Domain. The reliability for the Total Stress Score is .95. Test–retest reliability over 3-week and 3-month intervals was also quite high. The PSI is available through Pediatric Psychology Press, 320 Terrell Road West, Charlottesville, Virginia 22901.

2. In addition, measures of temperamental characteristics provided useful information regarding the child's difficultness, adaptability, demandingness, and other traits that impact the parent's response to the child as well as the child's capacity to respond to therapeutic intervention. Child temperament can be assessed using the PSI, although one may wish to use a child temperament

TABLE **2.2** Clinical Observations of Vestibular Dysfunction

Vestibular hypersensitivities:

1. Easily overwhelmed by movement (e.g., car sick)
2. Strong fear of falling and of heights
3. Does not enjoy playground equipment and avoids roughhousing play
4. Is anxious when feet leave ground
5. Dislikes having head upside down
6. Slow in movements such as getting onto therapy bench, or walking on an uneven surface
7. Slow in learning to walk up or down stairs and relies on railing longer than other children same age (for children with mild motor delays)

Underresponsiveness to movement:

1. Craves movement and does not feel dizziness when other children do
2. Likes to climb to high, precarious places
3. No sense of limits or controls
4. Is in constant movement, rocking, running about

scale such as the *Infant/Child Characteristics Questionnaire* (ICQ) (Bates, 1984). The questionnaires are reliable and easy to administer, and they provide a good indicator of difficult temperament. The ICQ consists of 24 items, answered on a 7-point scale. As an example, the four dimensions that the 6-month questionnaire assesses are fussy/difficult, unadaptable, dull, and unpredictable.

3. Once the child turns 2 years of age, the *Child Behavior Checklist* (Achenbach, 1989) may be used to assess behaviors. It may either be administered by an interviewer or self-administered. Separate interview forms are available for 2 to 3, and 4 to 5 year olds. Using clinical cutoff points, problems in the areas of social withdrawal, depression, sleep problems, somatic problems, aggression, and destructiveness may be ascertained. The Child Behavior Checklist is available by writing to Thomas M. Achenbach, University of Vermont, Department of Psychiatry, 1 South Prospect Street, Burlington, Vermont 05401.

4. The revised Conners' Rating Scales (Conners, 1997) is a comprehensive set of scales for parents, teachers, or self-report that can be used to measure psychopathology and problem behaviors in children and adolescents from ages 3 to 17 years. It has both long and short versions of each scale and can be used to assess attention-deficit/hyperactivity disorder as well as other behavioral problems. Of particular value is that the scales have separate scoring for males and females.

TABLE 2.3 Clinical Observations of Motor Control and Motor Planning Problems

Motor control:

1. Frequently breaks toys—cannot seem to judge how hard or soft to press when handling toys
2. Trips over obstacles or bumps into them
3. Falls frequently (after 18 months)
4. Slumped body posture when sitting or standing
5. Leans head on hand or arm
6. Prefers to lie down than sit, or to sit rather than stand
7. Has a loose grip on objects such as a pencil, scissors, or spoon, or grip is too tight on objects
8. Fatigues easily during physical activities
9. Is loose jointed and floppy; may sit with legs in a W
10. Has difficulty manipulating small objects, particularly fasteners
11. Eats in a sloppy manner

Motor planning:

1. Fear of trying new motor activities; likes things to be the same and predictable (e.g., routines)
2. Difficulty making transitions from one activity to next
3. Must be prepared in advance several times before change is introduced
4. Cannot plan sequences in activities, needing structure from an adult
5. Easily frustrated
6. Is very controlling of activities
7. Difficulty playing with peers
8. Aggressive or destructive in play
9. Temper tantrum easily
10. Did not crawl before starting to walk
11. Difficulty with dressing

SUSTAINED ATTENTION

Identification of attentional problems in infants and toddlers is difficult because tests of cognitive functioning in the first 2 years of life have been found to have little predictive value for later performance on intelligence tests in the school years for normal children (Bornstein & Sigman, 1986). It is often difficult to identify infants considered to be at high risk for later cognitive delays using current cognitive development scales (Ross, 1989), although infants with moderate to profound mental retardation can be successfully diagnosed in the first 2 years of life (Ross *et al.*, 1985; Siegel, 1981). Part of the problem lies in the limits of the cognitive assessment tools themselves (i.e., in what they are actually testing). Current standardized instruments that measure intelligence do not reflect a continuum of the same skills at different ages and instead tap a variety of behaviors (e.g., perceptual, language, fine motor). Fagan (1982) and Siegel (1981) have suggested that evaluations of intelligence should focus on behaviors such as discriminating different stimuli, categorizing, and retaining new information—which are processes common to both infants and older children.

Infants who are likely to develop later perceptual and learning difficulties by the preschool years are those with reported regulatory disorders during infancy, including problems in several of the following areas: behavioral disorganization, short attention span, sensory hypersensitivities, sleep and feeding disturbances, and hyperarousal (DeGangi *et al.*, 1993). These infants present a unique challenge to the clinician because they typically score well within the normal range on motor and cognitive developmental tests during infancy, yet, if left untreated, they are apt to develop attentional, behavioral, and developmental deficits by age 4 years. In addition to infants with regulatory disorders, infants who have suffered substance exposure *in utero* are at risk for attentional problems (Neisworth *et al.*, 1995) and should receive neurobehavioral assessment to appraise the type and extent of their atypical behavior.

With early identification, it may be possible to prevent serious long-term learning and cognitive delays. By assessing attentional processes in infants, special educators, psychologists, and occupational and physical therapists can design intervention programs that focus on the processes that underlie acquisition of developmental milestones. We now describe two instruments that measure attentional processes.

Parent Report Measures

In addition to clinical observations listed in Table 2.4 and items from the Infant–Toddler Symptom Checklist related to attention, the *Conners' Rating Scales—Revised* (CRS-R) (Conners, 1997) is useful in measuring ADHD in children from ages 3 through 17 years. Based on a large normative database, the CRS-R includes multidimensional scales that assess ADHD and comorbid disorders. It includes both teacher and parent report forms and long and short versions of the scale.

Instruments for Direct Clinical Observation of the Child

1. For young infants, there is a standardized instrument available to assess attentional abilities: the *Fagan Test of Infant Intelligence* (Fagan, 1982; Fagan *et al.*, Singer, Montie, & Shepherd, 1986; Fagan & Detterman, 1992). This test measures visual recognition memory in 3 to 7 month olds. It assesses the infant's ability to differentially attend to novel versus familiar stimuli in visual recognition tasks. The infant is presented with a novelty problem composed

TABLE 2.4 Clinical Observations of Attention

1. Vulnerable to distractions (e.g., sights or sounds), distracted at least three times during testing by environmental stimuli
2. High activity level, constantly running about and unable to sit still for an activity; attempts to leave table three or more times during testing; may stand up for parts of table top testing; may need several breaks from the testing
3. Plays only briefly with toy before wanting a new activity
4. Impulsive in handling materials, needing three or more reminders to wait before touching
5. Tunes out from activity, difficult to reengage; processing of directions is slow; urging needed to respond
6. Can't shift focus easily from one object or another after playing for long period of time
7. Gives up easily; is frustrated and needs urging to persist
8. Prefers only easy tasks
9. Wanders aimlessly without focused exploration
10. Depends on an adult to focus attention during play activities
11. Becomes excited when confronted with crowded, bustling settings such as a crowded supermarket or restaurant

of two pictures. The infant is first exposed to a stimulus, such as a picture of a woman's face, for a set period of time. The tester sits behind an apparatus out of the infant's view and observes the infant's visual fixations through a peephole. The tester records on a computer the length of time that the baby fixates on one of two pictures. After the infant has studied the familiarization picture for the standard study time, the tester withdraws the picture and presents the previously seen picture with a novel one. The two pictures are presented to the infant simultaneously for the test time, which usually spans 3 to 5 seconds. The computer is programmed to calculate a "novelty score," which consists of the amount of fixation on the novel pictures divided by the total fixation time on both novel and familiar pictures.

Interobserver reliability was found to be .96 to .99. Longitudinal studies of infants' visual preferences have confirmed the relationship between visual recognition memory and later intelligence (Fagan, 1982; Fagan & McGrath, 1981; Rose & Wallace, 1985). The Fagan Test of Infant Development was also found to accurately identify 91% of 54 normal children at 3 years of age (Fagan *et al.*, 1986).

2. Another assessment tool that has been developed to measure attention in infants is the *Test of Attention for Infants* (TAI) (DeGangi, 1995). The TAI measures sustained attention, which is reflected by how long an infant engages in various cognitive behaviors (e.g., visual inspection, manipulation). The TAI provides an overall measure of sustained attention in infants aged 7 to 30 months. The TAI specifically measures the infant's ability to: (1) initiate and sustain attention during novel and moderately complex events; (2) persist and maintain interest in a given task over time; (3) self-initiate organized

adaptive motor, visual, and social responses while sustaining attention; and (4) shift attention between stimuli and focus attention when competing stimuli are present. The test's four subdomains (subtests)—visual attention, tactile attention, auditory attention, and multisensory attention—were selected because of the clinical importance of processing information from the various sensory channels.

There are five age-specific versions of the Test of Attention for Infants (TAI) that are designed for 7 to 9 month olds, 10- to 12 month olds, 13–18 month olds, 19–24 month olds, and 25–30 month olds. There are between 16 and 23 items on the test, depending on the age version used. Many of the test items require that the infant press a switch plate to activate a battery switch-operated

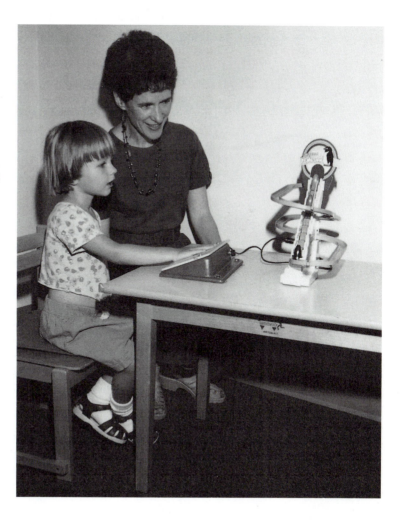

Child attending to visual attention task on the Test of Attention in Infants.

toy, thus minimizing motor responses that may confound test results should a motor delay be present. The subtests on the TAI include the following:

a. Visual–auditory attention in three tasks that measure interest in a simple light display, and two novel activities that involve movement of objects on a trajectory (e.g., penguin run and wildlife jump).

b. Tactile attention to two tactile–proprioceptive activities involving a vibrating doll and a vibrating pillow.

c. Auditory attention to a wind-up record player.

d. Multisensory attention to a five-feature busy box and a task with two competing stimuli, a drumming bear and a walking cow.

The test administration is videotaped and a range of behaviors are later coded. These behaviors include visual inspection, activation of the switch that denotes an understanding of causality, banging and fingering, social referencing, holding (doll and pillow items only), symbolic play (doll item only), and off-task attention. Observations of these various behaviors permit evaluation of complex attentional processes that occur while the infant is interested in a novel, moderately complex event. Total test administration time is less than 15 minutes. Scoring takes approximately 20 minutes.

In regard to construct validity, it was found that the total test score could be used for diagnosis with a false-normal error rate of 11.1 to 28.6% and a false-delayed error rate from 6.6 to 23.3%. Strong empirical support was evident for the four subdomains of sustained attention. Estimates of interobserver reliability were computed using three different observers and two independent samples of children. The generalizability coefficients for coded behaviors and total test scores were very reliable except for social referencing, which showed subjectivity. Interobserver reliability for subtest and total test scores ranged from .806 to .959. Decision-consistency reliability was high for all subtests and the total test, with the exception of the auditory attention subtest. A predictive validity study using the TAI and the McCarthy Scales of Children's Abilities (McCarthy, 1972) at 3 years showed that the TAI correlated with the perceptual motor subtests of the McCarthy as well as the general cognitive index. The TAI correctly predicted learning outcome in 61.5% of children tested (e.g., normal scores on the TAI predicted normal distribution of scores on the McCarthy); at-risk or deficit scores predicted potential learning disabilities (i.e., more than a 1- to 2-standard-deviation spread in scores on the McCarthy). Poor performance on the TAI also correlated with ratings of distractibility on the Parenting Stress Index (Abidin, 1986). Overall, this psychometric evidence, viewed in conjunction with the evidence previously gathered on the quality of the test, suggests that the total test scores can be used reliably and validly for diagnostic decisions.

3. In addition to the Fagan and the TAI, clinical observations of attention may be obtained through administration of the *Bayley Scales of Infant Development, Infant Behavior Record* (IBR) (Bayley, 1995). This descriptive rating scale of behaviors for children up through 4 years of age focuses on interpersonal and affective domains, motivational variables, and a child's interest in specific modes of sensory experience. Specifically, the IBR yields ratings in social orientation, cooperativeness, fearfulness, tension, general emotional tone, object orientation, goal directedness, attention span, endurance, activity, reactivity, sensory areas of interest displayed, energy and coordination for age, judgement of test, unusual or deviant behavior, and general evaluation of the child. The IBR provides a convenient form for recording qualitative observations and evaluations and concludes with a general evaluation of the child's overall performance. An examiner completes the IBR immediately after having administered the Mental and Motor Scales. It is completed by indicating the one statement that best describes the child's behavior. Additional space is provided for an examiner's comments, which can broaden the base on which to make clinical judgments about a child.

In addition to structured observations of attention, a checklist is provided in Table 2.4 that may be useful in making functional observations of attention in infants and young children.

PARENT–CHILD INTERACTIONS

The quality of the parent–child interaction and parent–child relationship is an important source of information about the child's functioning (Barnard & Kelly, 1980). Assessment of the child within the context of the parent–child relationship is important because it reflects how the infant responds to and copes with his or her primary relationship, that is, the caregiver (Stern, 1985). Research indicates that children with mothers who are socially responsive, who use elaborated and clear verbal teaching methods, and who encourage symbolic thinking tend to perform better on standardized measures of intelligence (Bornstein & Sigman, 1986). There is also evidence that infants and young children of parents who are depressed show delays in cognitive, language, and attentional skills as well as somber affect (Cogill, Caplan *et al.*, 1986; Lyons-Ruth *et al.*, 1986). Therefore, it is useful to combine a variety of measures in assessing emotional development, affect regulation, behavior, and play that engage both parent and child participation.

Any assessment of emotional development should include systematic play observations of parent–child interactions. Barnard (1979) has described some of the important components for adaptive interactions. These include the following: (a) social engagement, which includes child traits such as soothability, attention, and developmental competence, and parent traits such as ability to read and respond to the infant's signals; (b) contingency of responses, which is the capacity to respond to one another's signals appropriately; (c) richness of interactive content (e.g., range and content of play); and (d) adaptability of the dyad to change over time as both the parent and child mature.

1. The *Nursing Child Assessment Satellite Training* (NCAST) *Teaching and Feeding Scales*, developed by Barnard (1979), was based on these essential interactive capacities. Observations are made during feeding and during two developmentally taught tasks, one at the child's level, and the other slightly above the child's ability. Parent behaviors are scored for sensitivity to the child's cues, response to the child's distress, and fostering of cognitive and social–emotional growth. Child behaviors include clarity of cues and responsiveness to parents. The Teaching Scale of the NCAST has been found to be more strongly correlated with cognitive development than the Feeding Scale (Gross *et al.*, 1993).

2. The *Parent–Child Early Relational Assessment* (PCERA) (Clark, 1985) assesses the quality of parent–child relationships. It was developed with the primary purpose of evaluating parents and children in families at risk for, or who show, early relational disturbances. The infant or child is observed for 20 minutes in interaction with each parent during four 5-minute segments that include free play, a structured activity, feeding, and a separation–reunion period. Parents are rated on amount, duration, and intensity of positive and negative affective qualities such as sensitivity to infant's cues, visual regard of baby, structuring of the environment, tone of voice, intrusiveness, and inconsistency. The infant is rated for positive and negative affects and interactive behaviors, including such things as mood, attention, social initiative and responsiveness, and motor and communication skills. In addition, the dyad is rated on the quality of mutual involvement and joint attention to the task and amount of reciprocity and pleasure.

3. In addition, the *Functional Emotional Assessment Scale* (Greenspan & DeGangi, in press) is a scale that may be used to evaluate parent–child interaction patterns in children from 7 months through 4 years. A preliminary version of the FEAS appeared in a textbook by Greenspan (1992). The revised version of the instrument based on over 5 years of research by DeGangi appears in Appendix B. This scale is based on the assumption that stages of emotional

development can be observed through play interactions between the parent and child and that clinically relevant behaviors can be included within each stage. The FEAS focuses on the constitutional and maturational patterns of the child, the parent's capacity to sustain and support the child's interactions, and the dynamic interaction between parent and child. The caregiver is asked to play with the child as they might at home for 15 minutes. It is useful to ask the parent to play with his/her child in several different play situations to observe the child's varying play skills, interaction abilities, and the parent's capacity to facilitate the child's play skills. For this reason, it is suggested to observe the parent and child as they play with three different types of toys: symbolic toys, textured toys, and movement equipment. Symbolic play materials consist of age-appropriate toys such as a toy telephone, a large baby doll, bottle, toy cars, and plastic tableware with cups and plates. Textured toys that may be provided include plastic porcupine toys, textured balls, furry puppets, a paint brush, a heavy musical toy with balls on spokes, and a furry blanket. Movement play materials may include an inflatable bolster, a large plastic dome that tips side to side when the baby sits inside, and a rotating spinning board. Preschool children may be observed on equipment such as a trampoline, a suspended swing, or a scooter board.

The parent and child are observed playing with each set of toys for 5 minutes. These unstructured play observations may be videotaped. The infant and caregiver's behaviors are scored for six levels of emotional development including the following:

Child and mother playing with symbolic play toys during administration of the Functional Emotional Assessment Scale.

a. Regulation and interest in the world

b. Forming relationships (attachment)

c. Intentional two-way communication

d. Complex sense of self:

(1) Behavioral organization of sequential circles of communication

(2) Behavioral elaboration of feelings dealing with warmth, pleasure, assertion, exploration, protest, and anger

e. Emotional ideas: Representational capacity and elaboration of feelings and ideas that are expressed symbolically

f. Emotional thinking of complex intentions, wishes, and feelings in symbolic communication expressed through logically connected ideas

Aside from these six levels of emotional development, items on the FEAS

Child and mother playing with textured toys during administration of the Functional Emotional Assessment Scale.

measure the infant's or child's regulatory patterns and caregiver responsivity. The scale is intended for use with children with regulatory disorders, pervasive developmental disorders, emotional and behavioral problems such as oppositional behaviors or social withdrawal, and with children who have experienced physical or emotional abuse or neglect. Because each level of emotional development contains at least eight items, the scale also lends itself to measuring progress and developing treatment goals.

4. In addition to these scales, there is a play-based assessment, the *Transdisciplinary Play-Based Assessment* (Linder, 1990). It is a naturalistic, functional assessment of the child that is developmental in nature and is based on the observations of a transdisciplinary team consisting of parents and professionals alike. The assessment is designed to identify service needs, to develop intervention plans, and to evaluate progress in children who are functioning between 6 months and 6 years. Observation guidelines are presented in cognitive, social–emotional, communication and language, and sensorimotor development. These guidelines may be used to observe various play and interaction skills in addition to other areas of development. The assessment is available through Paul H. Brookes Publishing, Baltimore, Maryland.

CASE EXAMPLE OF ASSESSMENT PROCESS

The following case example involves of a 2-year-old child who had not been diagnosed yet but was showing features of pervasive developmental disorder. Children with PDD often show regulatory problems. However, during infancy the child with severe regulatory disorder may show features of PDD but, over time, seems to evolve out of these symptoms and develops warm attachments and relatedness. This example is of a child who, with adequate diagnosis and treatment, might be in the latter group. It depicts how one might evaluate a more difficult-to-test child using the various assessments described in this chapter.

Ethan was referred at age 2 years by a speech and language pathologist because of problems that he was having in the areas of social engagement, gestural communication, and attention.

Background History

Mr. and Mrs. M. attended the intake interview to discuss their presenting concerns and Ethan's background history. Ethan was born full term at 6 lb, 8 oz, with Apgars of 10. He had jaundice at birth, but since then has been healthy. The parents first noticed Ethan's problems after he turned 1 year of age. Although he crawled and walked on time, had good fine motor skills, and could babble, Ethan did not use words. He waved goodbye for a short while, but lost this skill. He did not point, but gestured when he wanted to be picked up and often led his parents to whatever he wanted. He put his parents' hands on objects that he wished to manipulate. Ethan seemed to understand many things that were said to him and could follow directions to Barney songs (e.g., marching along with music). He occasionally said "goodbye" when prompted by a computer program. Despite these receptive skills, Ethan didn't look at persons when he was called or spoken to. The only times that Ethan would look was when the person was very entertain-

An adequate support system is necessary to help a family cope with a difficult situation. More and more, parents are finding that they have no extended family in their geographic area and, as a result, have no one to help them or to provide a respite. Parent–baby groups have become an alternative support system for many families; however, many fussy babies cannot tolerate being in a play group situation, thus removing this option for the parent. Additionally, many parents take their children to baby gym or swim classes, although these activities are often too stimulating for the regulatory-disordered child. As a result, many parents feel even more isolated and removed from the typical activities in which parents engage with their children. Sometimes parents who try such options feel stigmatized by other parents because their child appears so out of control.

The experience of depression is often secondary to coping with the demands of parenting the fussy baby. Many mothers report feelings of inadequacy when normal parenting skills do not seem to work with their child. First-time parents often confuse their child's constitutional difficulties with parental inexperience, which exacerbates depression or feelings of helplessness. These feelings are compounded when the infant rejects being held and cuddled because of hypersensitivities to touch. Sometimes the parents learn to avoid sensorimotor activities that provoke their child's hypersensitive responses. For example, if the child dislikes swings and playground equipment because of extreme fearfulness of movement in space, a protective mother may guide her child away from movement activities. In some cases, the parents may experience similar hypersensitivities, which compounds their responses to their infant who shares these constitutional difficulties.

Below is a list of underlying assumptions that may be useful in thinking about how one works with families.

1. There is no one right way to work with families. There is more than one way to raise children and to stimulate a child's development. Remember that the range of normal is broad. There are also different styles of interacting. What works for one person may not for-another.

2. Understanding developmental tasks is important to the helping relationship. Helping caregivers understand their child's strengths and needs can be accomplished by emphasizing how their child is developing normally and what their child likes to do, while at the same time guiding them on what the next steps should be to help their child's development. It is also useful to explain to parents why certain intervention strategies are being used and how they relate to their child's developmental needs.

3. This parent and child belong together (except in instances of abuse or neglect). There is no better parent for this child and no better child for this parent, putting aside the challenges that parent and/or child may feel about one another. Some professionals may experience thoughts like, "If only this mother was different …," "If she did this instead, everything would be better,"

"If only I could take this child home for a weekend, I know I could …" As professionals, it is important to help the parent and child "be" together in emotionally healthy ways.

4. Recognize countertransference. It is very powerful. The feelings and reactions that are elicited in the therapist when working with a dyad often help in understanding the dynamics between parent and child. The countertransference may reflect feelings that the parent or child is projecting onto the other that in turn elicits a response in the therapist. Get support from a supervisor or your team in handling difficult feelings. The countertransference often provides important insights about the treatment process and what needs to happen next. We have all been helpless infants. Often we identify with the child in our work. Some of us are parents as well, which may help in empathizing with the parent's viewpoint.

5. This parent and child do have it within them to find the answers, but they need to discover what will work best for them. The relationship of parent and child is one of uncertainty and discovery. It is often hard for both parents and professionals to resist a "fix-it" model.

6. Respect the unconscious and defenses that might be there for the parent and child. Try to get in touch with the feelings that they have about themselves and each other. If an approach is not working, why not?

7. Strong feelings should be elicited in a therapist. This is important for empathy. The feelings may be very uncomfortable, such as feeling depleted, rejected, or angry. These feelings may be what the parent is experiencing.

In essence, a family-centered approach focuses on parental concerns, family stresses in coping with the difficult child, adaptive and maladaptive parent–child interaction patterns, and parental depression or marital conflicts that may be secondary to the child's constitutional difficulties. These issues may be addressed directly through parent guidance and the child-centered activity.

PARENT GUIDANCE

Structured developmental therapy approaches for infants with regulatory disorders involve a blend of behavioral management, supportive counseling, practical management techniques, sensorimotor activities, and developmental therapy to address specific constitutional problems (DeGangi *et al.*, 1991a). Parent guidance is an important component of the therapy process. It provides parents with emotional support in coping with their difficult child and is useful in developing effective strategies in setting limits, and management of their child's sleep, self-calming, and feeding problems. Although parent guidance is individualized, a variety of self-help books is often used to help parents manage specific problems such as sleep or dietary problems (Carey & McDevitt, 1995; Daws, 1989; Sears,

1985; Rapp, 1986; Turecki & Tonner, 1985). Although the relationship between food allergies and behaviors is controversial, the possibility of food allergies should be explored for those children who do not respond to behavioral management techniques. For example, it was recently reported that a significant number of infants who did not respond to behavioral techniques for sleeplessness did respond to a hypoallergenic diet that eliminated all milk products (Kahn *et al.*, 1989).

Sleep problems are addressed by a combination of methods, including developing appropriate sleep–wake routines (Ferber, 1984). Since sleep problems are often accompanied by separation anxiety, separation games are practiced (e.g., chase games, peek-a-boo). Techniques to console the irritable child include addressing the child's sensory hypersensitivities, developing the child's own capacity to self-calm, and reducing parental anxieties when crying occurs. Managing temper tantrums and helping the child accept limits focus not only on the child's difficulties in expressing frustration and negative affect but in helping parents develop a consistent plan in approaching the child's behaviors. Feeding problems focus on inhibiting tactile hypersensitivities of the face and mouth, expanding the child's repertoire of foods, and addressing behavioral feeding problems such as refusal to eat and food throwing. Attentional problems are addressed by structuring the environment, reducing the child's hyperarousal through sensory inhibition, and facilitating sustained attention by helping the child elaborate on his play. In addition, problems with communication and play are addressed through the structured intervention by explicitly teaching parents how to promote face-to-face engagement, reciprocal interactions, two-way communication, and gestural or vocal signaling. The chapters on sleep, feeding, irritability, and attention present more detail about the specific techniques that may be used to address these problems.

When therapy is initiated, the clinician seeks to help the parents understand their child's behaviors and how they as parents respond when the behaviors occur. The clinician discusses what techniques have already been tried by the parents in order to determine which ones may or may not have worked. Sometimes it becomes apparent that parental inexperience or mismanagement of behaviors exacerbates the child's regulatory difficulties, but when this appears to be the case it is important for the therapist to be supportive and nonjudgmental. It is also important to determine if discrepancies exist between the father and mother in managing their child's difficult behaviors.

Parent guidance takes the form of a working dialogue with the parent to develop the best match between the parent's concerns, the family lifestyle, and management techniques. Major emphasis is placed on developing problem-solving strategies from which the parents often develop insights about their child and themselves. For example, some parents may realize that they are overcontrolling and cannot tolerate their child's overly active and loud behaviors. It is important to help such parents understand what underlies their child's difficulties and develop strategies to help their child organize his behaviors before they become uncontrollable, yet at the same time provide opportunities for normal active exploration. Parent guidance blends the principles of behavioral management, supportive therapy, practical management techniques, brief psychodynamic therapy, family therapy principles, and sensory integrative treatment.

SENSORY INTEGRATIVE THERAPY APPROACH

To address the constitutional problems of the child, principles from sensory integrative therapy (Ayres, 1972, 1979; Fisher *et al.*, 1991) are used. Treatment techniques involve desensitizing hyperreactivities, organizing sustained attention, facilitating organized, purposeful activity, and promoting self-calming and modulation of arousal states through specific sensory inputs. The major principle underlying sensory integrative therapy is improvement of the child's ability to organize and process sensory input during self-directed, purposeful activities. The child's interest and motivation guide how the various sensory integrative tasks are provided. When tactile hypersensitivities are present, activities are used that involve firm deep pressure, proprioception (e.g., heavy objects), and exploration of textured objects. Vestibular stimulation is used to address problems including gravitational insecurity (e.g., fear of leaving earth's surface) and excessive craving for movement. Motor planning activities emphasize sequential movement in space and transitions in activities.

Sensory integrative therapy provides a foundation for children experiencing sensory processing and attentional deficits. It is provided within the context of the child-centered activity and parent guidance. Specific treatment techniques for desensitizing the hyperreactive child, organizing sustained attention and purposeful activity, and promoting self-calming and modulation of arousal states are derived from the sensory integrative treatment approach. In the next section, the basic tenets of this philosophical approach are described. More detailed is provided in Chapter 8.

The underlying premise of sensory integrative theory is that the ability of the central nervous system to take in, sort out, and interrelate information received from the environment is necessary to allow for purposeful, goal-directed responses. The major principle underlying sensory integrative treatment is improvement of an individual's ability to organize and process sensory input provided during meaningful events, thus allowing for an adaptive response to the environment. A child's ability to actively experience sensations while simultaneously engaging in self-directed, purposeful motor activity is essential to intervention. Sensory integrative therapy facilitates an individual's ability to make adaptive responses to environmental stimuli, and these responses facilitate organization in the central nervous system by providing sensory feedback about a goal-directed event.

Self-directed and self-initiated actions differentially enhance central nervous system function and maturation (Kandel & Schwartz, 1985). In essence, such approaches as child-centered activity allow a child to develop automatic functions of better self-organization and control. The child learns to develop appropriate motor responses to different sensory events based on neural feedback and central nervous system organization (Clark *et al.*, 1985).

CHILD-CENTERED ACTIVITY

Description of Child-Centered Activity (CCA)

Addressing the emotional aspects of the parent–child difficulties that exist between the regulatory-disordered child and the parents is central for treatment. This approach focuses on using the inner resources of the child and parent. Using an experiential model, child-centered activity is a form of infant psychotherapy that is adapted to the sensorimotor phase of development. The theoretical approach underlying child-centered therapy is based on ego psychology as described by Greenspan and colleagues (Greenspan, 1981, 1989, 1992, 1997; Greenspan & Greenspan, 1989) and an object relations theoretical framework (Winnicott, 1960). In this approach, infant psychotherapy focuses on the dynamics of the parent–infant interaction, insights gained by parents about their relationship with their child or issues from their past, as well as the emotional needs of parent and child during interactions (Lieberman & Pawl, 1993).

Others have applied principles of infant psychotherapy to the sensorimotor phase of development as well (Ostrov *et al.*, 1982; Mahrer *et al.*, 1976). Wesner *et al.* (1982) have described an approach that is similar to Greenspan's "floor time" that they term "Watch, Wait, and Wonder" (WWW). In this approach, the infant initiates all interactions and the parents seek to discover what it is that the child is seeking and needing from them and the environment. In this process, the parent may become attuned to her child's constitutional and emotional needs, how her child wishes to communicate and interact, as well as the quality of the parent–child relationship. Helping the parent recognize projective identifications with the child is considered an important aspect of the treatment process. The WWW approach has been used successfully with mentally retarded and developmentally delayed children (Mahoney, 1988; Mahoney & Powell, 1988). It has also been used as a method to focus on unresolved relational conflicts of the mother involving the mother's projective identification with her infant (Muir, 1992).

The child-centered activity (CCA) approach focuses on improving the developmental capacities of the child within the context of the parent–child relationship. Relevant stages of emotional development outlined by Greenspan (1989, 1992) are used to help guide this process. These stages include engagement and disengagement with objects and persons; organized, intentional signaling and communication on verbal and gestural levels; representational elaboration of shared meanings; and symbolic differentiation of affective–thematic experiences. In the child-centered approach, constitutional problems of the child such as irritability, sensory hypersensitivities, inattention, and other problems of self-regulation are addressed through the medium of play with the parent. Insights gained by parents about their relationship with their child or issues from their own past are addressed as they pertain to parenting and fostering the child's healthy emotional development and regulatory capacities.

In child-centered activity, the parent is taught to provide daily 15- to 20-minute sessions of focused nonjudgmental attention. During this time, the child is the initiator of all play and the parent is the interested observer and facilitator, elaborating and expanding on the child's own activity in whatever way the child seeks or needs from the parent (e.g., to imitate, admire, or facilitate). The parent is nonintrusive and nondirective in his or her interactions with the child. In this approach, the parent is instructed to "watch, wait, and wonder" with respect to what the child is seeking and needing both from the parent and the environment, and to then respond accordingly (Wesner *et al.*, 1982).

The child's attention span and activity level dictate the direction that the play takes, rather than an imposed structure or specific task demand presented by the parent. In this way, the child needs to refine his or her ability to attend and give effective signals, while the parent learns to become a more sensitive responder. If the child's gestural or vocal signals are nondifferentiated, the parent may reflect their nonspecificity by imitating, and then wait until the child can signal what he or she wants. The environment is organized to make toys and materials available that promote sensorimotor development and emotional themes in a safe area where there are no prohibitions or interruptions. For example, if a child has tactile hypersensitivities, textured toys and heavy objects are placed in the room along with other play materials. If the child has feeding problems, dolls and feeding utensils and mediums such as corn, dried beans, or water are set out. In general, the toys should be childproof and developmentally appropriate. For example, for a 6 to 12 month old the play materials may be tableware, blocks, dolls, and tactile materials such as Koosh balls, whereas toys for a toddler may be toy telephones, a cradle with a doll, toy trains and cars, blocks and balls. Extrinsic reinforcement, such as praise, are deemphasized. Instead, the parent reflects on the child's expressivity through expanding on facial gestures, affect, or language cues. The parent is given permission to be an observer of the child and to respond to the child's cues. The CCA medium offers the parent space to ponder the nature of their relationship with their child and minimizes the need to do to or for their child.

During the time that the parent and child engage, the therapist acts as an attentive observer. She or he models how to be a nonjudgmental observer of the parent–child relationship. In essence, the therapist provides to the parent what the parent provides for the child. Throughout the process, the therapist tries to convey a sense of respect for the caregiver's parenting ability.

Mother and child engaged in child-centered therapy.

During therapy sessions, CCA is practiced for 20 minutes followed by a discussion between therapist and parent about the process. For some parents, 20 minutes may be too long to tolerate this type of play with their child, in which case CCA should be attempted for as long as the parent is able. The parents may be asked what they observed about their child. In addition, they may be asked questions about what it was like for them to play with their infant in this special way and how they felt during playtime. The therapist's role is supportive while seeking to help clarify and reflect on the parent's responses to the child and what the child's behaviors might serve for the child. This process is important in order to address how the parents have adapted to the child's regulatory problems and to help parents become more aware of how their cues might be perceived by the child. Parental stress, depression, feelings of incompetence or displeasure with parenting, connections with the past (e.g., how parented), feelings elicited by the child's behavior, and family dynamics—including the impact of the child on marital relations—may be topics that emerge. If a parent is resistant to exploring their own issues and prefers to focus solely on the child, the therapist should be respectful of this wish. The therapist may gently raise concerns about how the child's behaviors affect the parents and family.

Unlike more structured therapy approaches, CCA is a process-oriented model rather than a technique to be mastered. Some parents need considerable help to allow their child to take the lead. They may have difficulty resisting the temptation to teach their child new skills, particularly when they are worried about lags in development. The therapist should seek to help the parents gain insights about their child's regulatory problems through what is expressed in the play context.

The underpinnings of this approach lie in the view that play, rather than direct instruction and skills training, is the medium by which a child learns, and that children learn best when actively engaged in the presence of a loving parent. As the child becomes the initiator of an interaction, intrinsic motivation and active participation in interactions and explorations are enhanced. The child experiences the parents' encouragement to act on his interests, which enhances the child's feelings of success, competence, and control. As a result, the child learns to develop internal control, and to engage in explorations with his environment and interactions with others.

Through the medium of CCA, parents become more sensitized to their child's behavioral style, developmental needs, and interests. For a child with significant sensory disturbances, this learning has far-reaching implications. For example, the infant with tactile hypersensitivities may avoid handling textured objects, reject new food textures, and experience physical discomfort when touched by others. Because of the underlying tactile hypersensitivities, the infant may exhibit difficulties in manipulating small objects, feeding, and playing with peers. In treatment, the mother may set out several types of textured toys (e.g., a large bin of styrofoam chips with many interesting toy figures buried inside the bin) during the time designated for child-centered activity. She waits and watches the child as he approaches the materials, facilitating exploration by taking turns. In this way, the child learns to explore the materials on his own terms, taking in only as much tactile information as his/her nervous system can handle. Aggressive behaviors may be channeled appropriately by providing the child with toys such as heavy pushcarts that he can lift and move or large nerf balls and bats that can be thrown and hit. These types of activities also serve to desensitize the child's overly sensitive tactile system.

The CCA approach has been applied by individuals in several disciplines to accomplish different goals. Speech and language therapists have used this approach to achieve balanced interactions between an adult and child through turn-taking. For example, a child initiates an action, and the adult imitates the action or vocalization, or responds by continuing the child's topic. This turn-taking exchange may continue for a number of turns, with variations in responses during each turn. It not only serves to facilitate communication but also increases attention to tasks.

Because the focus of the approach is on mastery for both parent and child, it is a highly positive and reinforcing experience for both parent and child. Preconceived notions that a child must be taught in order to learn are challenged, particularly for the parent who perceives the child as less competent than his peers. The parent's weaknesses and limitations are not considered detrimental to the treatment process; however, these difficulties and problems must be addressed. Some parents may not be able to embrace this approach. Since CCA expects parents to take a central role that may be anxiety provoking, parents with obsessive or rigid parenting styles may find the more reflective and responsive style of

Child pretending to feed the doll during child-centered therapy.

child-centered activity difficult. If it can be mastered, it may help parents develop less rigid patterns of interaction and allow for an expanded repertoire of parent behaviors that later enhance mental health. The child-centered activity is a natural foundation for listening skills.

Goals of CCA

The ultimate goals of the child-centered activity for an infant are to:

1. Provide the child with focused, nonjudgmental attention from the parent
2. Facilitate self-initiation and problem-solving by the child
3. Develop intentionality, motivation, curiosity, and exploration
4. Promote sustained and focused attention
5. Refine the child's signal giving
6. Enhance mastery of sensorimotor developmental challenges through the context of play
7. Broaden the repertoire of parent–infant interactions
8. Develop a secure and joyful attachment between parent and child
9. Enhance flexibility and range in interactive capacities

The goals for a parent are to:

1. Develop better signal reading of their child's cues and needs
2. Become more responsive or attuned to the child, allowing him to take the lead in the interaction

3. Develop a sense of parental competence as a facilitator rather than a director of their child's activity

4. Take pleasure in their child in a totally nonprohibitive setting

5. Appreciate their child's intrinsic drive for mastery and the various ways in which it is manifested

6. Change the parent's internal representation of himself/herself and the child to that of a competent parent and a competent child

Through the child-centered therapy process, parents who have felt overwhelmed by their children's difficulties may begin to acquire new ways of interacting and enjoying their child at home. By working through the parent–child relationship, the child's emotional and developmental competence is enhanced.

Instructions in How to Teach CCA

Below are some instructions that a therapist may use in guiding a parent to learn CCA:

1. Set aside 20 minutes a day when there are no interruptions. Be sure to do the play during a time when you and your child are well rested and you don't have other things to worry about, like something cooking on the stove or the doorbell ringing. Take the telephone off the hook or put the answering machine on. Be sure that your child's physical needs are met (e.g., toileting, feeding) so that you won't need to stop the play to take care of such needs. Put things out of reach that you don't want your child playing with (e.g., business papers, fragile objects). Use an area that is childproof, where there are no prohibitions or limits that you might have to set.

2. If you can, put out two sets of toys so that you can join in play with your child (e.g., two toy telephones, several trucks and blocks). Select toys that allow your child to explore and try new things that are more open-ended in nature. Avoid toys that require teaching or that are highly structured like board games, puzzles, or coloring. Your therapist will help you in picking out the best toys for playtime.

3. Let your child know that he or she is getting "special time" with you. Get on the floor with your child unless you are uncomfortable getting up and down off the floor. Try to stay close to your child so that he or she can see your face and you can see what he or she is doing.

4. Let your child take the lead and initiate what happens. Anything that your child does is okay, except for hurting himself or you or destroying toys and materials. If your child wants to throw toys, put out soft things that are okay to throw, like foam balls or bean bags. Play with your child however she or he wants to play. Discover what she or he wants from you during this time. Does he/she want you to admire him/her? To imitate him/her? Try out what

you think he/she wants from you and watch his/her reaction. See if your child starts to notice you and begin to interact more. Respond to what your child is doing, but don't take over the play.

5. Watch, wait, and wonder what your child is doing. Think about what your child is getting out of doing a particular activity. Enter their world and reflect on what their experience of it and you might be. Observing your child is the first step to providing a foundation for good listening.

6. Watch what your child seeks in play with you and try to pick materials each playtime that allow for those kinds of interactions. For example, if your child likes to bang and push toys, pick things that are okay to bang and push.

7. Avoid cleaning up toys that your child seems to be finished with until special time is over. Your child may return to those toys to play some more. Only clean up if your therapist suggests that your child is becoming overstimulated by the materials and needs less stimulation.

8. Talk with your child about what he's doing without leading the play or guiding what should happen next. For example, you may describe what she did ("What a big bounce you made with that ball," "Look how you like to run!"). With older children, you can ask questions about what is happening (e.g., "How come the baby doll is crying?" "What is the monster thinking of doing now?"). It is useful to help your child bridge play ideas, particularly if your child does something then moves onto the next play topic leaving a play idea hanging (e.g., "What happened to the dinosaur?" "I thought he wanted some food to eat.").

9. Have fun! This is very important. Try to enjoy playing with your child during "special time." If you find it boring, find the balance that will make the play fun and interesting for both of you.

10. Remember that "special time" is not a teaching time. Try to avoid praising your child or setting limits while you play. You want the motivation and pleasure of doing things together and exploring the world to come from within the child rather than because you are encouraging it through praise or reinforcement. There is no right or wrong way to play with toys.

11. Sometimes "special time" elicits uncomfortable feelings or strong reactions in parents. Reflect on what the play is eliciting in yourself. These reactions are useful to talk about with your therapist to understand what they mean for you and your relationship with your child. Should you feel overwhelmed by feelings, or try to be less involved and play the role of the interested observer. You may want to even take notes on what you notice about your child and shorten the playtime to 5 to 10 minutes if that is all you feel you can do. The important thing is that you are giving your child focused, nonjudgmental attention and the joy of interacting with you.

12. When "special time" is over, make it clear to your child that it is time to end. If your child shows frustration because it is difficult to end "special time,"

empathize with him and help him express his frustration. For example, "Wouldn't it be wonderful if we could do this all day long?" "I wish we could, but now it's time to stop and do something else." If your child should become tired during playtime, end it earlier. Clean up the toys and transition to something else—like a snack, reading a book, or some other activity.

13. Try to do "special time" every day, particularly during times when there are other stressors in the child's or family's life.

14. If there are other siblings, try to set aside time for focused interaction with them as well.

15. Take at least 20 minutes a day for yourself to rest, relax, and do something just for you. Things like catching up on household chores, food shopping, and other work don't count as time for yourself. This is your time to restore yourself.

The Process of Therapy

Child-centered activity is an experiential, process-oriented approach that involves an element of discovery about the parent and child and their relationship. It is often a difficult approach for parents and therapists to learn and do well. When the therapy is begun, the first few sessions should focus on the here and now—that is, what was noticed by the parent about their child and how the two of them interact, rather than how the parent felt about the experience. The therapist should avoid trying to coach too much while the parent is learning the approach, thus allowing the parent to find the way that they interact best with their child and to validate that their way of interacting is unique. The caregiver should be guided to take the role of the interested observer in the first few sessions to help them become more attuned to what their child is seeking and needing. Some parents report that they feel relieved that they do not have to constantly teach, organize, or redirect their child. The infant or child begins to learn to be more self-reliant and less dependent on the parents to self-regulate their activity and interactions. Through this model of discovering what will help both parent and child, the parent gradually learns that they don't have to have all the answers to solve their child's problems and that their child can be a problem solver too. Learning to cope and problem solve is often a major issue for the child with regulatory disorders.

Role of the Therapist in CCA

The role of the therapist is one of facilitator of the parent–child relationship by taking on the role of an observing ego toward parent and child. Although the therapist's role varies depending on what each dyad or family brings to the process, the therapist should try to avoid teaching or directing the process that occurs during child-centered activity. However, there are instances when the therapist needs to coach or reassure the parent, or modify the approach to be most effective. Here are a few examples of how that may happen. When parents have difficulty allowing their child to take the lead or they are overstimulating (e.g., too verbal, too active, or anticontingent to infant's response), the therapist may need to help the parent tune into the child's cues. In such cases, the therapist may cue the parent by saying things such as, "Let's see what she's doing here," or "It looks like she's changed the play topic to something else. Let's watch and see what she wants to do now." The therapist may also be more directive when the child's developmental needs are especially challenging, such as with a child who has autism.

While doing CCA, the therapist should be careful about where she sits so that the child does not seek to interact with her. Sitting slightly behind and to one side of the caregiver is often a good position. Should the child approach the therapist, she or he may smile, then look to the caregiver, referring the child back to the parent on a gestural level. Sometimes the child hands toys to the therapist. If this occurs, the therapist may offer the toy to the parent. If the child talks to the therapist, she or he should try to find a way to put the interaction back between caregiver and child. The therapist may turn to the caregiver and say things that bring them back into interaction with their child. Here are a few examples: "He has a lot of good ideas about trucks," or "What do you think he's telling us?" The therapist may also say to the child, "I wonder what mommy would do with you with that toy?" or "Go see what mommy thinks about that."

Therapeutic Challenges in Application of CCA

There are a number of challenges that arise in doing child-centered therapy. Lieberman and Pawl (1993) describe some common therapeutic mistakes in working through the parent–child relationship. Some of the things they describe include the therapist who may become so involved in the parent's experience that he or she overlooks the baby's contribution, or the therapist who colludes with the parent in maltreating the child, or the therapist who overidentifies with the child's experience and finds it difficult to become empathically attuned to the parent.

Some parents cannot see the value of doing this type of therapy, particularly when the child is demanding and won't listen to limits. They may say things like, "Won't this make him even more demanding of me if I give him more time?" It is useful to explain that during this time the child learns how to exert control in a healthy, adaptive way while getting their emotional needs met for attention, which will make accepting limits easier at other times of the day. When this is the issue, it is useful to practice limit-setting after doing CCA by cleaning up the toys, then embarking on an activity that may evoke conflict (e.g., sitting at the table for a meal, walking to a car without running into the street), all the while helping the parent and child balance limits and share control.

Some parents resist doing CCA when they view development in their child as something that should be taught. It is often hard for them to stop the urge to teach skills or direct play during CCA. It is important to acknowledge how the parent may be a "natural-born teacher" and have many good things to offer their child, but that there are certain things that cannot be taught explicitly. Referring back to the goals of CCA for the child is important in helping the parent understand the process and why this is different from a teaching time.

Mothers with mild to moderate depression often find that CCA provides them with something to work on with their child. Once a depressed mother begins to see progress in her child's behaviors, the mother often feels improved self-esteem and effectiveness as a parent. In working with a depressed mother, it is sometimes useful for the therapist to narrate aloud what the child is doing, speaking through the child so that the mother can remain more engaged in the process. For example, a baby may be banging cups on a container, then glancing up at mother to see what her reaction is. The therapist may say aloud, "Hey, mom, I like banging this cup with you." If the mother is not tactually defensive or resistant to being touched, it may help the mother to be touched gently on the shoulder or back by the therapist to keep a connection going between therapist and mother. The therapist should accompany these gentle touches with comments that reflect the process such as, "See how she smiles at you when you hold the toy out to her." Nurturing the parent in this way is especially important when the mother feels depressed and has difficulty engaging on any level with her child.

Debriefing about the Process

In the first few sessions, it is often useful to ask the parent questions about their experience of playing with their child. Some questions that may be useful are, "What have you noticed this week with your child?" "What do you think was happening when your child did x (or wanted you to do x)?" "How did you feel when you and your child were doing x together?" "How easy or difficult was it for you to do this play with your child?" As the caregiver becomes more comfortable with the process and in talking with the therapist about their reactions, feelings and projections from the past may be further explored. The therapist may ask things such as, "How did you play as a child with your parents?" "Does playing with your child remind you in any way of your experiences with your own parents?" It is not necessary that the parent make connections with their own past or feelings and reactions to their child in order for CCA to be successful, although insights are useful to the process. As the therapy process unfolds, the parent may talk more about observations that they made about their child as they did the playtime at home. They may also discuss how they might have been surprised by the child's responses, which were quite different than they had expected.

It is important to avoid intellectualizing the play experience, focusing too much on questions about why the child did something, or asking the parent too many questions about what happened. The parent may express emotions such as feeling rejected by the child turning his or her back to the parent. The therapist may normalize those feelings by expressing that many parents feel as they do when similar things happen. Empathizing with their position in a nonjudgmental way is very important. With parents who become preoccupied about their reactions to their child or who need to talk at length about themselves and their own past, the therapist may wish to refocus attention onto what happened that day between parent and child. In such cases, it is often useful for the parent to receive individual counseling around their own needs rather than diluting attention away from the relationship between parent and child.

Sometimes the parent expresses feelings of resentment or anger toward their child, or of feeling depleted when they give their child attention during CCA. It is important for the therapist to acknowledge these feelings, nurturing the parent so that they feel less depleted. It is often useful to spend the first few sessions attending to the parent's needs, listening to them and acknowledging how they feel in a nonjudgmental way. As the parent feels more "filled up" by the therapist's focused attention, it may be possible to try CCA in small doses. In such cases, the parent often needs to play with the toys themselves because they did not get to play as a child. The therapist should set out two sets of toys, one for the parent and one for the child. In addition to allowing the parent time to play, the therapist may nurture him or her further by providing a snack to "feed" both parent and child.

As the therapist processes the experience of what happened in the session, it is useful to focus on positive interchanges. Often parents with regulatory-disordered children do not see the positive aspects of their relationship with their child and need help to see what is going right. For example, the therapist might comment, "You looked like you were really enjoying each other when you were playing together in the pup tent." The therapist should be careful when sharing his or her observations so as not to interject interpretations or projections about the process. This creates a dynamic between the therapist and parents whereby the therapist is the "wise therapist" who expresses opinions about the parent and child. To validate the parent's own discoveries and learning process, it is better to elicit the parent's interpretations and help bridge their feelings and reactions with what is actually happening in the relationship. Comments made by the therapist may be things like, "I wonder what you were experiencing when x wanted you to hide," or "Did you notice that x seemed to watch you more when you did x?"

Modifications of CCA to Accommodate Family and Child Needs

It is very useful to practice the CCA approach with whomever the important caregivers are in the child's life. For example, if a grandmother is the primary caregiver, she should be involved in the therapy as well as the biological mother. When possible, both parents should participate in the therapy, helping them see how each have a unique relationship with their child. Sometimes there is a competition between mother and father, one of whom may feel they know what is best for the child and that the other should do it that way. The process of CCA helps parents to allow one another to find the way that they interact best with their child and to permit differences in parenting styles. When both parents come to the therapy session, it is useful to have each parent take a turn practicing CCA with their child while the other is an observer of the process. Often this way of working helps to address couples and family issues that may impact on the child. In some instances, a clinical decision may be made to teach the nanny or babysitter how to do CCA, especially if the parent is unable to provide emotionally healthy interactions for the child due to a major mental illness, significant medical problems, or other reasons that place the child at risk for neglect or abuse.

Father and child playing with furry puppet.

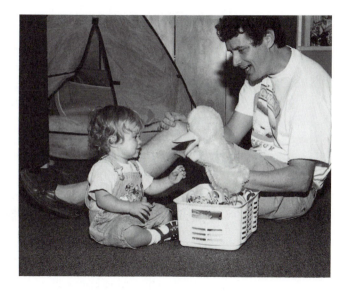

There are many modifications that can be made in the CCA approach (Seligman, 1994). The entire family may participate in doing CCA. In a two-parent two-child family, one parent may be "assigned" to one child at a time, the therapist observing and supporting interactions with one parent–child dyad at a time for 10 minutes each. One may construct a group in a school or day-care setting when parents come in during "free play" to practice CCA with their child. Classroom models of CCA need to be carefully monitored so that parents do not engage in teaching activities with their child because of the context and types of materials that are available. One may set up special groups that use CCA, such as first-time mothers, dads only, teen mothers, or single mothers in a drug treatment program.

Whatever model is used, the staff needs to be well versed in CCA and to think through the best way to do the therapy while having enough time to discuss the treatment process with families in a protected and safe environment. Another modification that is useful with multiproblem families or high-risk parent–child dyads is a two-clinician model. After practicing CCA, one clinician may debrief with the caregiver while the other clinician plays with the child. This model must be carefully thought out so that the parent does not feel threatened by another person playing with their child, especially after it has been emphasized how the parent and child are unique and special to one another.

Examples of Responses Parents Have Had to CCA

Here are a few of the varied responses have been elicited by parents who have used CCA:

- "I used to carry my 18 month old all day long. She breast fed at least 12 times a day. I even slept with her with my breast in her mouth through the night. The special time helped me to realize that she could be alone without needing me all the time. I could see that she was ready to separate from me by the way she played, like hide-and-seek, and wanting me to stay in one place while she moved away, then returning to my side. One day I suddenly took a look at my family and thought how my other child was missing out on what he needed and how I never spent any time with my husband anymore. I began to feel like a person again. The therapy helped sort out what our family needed."

- "I used to hate spending time with my child and couldn't wait to get away from him, all that fussing and crying. I went back to work to get away from him and dreaded coming home at night. I hate to say this, but I didn't like my own child. I thought he was a monster, and I was becoming one, too, the way I screamed at him all the time. Now we have so much fun together, and I realize that my reactions to his crying just set him off even more. Now I really miss him when I'm away from him. I feel like I got my baby back."

- "I was afraid that my child would hit or bite me. I was scared to even go to sleep at night that he might attack me. Imagine that! A big woman like me afraid of a 5 year old. It took me a long time to get used to him playing like he does, wanting to pull and push on things the way he does. But now I understand that he needs to do this because of his tactile defensiveness, his high need for physical contact, and his getting overstimulated so easily. Once I relaxed about him needing a rough kind of play, I started to think of ways to do it with him that felt okay for both of us. It seemed amazing to me when he stopped the hitting and biting. We're both a lot happier now."

- "I used to sit over on that sofa and look out the window, thinking how I just wanted to get out of here and take drugs—anything to not be with my kid. I hated the therapist at first, her talking about taking turns with my baby, following his lead, all that therapist talk. I would have preferred to have taken out the garbage than play with my kid, but somehow she figured that out. One day it just clicked for me. I realized that he was going to turn out just like me—on drugs, depressed, no one to love him, and feeling alone all the time. Now we have each other, and I'm proud that I know how to play with him, something I never got from anyone else. No one could have done it except me. I have to say that the therapist is A-okay."

- "My child was so developmentally delayed that I couldn't let up for a single minute. I did therapy with him all day long. Even when he was feeding, I used to stretch his heel cords so that I could fit everything in that he needed. After doing CCA, I realized what a relief it was not to be his therapist. Only I could be his mom. No one else could be this for my child. I also discovered that all the early intervention services that were supposed to be "family-centered" were not really "family-centered." The special time that I learned helped me figure out that no one in our family was happy. We just drove from one therapy appointment to the next, doing things all day long for Asher. Nancy, our older daughter was always left out. Now we spend time together as a family, having fun, and Asher is making all kinds of progress that no other therapy could have done for him. I think what did it for him is that he's finally motivated to move and learn. And I'm happy as a mom, and that's good for the whole family."

These quotes give a glimmer of some of the reactions that different parents have had from doing CCA. They are useful in understanding the struggles that parents go through in learning how to do the therapy. But what is so striking about their comments is how powerful the intervention became for them in changing the course of things for their child and family.

The next section presents research investigating the effectiveness of CCA. This is followed by two case examples: one involving a very difficult case where CCA had to be modified to meet the needs of the mother, and one with an irritable child who was developmentally delayed.

RESEARCH EXAMINING THE EFFECTIVENESS OF TREATMENT APPROACHES

There is a paucity of research investigating the outcome of therapy approaches for infants and toddlers with regulatory disorders. Because valid diagnostic criteria for young children are lacking, few systematic studies have been conducted. When infants are used as subjects, normal maturation often confounds the effects of therapy over time. In addition, outcome measures are often based on therapist ratings rather than objective and valid observations. These methodological problems have confounded or negatively affected the results of many studies (Weisz & Weiss, 1993).

There are few studies examining the benefits of interventions suitable for children with regulatory disorders. Cramer and his colleagues (1990) contrasted the Fraiberg (1980) method of mother–infant psychotherapy and noninterpretive interactional guidance (MacDonough, 1989) with infants under 30 months of age showing behavioral disturbances. They found no differences in the two approaches; however, short-term gains were reported in symptom relief or removal and there were more harmonious mother–child interactions and better projective identification in as few as 10 treatment sessions provided once weekly.

Using a methodology that focused on the quality of attachment, Lieberman *et al.* (1991) found that anxiously attached dyads receiving infant–parent psychotherapy improved in maternal empathy, security of infant attachment, and mother–child partnership. They found that the mother's emotional connection with the therapist significantly correlated with the mother's empathy toward the infant. Mothers who were more able to use the parent–infant psychotherapy to explore their own feelings toward themselves and their child were more empathic and more engaged with their toddlers at outcome than those who did not develop insights. In addition, their children showed more secure attachment, more reciprocity, and less anger and avoidance toward their mothers.

Infant-led psychotherapy (e.g., Watch, Wait, and Wonder) and traditional psychotherapy was compared in a study with 67 clinically referred infants and their mothers (Cohen *et al.*, in press). Treatment was provided once weekly for 5 months. Dyads receiving the WWW approach showed more organized or secure attachment relationships and greater gains in cognitive development and emotion regulation than infants in the psychotherapy group. Mothers in the WWW group also reported greater parent satisfaction and competence and a decrease in depression compared to mothers in the psychotherapy group. Both methods of treatment helped in reducing the infant's presenting problems, decreasing parent stress, and reducing maternal intrusiveness.

We conducted a study that examined the relative benefits of a child-centered infant psychotherapy approach versus a structured developmental parent guidance approach in the treatment of irritability and inattention (DeGangi & Greenspan, 1997). By contrasting these two interventions, we hoped to examine the contribution and role of parent and child in addressing the child's self-regulatory needs. In particular, we wished to examine how the child's locus of control (internally initiated versus externally directed) would impact regulatory capacities and function. Subjects consisted of 24 infants between the ages of 14 and 30 months who had disorders of regulation, including high irritability, sensory hypersensitivities, and a short attention span. There were three groups of eight subjects, matched for age and symptoms. Twenty-four subjects had irritability and 21 had attentional problems. Subjects receiving treatment had a pretest—6 weeks of either intervention A or B provided once weekly for an hour's session—followed by a retest 4 months after intervention. Subjects in the no-treatment group were retested between 4 and 6 months after initial testing. We used formalized assessment procedures of development, attention, and self-regulation to systemize the change that might occur over time.

Our results showed that child-centered therapy (CCA) was more effective than structured therapy (STR) and no treatment in treating inattention and irritability. Seventy-five percent of subjects resolved in their attentional problems after receiving CCA, in contrast to 37.5% after STR and 0% after no treatment. In addition, 57% of subjects resolved in their irritability after CCA, 28% after STR, and 0% after no treatment. An important finding of this study was that children with regulatory problems can make progress in resolving problems related to inattention and irritability in 6 weeks of intervention using a child-centered therapy approach. The fact that these basic skills of self-regulation (e.g., organizing attention and regulating mood) were responsive to short-term intervention using CCA suggests that therapies focusing on the relationship between parent and child are more useful than interventions that stress concrete developmental skills.

In a prospective study including 39 infants with regulatory disorders (e.g., high irritability and sensory processing problems during infancy) who were retested at 3 years of age, subjects who had received parent–child psychotherapy showed more motor and sensory integration problems than untreated subjects at 3 years of age (DeGangi *et al.*, 1996). However, despite having more constitutional problems, they did not show the emotional and behavioral problems that were found in the untreated group. In a study examining the effects of infant temperamental traits and early home-based intervention on psychiatric symptoms in adolescence, it was found that early intervention focusing on the parent–child relationship helped to protect subjects from developing psychiatric symptoms in adolescence (Teerikangas *et al.*, 1998). These studies point to the importance of improving the parent–child relationship in preventing long-term emotional and behavioral problems in children at risk.

CASE EXAMPLES

In this last section, we present two case examples that exemplify the treatment approaches used for children with different regulatory problems and for families with different types of dynamics.

Case #1: A Challenging Case Example of a Child With Attachment Disorder

Ms. N. was participating in a residential drug detoxification program and was seen for therapy with me once a week to help her with parenting skills with her 8-month-old baby. She was also participating in a parent–child therapy group three times a week at our center. The group comprised several single mothers with young children, two of whom also attended the same drug detoxification program. The parents received group therapy, individual counseling, and parent guidance as part of their program.

Ms. N. was a 25-year-old single mother who had abused cocaine and alcohol during her teen and early adult years, but she had worked on and off as a secretary for the past few years. She claimed that she was drug and alcohol free during the pregnancy, but the neonatalogist diagnosed Kelly as having cocaine exposure *in utero*. Ms. N. felt that she was not attached to her baby and did not want her child to have the same relationship with her that she had had with her mother. The pregnancy was difficult. When Kelly was born, she had infantile seizures. Ms. N. was told by the pediatrician that it would be likely that Kelly would have developmental delays.

Ms. N. described how she often felt frazzled and overwrought when around her baby. She wanted help in learning how to play with the baby and in how to be with her without feeling that she was going to harm her. There were times when Kelly cried and Ms. N. felt the impulse to shake her baby to quiet her, but thus far she had been able to resist this urge.

Ms. N. had been participating in the drug detoxification program for the past 2 months and was, at the time of the treatment, drug free. Plans were for her to resume her regular living arrangements in another 2 months. She normally lived with her mother, who helped take care of her baby when she was working. Ms. N. was unsure who Kelly's father was. I spent the first session taking a history, ending with a brief introduction to the infant-led intervention. As she gave the history, mother held Kelly in her lap briefly, then let her down on the floor. Ms. N. seemed distraught, crying frequently, looking out the window, and twisting a kleenex to shreds. As she reported her history, I was struck by the feeling as if Ms. N. were giving details about someone other than herself. Kelly and her mother seemed detached from one another. Kelly rarely looked at her mother, seeming content to play alone. When her mother held her, Kelly rarely touched or looked at her mother.

History

Ms. N. was a single parent and had not wanted a baby initially, but after she became pregnant she decided to go through with it. Kelly was a biracial baby, born full term after a difficult pregnancy with questionable cocaine addiction at birth. In midpregnancy there were concerns that Kelly was not growing. As the pregnancy neared the end, Ms. N. became diabetic, and labor was eventually induced at 38 weeks gestational age. Kelly had several infantile seizures within the first week of life. After a difficult early neonatal course, Kelly seemed to show remarkable recovery, becoming alert and interested in the world. At first her movements were jittery and her muscles felt tense. She sometimes became agitated when held, but as she grew sensitivities to touch resolved, muscle tone improved, and she showed good development in all areas.

In the first few months of life, Kelly insisted on her mother carrying and holding her all the time. She hated being placed in a car seat or carriage and would cry until she was held again. A sensory history seemed to suggest that the source of these problems was related to separation anxiety, although there appeared to be some mild tactile hypersensitivities. She often followed her mother, crawling after her if she walked away from her. At 8 months, she could crawl and climb up on her mother's lap and had just begun to say "mama." Mother reported that Kelly was a happy baby and seemed connected to her, but I sensed a detachment between them. Kelly rarely looked at her mother as she spoke, and the only times that Ms. N. reached for Kelly were when Kelly needed her nose wiped.

A family history was taken to help understand some of the issues that Ms. N. had in parenting Kelly. There was considerable mental illness in her family of origin. Ms. N. described her mother as having obsessive–compulsive disorder. The grandmother was able to work as a housekeeper but had difficulties with the task of parenting. Her fixation on having things done a certain way made it difficult for her children to do things differently from her. Ms. N.'s father was an alcoholic and had traits of manic-depression. He went from one job to the next, working as a maintenance man, a car salesman, and a postal carrier. During the day, he was better able to function, but in the evening he drank. When Ms. N. was in high school, she began taking cocaine on weekends, using money she had earned as a store clerk. She also drank her father's alcohol without his knowledge. By the time Ms. N. was 19 years of age, she had participated in several drug and alcohol detoxification programs, only staying drug and alcohol free for several months at a time before resuming old habits. Home life was chaotic, with fighting and violence. Ms. N. reported that as a teen she sometimes felt "crazy" (e.g., fearful that bad things were in the house that would hurt her; experiencing memory lapses for events that had happened). She thought that she might have been trying to self-medicate through drugs and alcohol. She was able to seek support from teachers and friends, who provided her with good role models. She had been receiving counseling for the past few years through the drug detoxification program.

Ms. N. described her relationship with her mother as one of rejection. She felt that her mother was vicious and intrusive, but in public her mother would praise her accomplishments. Ms. N. was a good student and finished high school, something that her mother valued. In growing up, Ms. N. tried to insulate herself from the fighting at home by going to other people's houses to find solace. As Ms. N. reported this, she seemed agitated, shaking her foot, looking out the window, and squeezing a kleenex to shreds. Ms. N. stated that she didn't know what to do now that Kelly was starting to move away from her. It seemed that Ms. N. did better with Kelly when she was a helpless infant, but now that Kelly was becoming more independent, it was difficult for her to allow Kelly to become her own person.

4. Parent support:

    a. Provide support to mother in a nonjudgmental way, allowing her to express feelings about herself, her relationship with Julie, and Julie's demandingness and developmental problems.

    b. Help the mother find ways to restore her energy and do things for herself as well as her family so that she might feel more available to meet the many demands of her children and family.

Julie and her mother were seen as part of the research project described earlier in this chapter that provided 12 weeks of intervention on a once-a-week basis. Julie's treatment began with structured intervention. This was followed by child-centered activity for another 6 weeks. The therapists in this case were two clinical developmental psychologists, one with background in special education and the other with expertise as an occupational therapist as well. Mrs. T. attended all sessions.

As we began the treatment, we confronted several challenges that affected the treatment process. Mother had an unrealistic view of Julie's problems, thinking that she would be fully normal if only she would talk and get better balance. Mother was also very intrusive with Julie, constantly trying to teach her new skills because she felt that Julie "had a lot of catching up to do." Her style was often frantic, so that Julie could not respond or self-initiate any responses. Mother was also feeling overwhelmed and depressed. It was very important that we address mother's needs in a way that she would find supportive and nurturing.

Session 1

In the first session, Julie had difficulty transitioning from the waiting room to the playroom. She was extremely fussy and could not explore the room on her own. She spent the session in her mother's lap or by her mother's side. Mrs. T. talked about how stressed she felt that Julie constantly needed her attention. Mother began talking about her many concerns for Julie—her poor attention to tasks and people, feeding problems, night wakings, immature play skills with mouthing and banging toys, no verbal and little gestural communication, and no ability to self-soothe.

We tried several activities in this session to help Julie and mother engage in reciprocal interactions. The goals were to help Julie focus her attention on the task or her mother, to initiate exploration with the activity, then to respond to mother's cues in a reciprocal manner. Linear vestibular movement (e.g., rocking in a rocking chair) while providing firm deep pressure (holding Julie securely in mother's lap) was used to help soothe and calm both mother and child. The following activities were tried with mother, and suggestions were written down for mother to take home with her:

1. Find a quiet time to sit with Julie. Put out only a few toys. Perhaps put on quiet rhythmic music in the background. Start out soothed and calm. Slowly rock Julie on your lap.

2. Have Julie sitting on your lap while you rock. Have a blanket, dried beans, corn, or uncooked macaroni in a bowl. Mom should play with the materials first to capture Julie's attention.

3. Then try letting Julie take the first step. Imitate her, then let her take another turn. It should be like a circle—Julie does, you do, Julie plays more—all in the same activity.

4. Make up a game with your body like stamping your feet to the music or playing peek-a-boo. Have some fun.

During these activities, there appeared to be little pleasure in mother and child's interaction. Mrs. T. was highly intrusive. She could not allow Julie to take a turn or wait for Julie's responses to occur. We noticed that Mrs. T. seemed averse to having Julie sit on her lap, but this became more palatable if there was a pillow between herself and Julie. The therapists were very soothing and calm, praising Mrs. T. for trying the activities suggested and encouraging her to try these things out at home. The session was spent discussing Mrs. T.'s concerns and working with the dyad to establish attention and engagement through gentle rocking; tactile stimulation with the corn, furry rug, and pillows; and soft rhythmic music. We tried to think of activities that provided calming for both mother and child because they both seemed to need this. Suggestions were made to mother to modify her verbal input to Julie, relying less on words and more on gesture and intonation. Finally, we worked on following Julie's lead, and opening and closing circles of communication. We found mother to be a very likable, highly motivated, energetic woman who engaged easily with the therapists. She appeared enthusiastic about the treatment.

Session 2

Mrs. T. expressed similar concerns to last week, although she felt Julie was using more gestures. In this session, we continued to help Julie acclimate and focus, sitting next to mom and rocking with her as she held her child, listening to music on the tape player. We encouraged Mrs. T. to be more passive in her interactions while Julie took more initiative during sensory play with tactile materials (e.g., Koosh balls, corn, furry rug). We talked with Mrs. T. about allowing herself to be a secure home base while Julie explored a little on her own. We discussed how this was different from teaching Julie specific skills. This week our suggestions for home included the following:

1. Put a pillow on your lap, then encourage Julie to sit with you, giving her pillow "hugs" while you watch a video together.

2. Play with water, using brushes. Paint her feet and hands with the water and brush. You might put a doll in the bathtub so that Julie could paint the doll with the brush too.

3. Continue playing with the corn and the dried beans.

4. Always let Julie take the lead. Make a circle of communication: Julie starts, mom joins in, Julie takes another turn, then mom joins again. Always let Julie end the turn so that she can close off the circle of communication.

5. Try music and rocking for soothing.

During these activities, we noticed that mother had a high need to play with the toys, just as much as Julie. We speculated to ourselves that Mrs. T. had had a deprived childhood and needed to revisit the experience of play for herself. We were very aware that we were reparenting Mrs. T., providing her with aspects of nurturance that she may not have had early in life.

At the end of the session, Mrs. T. expressed how she was experiencing burnout and had difficulty getting any time for herself to physically and emotionally refuel. We encouraged her to spend some time alone each day, just for herself. Mrs. T. was able to say that she felt anxious about taking time for herself because there was so much to do at home, and she felt guilty whenever she tried to take time to relax. We emphasized the importance of her needing to refuel so that she would be more available for her family.

Session 3

Mrs. T. reported some positive changes. Mom was faithfully doing "quiet play" with Julie 20 minutes a day. She talked of her concerns about Julie's stubbornness, short attention span, and inability to play independently. She wondered how Julie would adjust to a kindergarten routine in a few years. In this session, Julie was more organized and focused. The media that we used included water play and vestibular stimulation on a large bolster (e.g., rocking and bouncing). Julie also engaged in very nice reciprocal play with her mother, using a tunnel to play peek-a-boo.

Session 4

This week we noticed that Julie was able to organize several sequences of behavior with one toy, thus showing the beginnings of more elaborated play. She tolerated the swing nicely and was engaged with her mother around music and movement. We worked with Mrs. T. on reading Julie's nonverbal cues and reducing her own verbal barrage, being very careful to be nurturing toward mother as we gave her feedback.

Mrs. T. opened up about her own exhaustion and depression. She felt that she must maintain a facade, a "happy face," on the outside in order to get through the day. In addition, she felt conflicted by the competing demands of her three children, taking little time for herself. We strongly encouraged her to take time out for herself as we had before.

Session 5

The next week, mom came in very positive about Julie's progress. She felt that Julie was more organized, communicating more purposefully, and better able to sustain some independent play. During "quiet play" at home, Julie was focusing on some fine motor tasks using keys, which mom had encouraged her to do. We strongly reinforced the good work both were doing and stressed how important mom was to Julie's growth. In this session, we worked on oral–motor and feeding skills using yogurt and crunchy granola, and vestibular activity on the swing and inner tube. Julie initiated play and Mrs. T. was able to engage her in a reciprocal game around bouncing on the inner tube. Julie seemed to focus her attention better when deep proprioceptive input was provided (e.g., pressing on her hips while bouncing on the ball). We counseled mom to try this and other movement activities at home, and Mrs. T. appeared to be very motivated to do. The program that we gave her to try included the following:

1. Try rocking and singing with Julie on your lap. Use a little pillow to put on Julie's stomach or back if she likes this.
2. Put out dried beans and macaroni in a box for Julie to explore. Let her take her shoes off to put her feet in the box. Also try Play Doh.
3. Pull Julie in a wagon. At the playground, encourage her to swing.
4. After movement activities such as the swinging, encourage Julie to sit down and do fine motor activities.
5. After her bath, pat Julie with the towel. Use lotion on her body, applying with firm pressure. Watch how she acts. If she pulls away, it means that she is not processing the touch in a positive way.

Session 6

Mrs. T. brought the maternal grandmother and the 12-month-old brother to the session. Julie was very unfocused and overstimulated and was unable to play in the bath of plastic balls. Her play was very fleeting. Eventually she organized herself to sit in a nest of pillows and listen to rhythmic rocking music.

Despite feeling more positive in the prior few weeks about Julie's progress, Mrs. T. came to this session expressing a good deal of frustration with Julie's slow progress. She continued to have an unrealistic picture of Julie's abilities, expressing relief in her belief that Julie was not mentally retarded or emotionally disturbed. Again Mrs. T. felt depleted, and again we encouraged her to take refueling breaks for herself.

Session 7

Child-centered play therapy was introduced after the first six sessions of the structured program. When the child-centered therapy began, Mrs. T. was suspicious about whether this type of intervention would work. She felt that Julie must be taught how to learn different skills and did not think that giving Julie the initiative in the play would work, although we had been teaching mother to try this all along. However, because Mrs. T. had developed a strong therapeutic alliance with her therapists, she was willing to try this therapy.

In the first session of child-centered therapy, we observed that Julie initiated a lot of proprioceptive stimulation—stamping her feet, butting mom with her head, and bouncing while sitting on the inner tube in a fairly well-organized sequence. Her play was immature but focused. It appeared that Julie needed to be grounded by the tactile play with her mother to help her focus her attention. Despite mother's worries that were expressed prior to the play, there was positive affect between mother and Julie. Mom seemed fairly relaxed with the child-centered play, although she needed to restrain herself from structuring turns and making verbal demands. Written notes were provided to the mother about child-centered therapy. These included the following:

1. Find toys that make noise or music such as a tape recorder or the pop-up tunes toy.
2. Use toys that Julie can pound, hit, or bang, such as a pounding bench with hammer or a chair to push.
3. Give her places where she can sit inside, such as a nest of pillows.
4. Let Julie take the lead but stay next to her.
5. Give her all your attention for a concentrated time—up to 15 minutes if you can.
6. Julie likes seeing what she can make you do—to sit down, now run with me, now jump. Go with it.
7. Let Julie do most of the work and to show you what she wants.

Mrs. T. appeared to be dealing more with the reality of Julie's delays. The early intervention program staff had been discussing a placement in the fall for Julie at a school for children with significant communication disorders and cognitive delays. Mrs. T. was concerned about Julie's diagnosis and what the future held for her. At a personal level, Mrs. T. discussed how isolated she felt from her peers, how different her experience of mothering was from her friends, and how her friends were unable to empathize with her. In addition, Julie had been ill with a skin irritation and a fever. Mrs. T. had been feeling very tired. We suggested that she set a schedule that included "special time" for herself, free of distractions. We began the child-centered therapy with mother and child after mother had time to discuss her many concerns.

During processing after mother practiced the child-centered therapy, Mrs. T. discussed tensions in her role and relationship with own mother, who was very critical of her. There is a very strong work ethic in the family, with high demands on the mother to meet all the needs of the children and husband. Mrs. T. stated that even if she had time for herself she would feel guilty about it. In addition, she felt that her mother was critical of the way in which she parented her children.

Session 8

We noticed that this week Julie looked regressed in her play, unable to engage with objects or sequenced activities. The main focus was trying to engage mom in the therapeutic process and to help her understand that Julie needed to be the initiator of the play. With this guidance, Mrs. T. was able to respond appropriately to Julie without being overly intrusive, and the affective engagement in the dyad was very positive.

Mrs. T. expressed doubts about the child-centered therapy. Julie seemed to be going "backward" in her view since she was not teaching her specific skills when she did the child-centered therapy. Mrs. T. reported that "special time" consisted of her putting out toys that were good for her child's cognitive level, which Julie showed little interest in. At the same time, Mrs. T. was feeling exhausted. She did take an hour for herself but admitted that she felt guilty asking for relief from her husband since this was frowned on by her mother. We reinforced the need for her to get respite and to have some pleasure in her own life

Session 9

The play was consistent with previous weeks in that Julie craved the tactile grounding in order to focus. Julie spent time flitting from the inner tube to the big box enclosure to rocking activities. Julie was especially interested in pulling her mother's hand and tugging mom along as she moved about her environment. Her mother responded by trying to fend off Julie's demands, stating, "What do you want?" The therapist's presence in the room at this point was somewhat counterproductive in that Mrs. T. needed to talk about her concerns, which took her away from Julie. We suggested the possibility of finding someone for her to talk with privately as a future option. During the actual treatment session, we found that it was better to allow Mrs. T. to practice the child-centered therapy while we went into the observation booth for about 15 minutes.

Mrs. T. was able to take our suggestions and had been negotiating how her needs were separate from Julie's. She acknowledged that she was loosening up on her usual involvement with the oldest child's schoolwork and in doing things constantly for Julie. There was a birthday party for the young baby, in whom mom took great pleasure. She talked about the fun times she and her husband had begun to take for themselves after their long work day. All of these changes were occurring under the critical eye of her mother, who referred to Mrs. T. as being selfish. At the same time, Mrs. T. was worrying about not setting enough limits on Julie, particularly her high need for constant attention.

Session 10

Mrs. T. came in looking very attractive and upbeat. She reported that Julie seemed better able to play by herself and able to separate more easily from mom. We continued to reinforce the idea that a big dose of child-centered play with mom could go a long way toward independence in other contexts. We contrasted again the difference between structured teaching and child-initiated activity. In Julie's case, the essential need was for both types of interventions because of the seriousness of her delays.

Julie continued with her sensory play while attempting to control her mother's involvement with her activities, pulling and tugging mom to come along with her. The dyadic play was positive and well modulated; mom was responsive and nonintrusive.

It was interesting that the early intervention staff from Julie's center called during this week to discuss Julie's wonderful progress. They no longer found Julie to be irritable and demanding, and found that she could join into circle time, snack, and other activities without any difficulty. She was showing increased gestures, intentional communication, fewer problems with hypersensitivities to touch and movement activities, and better-focused attention. They asked what we were doing that was working so well.

Session 11

We noticed that Julie's mood regulation was better, with less whining and more autonomy. After some reminders about letting Julie take the lead, the dyadic play went well. Mother needed repeated reminders to allow the play to be child-initiated. It was not something that came naturally to her. Julie engaged in the same tactile–proprioceptive activities of previous weeks, but we noted better organized sequences of play and very positive affect between mother and child.

Mrs. T. reported major changes in the family's sleeping arrangements. Julie was now sleeping in the older sister's bedroom and the baby was in a separate room. Although this was not shared with the therapists before, Julie had been sleeping in the parent's bed. Mrs. T. stated that she and her husband slept alone together ("I'm back with my husband and now we're having special time!"). At home Julie was apparently observing and imitating her 1-year-old brother and experimenting more on her own. Mother described herself as standing by while Julie did things for herself.

Session 12

At the last session, Julie engaged in considerable tactile–proprioceptive play, laughing and smiling as her mother followed along with her. During this play, we observed Julie to gesture using signs while vocalizing with a few new words that she had just attained (e.g., up, more). Her sequences of play were intentional and organized. It was clear what Julie wanted to do in her play. In addition, she was able to use the sensory play to help organize her attention for a focused fine motor task. Julie indicated that she wanted to sit in a chair with a table in front of her. She pointed to the puzzle, signed "more," and clapped as her mother placed the puzzle on the table for her to do. She then proceeded to work at this task for at least ten minutes.

We reinforced Mrs. T.'s observation that Julie was happier when mom could give her a dose of full attention, even if only briefly. Julie was now able to play independently for 10 minutes at a time. Mother was in the throes of planning for Julie's fall school placement, getting financial support, negotiating with her husband on the best plans for Julie, and accepting the fact that Julie was a "special needs" child. We discussed termination and our work together. We emphasized again the need to try to build in a support for mom when she moved into another setting. We reviewed with Mrs. T. the activities that Julie liked and needed. In addition, we stressed the important role that mom played in facilitating the changes that we observed with Julie. Her playing with Julie, giving focused attention while Julie took the lead, and letting Julie show her what she wanted were important to the progress that she made.

Conclusion of Treatment

At the conclusion of the therapy program, many of Julie's problems had resolved. Sleep and feeding problems were no longer a concern. Chronic irritability had diminished significantly. This appeared related to Julie's capacity to refine her gestures and vocalizations to communicate her needs, her ability to play by herself for short periods of time, and her mother's changed perception of Julie as a child who could master new skills. Difficulties separating from mother had improved when Mrs. T. set aside playtime with Julie to fulfill her needs for focused, one-to-one attention. Julie was more animated and happier and was more able to play by herself at home. Her mother found her to be far less clingy and needy, although Julie remained fairly demanding, requiring help to play with objects for any sustained period of time. Julie's play skills showed more organization and range in terms of variety. Julie was beginning to develop autonomy and had her own opinions about toy and activity preferences. Attentional skills had improved dramatically, particularly when tactile–proprioceptive or movement activities had been used prior to tasks that required focused cognitive, language, or perceptual thinking.

Treatment of Irritability and Other Mood-Regulation Problems

I can't stand our child's crying another minute! This has been going on since he was born. He's the baby from hell! My husband told me that if I didn't fix his crying, he was leaving home. We can't find any babysitters to take care of him because he is so irritable. I worry that someone else might abuse him because they wouldn't love him like I do. I'm exhausted and at my wit's end!

These words, spoken by a parent with an irritable child, are depictive of the tremendous impact that an irritable child can have on the parent–child relationship and family life. Parents become frantic in their attempts to console their child. When nothing works, parents often feel ineffective. They may worry that their child appears unhappy most of the time. For the child, it is an unsettling experience to be chronically unregulated when things like transitions in activities and small frustrations set them off. They learn to depend on their parents to soothe them because they lack strategies for self-calming. And because they are irritable most of the time, they may not experience pleasurable interactions with others.

There are many reasons why a child is irritable or has mood-regulation problems. To treat these problems most effectively, it is important to understand the way in which emotion regulation develops in the young child. This chapter begins with an overview of different views of emotion to provide a framework for treating irritability and other disorders of mood regulation. Since a major aspect of mood regulation relates to how emotions are socialized, a developmental–structuralist framework is presented. A case example is presented that depicts psychosocial functioning of a child with mood-regulation problems using the developmental–structuralist model. Finally, suggestions for treatment of different problems related to mood regulation and irritability are described, along with a detailed case example.

WHAT IS AN EMOTION?

Emotions have a powerful impact on our experience of the world around us. Emotional expression provides a window into an individual's internal experience of the world. Emotions motivate our actions and affect the way in which we interact with others and our environment. Emotions provide life experiences with meaning. By guiding our thoughts and actions, emotions have a regulatory function, thus helping us to acquire adaptive behavior patterns (Dodge & Garber, 1991). Through the expression of emotion, we can learn about how a person perceives him or herself and others, and how well they self-regulate when presented with challenging situations.

There are many individual differences in how people experience and express emotions and interact with others. Many people are predominantly happy, content, and curious. Others may be often withdrawn, sad, and depressed. Still others appear angry, destructive, and disorganized. Most people display different emotions and act differently depending on the situation and their underlying mood at the time. But when a person is predominantly withdrawn, avoids other people, and has no interest in learning most of the time, it can affect their development and adaptability. Similarly, the person who is angry, destructive, and overly aggressive will have difficulty engaging in appropriate interactions with others and in modulating their activity in everyday life.

Over the years, there has been considerable debate about what constitutes an emotion. Is it a subjective state such as feeling "depressed," "content," or "anxious"? Is it what motivates our interest in the world and guides our social interactions? Is emotion the outward motor expression of feelings—the smile; the scowl; the loud, stern voice; or the uplifted buoyant body posture? How much of emotion is affected by cognitive appraisal of a situation, event, or stimulus and how much by physical or autonomic responses (e.g., heart racing, cold clammy hands) that are experienced during anger, pleasure, or other emotional states? Most current views of emotion embrace all of these components. A broader view is generally accepted by emotion theorists who consider emotion to be the interface between the individual and his environment. Emotions mediate the individual's capacity to adapt or respond to a variety of experiences.

There are five major areas related to emotional regulation. These include:

1. *Cognitive appraisal*: Before, during, and after an emotion is experienced, the individual engages in cognitive appraisal. This process of evaluating the situation on a cognitive level determines what emotions are elicited. Some of the things that impact cognitive appraisal include

    a. *Reading and understanding social cues*: The irritable child may not be able to read and understand social situations and evaluate whether they should approach or withdraw. They may react in an unpredictable manner because of this difficulty.

    b. *Perception, including face recognition and discrimination of affects*: Some children have difficulty reading facial and gestural signals. As a result, they may misconstrue what a person is trying to convey. Because of this problem, it is often difficult for them to understand when firm limits are placed on them.

    c. *Predicting one's own behavior and that of others*: A major goal for the child with mood-regulation problems is to begin to predict their own behavior and modify it in response to different situational demands. Learning that certain behaviors have consequences is important to this process.

2. *Physiological aspects of emotions*: One of the things that helps us to link meaning to emotions are our physiological responses. As cognitive appraisal takes place, physiological responses activate arousal to allow the person to respond accordingly. This is important to prepare the person for action. For example, in dangerous situations, the person needs to be ready to flee. Without

physiological readiness, the person may not survive. Both neuroendocrine and autonomic states contribute to the physiological activation of emotions. Many irritable children are in a state of hyperarousal and, therefore, do not have the typical physiological responses one needs to react in a calm and focused manner.

3. *Expression of emotion*: Communication of reactions, feelings, or intentions to others during social interactions is an important component of emotion. The motor expression of emotion is manifested through the neuromuscular system and consists of facial patterning, postures, and gestures. Frequently the irritable child expresses intense negative emotions (e.g., anger, distress, frustration). They often have difficulty communicating more subtle ranges of emotions (e.g., express through words or facial expressions that they are beginning to feel frustrated versus tantrumming), and they may have little opportunity to express more positive emotions.

4. *Socialization of emotions*: As children develop, they are reinforced to express certain emotional displays. This process occurs first through the parent–child relationship, but if this relationship is affected by the child's irritability and mood-regulation problems, it is more difficult for the parent to provide social feedback.

5. *Modulation of emotion and mood states*: Learning how to modulate emotions in response to internal states, situational demands, and the social context is a very important skill. How an individual perceives the experience of the emotion during and after its expression relates to the subjective feelings associated with emotions. Cognitive factors such as memory and imagination play an important role in defining the subjective experience of emotions.

These components of emotion do not necessarily occur in this sequence; however, there is general agreement that the concept of emotion should include these five elements (Scherer, 1984). Understanding the various elements of emotion regulation is important for treatment planning in working with children with regulatory disorders. The next section details the different components of emotion regulation, with emphasis on how problems in each area may be observed and treated.

COGNITIVE APPRAISAL

Reading of Social Cues

When faced with a situation, an individual makes a cognitive appraisal that affects the intensity and quality of the emotional reaction. The individual relies on already acquired knowledge about similar situations, memories of past experiences, perceptual skills in reading signals or cues from the environment, as well as analytical skills in appraising the situation. This appraisal process is ongoing and may be manifested in a number of different emotional responses over time as the individual reflects on past and current experiences. For instance, suppose the child thinks that a situation is very demanding. At first, the child may experience much apprehension and fear. If the child remembers that he was successful in a similar difficult situation in the past, he may feel challenged and excited after his initial response. However, if he experienced extreme frustration and feelings of incompetence in the past, he may seek to avoid another such experience and exhibit negative emotions.

How cognitive appraisal might impact a child with mood-regulation problems is depicted by Owen, a 4-year-old child who was struggling at preschool. He often became irritable when there were transitions in activities, his space was invaded by other children, activities were more rambunctious, or when the classroom noise level became loud. He felt that he wasn't ready to move on to the next activity when the children were expected to do so. Although he was a very competent child, he had trouble adjusting to change and would become distressed when expected to do certain tasks such as share toys with other children or clean up his toys to get ready for a snack. Usually after about 2 hours at school, Owen would begin to show his distress by hitting or biting other children or by withdrawing. His responses were very unpredictable, with some good days followed by several days with multiple incidents. Each time he bit a child, he was sent home from school. Within a month, he was being sent home so frequently that his parents chose to keep him at home to give him a break from the stress of school.

As we tried to work out a viable solution to the problem (e.g., getting a full-time aide to help him make transitions, to stop him before he bit another child, and to organize him when he appeared distressed), Owen began to make comments that he never wanted to go back to school again. In the month that it took to find an aide, we saw Owen regress. With each day that he stayed home from school, he became increasingly more agitated, refusing to change his clothes, wanting to isolate himself in his bedroom, and screaming at his parents whenever they made the simplest of requests. As we reintroduced Owen to school, we had to change his cognitive appraisal of school and himself to a more positive one. We were able to accomplish this by beginning with a short school day and a shortened week of school and using positive reinforcement from his aide for accomplishing tasks. We provided scheduled breaks during the day when he could reorganize himself (e.g., calming by sitting in a bean bag chair and looking at books, sucking on ice pops, or building a fort that he could go inside). We instituted a school and home program that reinforced good behavior and compliance, for playing friendly (e.g., not biting other children), making transitions (e.g., cleaning up toys when time for a snack), and self-calming when agitated (e.g., asking for time alone in bean bag chair). Within a few months, he became much more compliant both at home and school and was beginning to make more positive self-statements (e.g.,

Some individuals seem to have a great deal of difficulty in recognizing the autonomic responses that accompany emotions. As a result, they may not perceive that they are getting angry or upset until they suddenly blow up. This has important implications for parents who may be at risk for abusing their children. It is important to teach them how to recognize the bodily signals that mean they are getting angry (e.g., stiffening of muscles, skin getting hot, stomach churning) so they can cool off before they explode at their child. By tuning into these body signals, the person can learn to control their behavior better.

The task of learning how to read body signals was a major piece of intervention with 9-year-old Alexis. She had a short fuse and would explode, screaming at her parents and throwing things, whenever she experienced the slightest bit of frustration. Her tantrums would go on for several hours, which resulted in the whole family being up all hours of the night trying to console her. Her parents thought that Alexis looked like a wild animal with hair falling in her face, her body slumped over and hands clawing at the air like a tiger. Alexis would also shut down when she became depressed, hiding under a table or sitting inside her closet for hours on end. These mood changes would come on suddenly, and, once in an intense mood state, Alexis had considerable difficulty coming out of it. Although she was a child who was helped by medication, through therapy Alexis began to be able to recognize when she could feel her mood shifting to anger, frustration, or sadness. When she felt herself becoming upset by things, she could focus on what her body was telling her, then take steps to soothe herself before her mood state progressed too far. Doing things like jumping on a trampoline, kicking a soccer ball, or playing piano helped her to self-calm. Alexis also talked with me about her "Tantrum Warning Device" (Figure 4.1), a concept that we used to help her predict what situations caused her to become upset. For instance, doing homework almost always caused her warning meter to go up to a "medium sizzle." Not getting to stay up late and play Nintendo would make her get "boiling mad." The object of the warning device was to recognize when her mood was moving from mild to mild–medium or medium anger and get it back down again by calming herself.

EXPRESSION OF EMOTION

The expression of emotion involves facial expressions, gestures, posture, movements, and vocal responses. This outward display of emotion, also called "affective expression," is linked to our inner emotional experience. The expression of emotion is primarily facial. Because the facial musculature has greater sensory and motor innervation than postural muscles or visceral organs (e.g., heart), expression of emotion through the face is much more specific. Facial expressions provide information or meaning about the emotional experience of the sender to other persons. They also provide internal feedback to the person emitting the facial expression.

FIGURE 4.1

"Tantrum Warning Device"
developed by child.

In order for an emotional signal to capture someone's attention, it should involve as many dimensions as possible. The toddler who sees his parent frown, stomp his foot, point with his finger, and firmly state "NO!" knows that his parent means business. In contrast, parents who have difficulty setting limits may display weak or even discrepant signals that are difficult to read and are confusing to the toddler. An ambivalent parent may smile as they say, "Now, don't throw your food, honey!" Some toddlers may be confused by this mismatch of signals. Others may know what is expected of them but continue on with their disruptive activity, suspecting that there are no consequences to their actions.

Universality of Emotional Expression

For many years, there has been an argument about whether facial expressions are universal or specific to cultures. One way to study this is by observing cultures that have had little contact with other cultures. Although people in such cultures do not display any facial expressions that are not observable in other cultures, there are certain standards or norms that individuals follow in expressing emotions. Ekman and Friesen (1969) have termed these "display rules." These are cultural norms that are internalized about when, where, and how an emotion is displayed. Therefore, affective expression will vary considerably depending on socialization and cultural norms. For example, in Western cultures, males are not expected to cry and females are generally expected not to display anger. In some societies, joy may be expressed through an uplifted body posture, laughing, large body movements, and loud vocal exclamations, while in others a simple smile may be all that is observed. Regardless of culture, there are certain facial expressions of emotion that are universal (Izard, 1971). The facial expressions that are universal to all cultures are fear, surprise, anger, disgust, distress, and happiness. There is less universality for interest, contempt, and shame.

of the top three or four targeted behaviors, the parents should leave it alone, letting the child do it their way. Compliance and good behavior should be reinforced with praise. Some families like using praise coupled with tangible reinforcers such as stickers, checks on a chart, a cookie, or a visit to the "Mommy Treat Bag" at the end of the day.

8. *Help the child become more self-reliant*: Many parents complain that their child is constantly whining and demanding their attention. To help build the child's capacity to organize himself and decrease reliance on the parent to entertain him, the caregiver should try playing with the child for about 10 to 15 minutes using the child's favorite toys. After the child is playing well, the parent should encourage the child to keep playing while they do a small chore or activity in the same room. Every few minutes, the parent should reassure and praise the child, "Good playing alone!" Mom or dad may try to keep the connection between them and their child by singing a song from across the room while they work.

Whenever the parent is involved in a task such as cooking a meal, it is wise to offer the child some pots and pans, plastic containers, and small objects to use in filling, dumping, stirring, and the like, so that the child can play and imitate the parent cooking. If the child complains, the parent should try to redirect him physically or verbally. The parent should be clear to the child about when it is time to pick them up and when it isn't because their hands are tied up. As soon as mom or dad are finished with their chore, they should reward their child by sitting with them to read a story or playing with him briefly to reward his playing alone. Young babies may be carried about in a sling or backpack while the parent does household chores so that he or she can see what mom or dad is doing.

With preschool and school-aged children, it is helpful to teach the child to label emotions and read bodily signals so that they can implement calm-down strategies on their own. Sometimes children respond to ideas like a traffic light or mood meter, with red colors denoting the time to put on the brakes or mad or angry feelings, and green or blue colors for calm and focused feelings. Other children respond well to thinking about "how their engine is running." A good resource book for therapists is the program on this topic developed by Williams and Shellenberger (1994).

9. *Develop tolerance for frustration and a sense of mastery*: Using child-centered play, parents can work with their child to develop the capacity to tolerate frustration. For example, suppose the child is trying to fit a toy into a container and is getting frustrated. The parent might reflect, "Yes, it doesn't fit!" rather than immediately help the child solve the problem. Mom or dad might gently reposition the container for better success, but should avoid taking the object from the child and solving the problem for him. It is a good idea to wait for the child to look to the parent for help. In this way, the child learns to

coordinate communication with others when frustrated. The parent may want to first reassure the child, "You can do it, keep trying." If this is not enough, the parent may help the child solve the problem through physical or verbal guidance.

Developing a sense of mastery is important to help the irritable child feel that he can overcome frustrations and gain pleasure from his own accomplishments. This can be done by giving the child small "jobs," like turning the lights on and off when leaving or entering the room, closing the dishwasher, or pushing a drawer shut. If these things are done everyday, it will help the child feel that he contributes to the family and is a big help. The child should also be encouraged to do age-appropriate activities that he can master such as stirring with a spoon to make pudding or playing with pull-apart toys like pop beads.

10. *Support the parents in feelings of isolation and provide respite*: Parents of irritable children can feel very isolated because normal parenting experiences are often precluded. For example, many parents report that they cannot take their child to play groups, birthday parties, or other family gatherings because their child will fall apart. Parents often express the fear that other caregivers may abuse their overly distressed baby, thus resulting in the parents never leaving their child with other caregivers when respite is sorely needed. When parents must cope with an infant who cries in excess of 2 hours a day or a child who is highly irritable, respite should be explored to help parents restore their capacity to deal with their overly fussy infant. The caregivers should give themselves a break before they explode at their child. Parents should be encouraged to put their child in a safe play area (not the crib or bedroom where he sleeps), and leave him for a few minutes so that he can calm down while the parents take a break for themselves as well.

11. *Address the parent's anxieties about the child's behavior*: It is important to talk with the parents to address their own anxieties and perceptions as to why child is crying or is irritable. For example, one set of parents believed that their young baby felt abandoned when she cried despite the fact that her parents were by her side almost constantly. As we explored this, it became apparent that both parents had issues around being emotionally neglected by their own parents. Once they learned ways of maintaining healthy connections with their child and became comfortable separating from their child, both parents and child became less anxious when together and apart.

It is often useful to help the parents become more attuned to their own reactions to their child's irritability. For example, if the child is anxious or angry, some parents may resonate to the child's emotion, becoming almost contagious to the same emotion. Instead of organizing or calming the child, the parents' reactions may cause emotions to escalate. As a result, sometimes irritable children end up having irritable parents and the irritable mood pervades the household.

12. *Help the parent to differentiate what the crying or irritability means*: Part of the therapy should focus on helping the parent observe when the child's cry or irritability is changing and recognize when and how the child self-soothes. Sometimes parents misconstrue normal babbling sounds as whining or they may view the child as constantly irritable when in fact the child is not. The therapist should empathize with how bad the crying or whining feels for the parents, then help them to read their child's signals. For example, the therapist might guide the parent, "Let's listen and see if we can tell what your child is telling us right now." By taking on a "watch, wait, and wonder" stance, the parent can step back from the experience momentarily to better read the child's vocal and gestural signals. The therapist can then help the parent distinguish between frustration, poor self-consoling, and expression of negative affects (e.g., aggression, discontent). In addition, the therapist should try to help the parents in grieving that they didn't get the child that they might have wanted and instead have one who is difficult, irritable, and demanding. Sometimes it is important to help the parents learn to accept that their child will always be more demanding and irritable in nature than other "easy children."

Case Example

Tommy was referred at 17 months of age because of high irritability. When Tommy was seen for the initial interview session, he was crying uncontrollably in his mother's arms in the waiting room. He cried throughout most of the session, only occasionally quieting down and wandering about to explore the toys in the office. Even when spoken to softly, he began to cry again inconsolably.

Mother's chief concerns were that Tommy was different from other babies and was very hard to handle. Tommy was recognized as different soon after birth. On his second day of life, a nurse from the newborn nursery approached his mother saying, "Mrs. G., you are going to have to do something about Thomas. He's keeping all the other babies awake." When he first came home from the hospital he was sleeping approximately 12 out of every 24 hours, and screamed most of the time that he wasn't asleep.

Earliest interventions were with a pediatrician, who diagnosed the baby as having "colic" and prescribed Donnatol when he was 4 weeks old. Neither parent wanted the baby to be medicated, so mother instead got a referral to a nurse practitioner. She explained that Tommy was very easily overstimulated—even by such things as faces, lights and noises. She recommended decreasing stimulation by doing such things as holding him facing away from mother when feeding and soundproofing his sleep environment.

Mother reported that during the child's first year he had otitis several times, which was then used as the explanation for his persistent crankiness. There was no current evidence of chronic ear pathology, and the remainder of his medical history was negative. He had good weight gain on breastfeeding, but was weaned at 3½ months of age because he kicked and punched, which the mother interpreted as his way of fighting being held. Once on bottle feedings, he slept through the night.

Mother tried to return to working part time when Tommy was 3½ months old. He was placed in a family day care, where he was with two other children. The caretaker described Tommy as "sensitive" and often reported to Mrs. G. that he was "cranky all day." Mother gave up going to work when the babysitter decided to take in more children. Although mother wanted to return to work, she felt that Tommy's fussiness could cause a caretaker who didn't really love him to abuse him. The parents had a limited support system to provide respite. Father's parents watched Tommy briefly on a few occasions, and a teenage babysitter was employed for a few hours in the daytime.

Mother reported that she felt that father had always been able to soothe Tommy a little better than she could and that he was the preferred person. Whenever she felt frustrated with Tommy, she gave him to her husband. At times, she reported, her husband had pointed out to her that she was acting irritable and/or tense with the child. Mother admitted having a great personal struggle with her current feelings about this child, which she described as being doubtful of her capacity to be a mother. She reported having felt this way even before Tommy was born, mainly because she felt she lacked the experience to be a good mother. She felt publicly embarrassed by his unsoothable crying.

Diagnostic Work-Up

Developmental testing, using the Bayley Scales of Infant Development, Mental Scale, was conducted, and Tommy was found to be functioning at age level. Despite his age-appropriate cognitive level of functioning, he exhibited definite evidence of an expressive language delay but no receptive language difficulties. In addition, he was unable to sit and play with toys, had difficulties initiating planned and purposeful actions, and demonstrated slow processing time during attentional tasks. On the Test of Sensory Functions in Infants, Tommy demonstrated severe hypersensitivities to touch and movement and an inability to plan simple motor actions in response to a sensory stimulus (e.g., textured mitt placed on his foot). His primary interests were gross motor tasks, but he had begun to like to look at pictures and magazines. His balance was poor, with falling, instability, and low muscle tone in his movement quality. Overall, Tommy exhibited delays in expressive language and in balance and muscle tone, was hypersensitive to touch, sound, and movement, and had attentional difficulties. In spite of mother's feelings of inadequacy, at every meeting she was gentle and supportive of him. On parent–child interaction measures, the mother was observed to be understimulating and at times somewhat withdrawn when Tommy played quietly. Mrs. G. was aware of this to the extent that she described not wanting to "rock the boat" when he was calm. Mother's interactions centered around assisting Tommy to obtain a toy out of reach or to introduce a new toy when he became fussy or distracted. No symbolic play or reciprocal interactions were observed. Tommy's manipulation of toys was stereotypic and immature for his age (e.g., taking toys in and out of box, shaking, banging).

Treatment Process

The treatment sessions focused on decreasing the tension between Tommy and his mother, and in the context of unpressured play with her, developing initiative, reciprocal interactions, purposeful manipulation of toys, regulation of mood state, and desensitizing responses to touch and movement. During the child-centered activity, Tommy spent a considerable amount of time lifting heavy push carts, pounding and pushing them on the floor, thus providing himself with heavy proprioceptive input and desensitizing his responses to loud noises. Mother discovered that when she gently imitated him his pleasure and length of time playing increased. In the first week of treatment, Mother was encouraged to allow Tommy to play in a large bin of styrofoam chips and to explore textured objects (e.g., slinky, rough hairbrushes), tactile activities that Tommy soon began to crave.

Within a very short period of time, Tommy developed a strong interest in interacting with both his parents. He appeared to derive enormous pleasure out of reciprocal interactions with them. His father began to attend our sessions and shared more excitement and involvement with his son. By the third week of treatment, Tommy's crying behavior was much diminished. The critical break appeared to occur once Tommy was able to express himself through gestures and he could tolerate touch, sounds, and movement. Tommy became much less reliant on his close-to-the-ground positions, including the W sitting posture and using trunk rotation in transitional movements, and fell much less often when walking. Moreover, he became very interested in looking at pictures and wanted to know the names of everything.

After a short-term intervention, Tommy was referred to the local public school's early identification program for enrollment. Furthermore, individualized speech and language therapy and occupational therapy were indicated. As Tommy improved, his mother began to talk about the contribution her self-doubts and depression had made to their difficulties.

Follow-Up

By the time Tommy was 4 years of age, he had made substantial progress in all areas of development. On testing, we found Tommy to be a very bright and verbal child. He was sociable and engaging. At school he had friends and home life was going well, although his mother found that she needed to adhere to predictable routines and to avoid introducing too many changes. The only intervention that was needed at the time was sensory integration therapy to address problems with motor planning, coordination, and balance. When Tommy reached third grade, the demands of school and homework became difficult for him, and he needed tutoring, but overall he did well in his development as he aged. Tommy is an example of a child who was highly irritable at birth and how this might impact him through the course of his development.

SUMMARY

In this chapter, the different ways in which constitutional and emotional factors contribute to emotional disorders were described. As demonstrated by the review of the literature and case scenarios, it is important to take into account the various ways that emotion regulation occurs and is manifested. The developmental–structuralist model described by Greenspan suggests that both adaptation and psychopathology can be described by the way in which sensory and affective–thematic experiences are organized. A comprehensive treatment model incorporates how the individual functions in his environment with focusing on helping the child develop the capacity to engage and self-regulate, to organize purposeful social communication and interactions with others, and to express emotional ideas and feelings while learning to self-monitor and evaluate the appropriateness of their responses. Therapeutic approaches need to address the child and family functioning, environmental modifications that support self-calming and organization, as well as parent–child interactions.

REFERENCES

Brazelton, T., Koslowski, B., & Main, M. (1974). The origins of reciprocity: The early mother–infant interaction. In M. Lewis & L. Rosenblum (Eds.), *The effect of the infant on its caregiver*. New York: Wiley.

Cannon, W. B. (1927). The James–Lange theory of emotions: A critical examination and an alternative theory. *American Journal of Psychology, 39*, 106–124.

Darwin, C. (1872). *The expression of the emotions in man and animals*. London: John Murray. (Reprinted 1965, Chicago: University of Chicago Press.)

Davidson, R. J. (1984). Hemispheric asymmetry and emotion. In K. R. Scherer & P. Ekman, (Eds.), *Approaches to Emotion* (pp. 39–58). Hillsdale, NJ: Erlbaum.

Some children have difficulty settling for sleep because of problems such as hyperactivity or sensory defensiveness that make it hard for the child to self-calm, to become physically comfortable in bed, or to screen noises from the environment. When this occurs, the child may need certain props in the bedroom to help him sleep. This will be discussed in detail in the treatment section of this chapter.

A home environment that is noisy and stimulating with few established routines will be less conducive to sleep than one that provides balanced levels of stimulation and calming, regularity in routines, an organized bedtime ritual, and a sleep environment that helps the child feel secure and calm. If the bedroom is very stimulating with Mickey Mouse portraits or high-intensity colors on the wall and with disorganization in the room (e.g., toys strewn around the floor), the child will be less able to decrease his arousal level for sleep. Likewise, the child will be affected by a home environment that is busy or very noisy. For example, there may be other children sharing the bedroom and making noise, the TV may be on after the child has tried to go to sleep, or adults in the house may have different sleep schedules because of their work life.

Where the parents choose to have the child sleep is often a very important piece of information that helps to understand the attachment process. Oftentimes this information is best obtained during a home visit. Sometimes parents may be reluctant to create separate space for a child because of their own need to have the child remain in their bedroom. This was demonstrated with 18-month-old Emily, who was sleeping with her parents but was giving signals that she would like her own space and separateness, playing games when she would leave her parents' side to go find things elsewhere in the room. When we did the home visit, we asked if Mrs. C. could show us Emily's bedroom. It turned out that Emily did not have a bedroom of her own despite the fact that the family had a three-bedroom home with only one child. One bedroom was the room where the parents slept with Emily; the other two bedrooms had been converted to a home office and a room for Mrs. C.'s weaving loom, yarns, and quilt projects. We talked about the importance of Emily having her own place and suggested that perhaps mother's project room might become Emily's bedroom. Mrs. C. then complained, saying, "Where will I do my projects?" In another situation that we found particularly disturbing, we learned that Maya, an adopted 9-month-old baby, slept downstairs our of earshot of the parents' bedroom in the dining room because her parents could not tolerate her screaming through the night. Mr. and Mrs. T. were ambivalent about adopting Maya, particularly when they discovered that she had a hearing impairment. They were pondering whether to send her back to her country of origin. As we worked with the family on attachment and understanding Maya's developmental needs, her screaming at night lessened. We felt that we had achieved a major breakthrough in their relationship with Maya when they created a bedroom for her next to their own bedroom, showed genuine signs of affection for Maya, and became interested in learning how to use simple signs to communicate with her.

When children sleep with their parents, the preschool or school-aged child may become aroused by the physical contact but not know how to handle these impulses. Some children become aggressive toward their parents, siblings, or peers during the daytime as a way of trying to discharge these impulses. The child may have difficulty accepting limits, complying with requests, and tolerating distress because of the lack of boundaries at nighttime. In addition, the child may witness sexual activity between the parents that they do not know how to handle emotionally. Usually the child misconstrues the sexual activity as aggressive. Addressing the sleep problem becomes more than simply one of working on separation and individuation, but one that is tied up in physical and emotional boundaries.

TYPES OF SLEEP DISORDERS IN CHILDREN

What constitutes a sleep disorder? There are several different types of sleep problems, some more common at different ages. The most common sleep problem is insomnia, when the child has trouble falling and staying asleep. Occasionally one sees children with excessive somnolence who sleep many hours of the day and night. As children develop, they may develop unusual sleep behaviors such as recurring night terrors or nightmares. The child may have an unusual sleep cycle, sleeping for a few hours at a time, then fully awakening. Of course, whenever sleep problems are present, it is important to rule out medical problems—including sleep apnea, such painful conditions as reflux, or severe ear infections and allergies (e.g., milk intolerance)—that may contribute to the sleep problem. The next section describes the problems of insomnia or excessive somnolence in detail as they relate to different regulatory and sensory profiles. These two types of sleep problems are emphasized because they are more likely to occur in children with regulatory disorders.

The Hypersensitive Child

Children with sensory integrative dysfunction related to hypersensitivities to touch and sound may experience sleep problems because they are easily hyper-aroused and find it difficult to get comfortable and settle for sleep. A child with this problem may become agitated with the bed sheets laying on their body or fuss with the way their pajamas feel. Sometimes the tactually defensive child falls asleep more easily if he has the body contact of a parent lying next to him, which in turn reinforces the child needing a parent to lie nearby to fall asleep.

A 4-year-old boy named Sam had this problem. Ever since he was an infant, he insisted that his parents go through a series of bedtime rituals. First, his mother would give him a 15-minute massage and get him dressed, but only after Sam changed his nightclothes several times before finding just the right one. This was followed by three bedtime stories with dad. Mr. N. would then lie down next to Sam and sing several songs while Sam would shine his flashlight at the glow-in-the-dark stars on his ceiling. Mrs. N. would return to the bedroom and lie down next to Sam. He would fall asleep while twirling his mother's hair in tight knots for almost 30 minutes. This routine took about 2 hours each night. Sam often reawakened in the night and wanted parts of the routine to settle him back to sleep. His parents eventually gave up and began taking turns sleeping in Sam's room but remained exhausted by their child's obsessive needs for settling that centered around his sensory and emotional needs.

Hypersensitivities to sound may result in the child having difficulty screening out noises in the environment to allow for sleep. The slightest noise agitates them or causes them to reawaken. The problem is aggravated when the household tends to be very noisy (e.g., several children in close quarters, the television on constantly) or full of activity. Children with hypersensitivities to sound often do well when provided with white noise.

In rare instances, the child who is extremely hypersensitive may shut down and sleep for long periods of time when overwhelmed by stimulation. Some parents misconstrue the child's need for sleep as simply a high need for rest. Ian, at 12 months, slept about 18 hours a day. When he was evaluated, we found that he was delayed in his developmental milestones, but that he was also severely hypersensitive to all stimulation. By decreasing the level of stimulation at home and keeping a calm environment for him, he became more interested in participating in activities and accommodated fairly quickly to a normal sleep–wake schedule. He quickly developed many skills, catching up in all areas except language. In another instance, 3-year-old Courtney came home after 6 hours in day care and would take a 3-hour nap, then wish to go to sleep by 7:00 p.m., sleeping through to 6:00 a.m. She, too, was hypersensitive to touch and was not only shutting down when she came home but was becoming aggressive at day care, biting and hitting other children who came near her. Both sleep patterns and aggression improved with a program that included sensory integration activities to address her tactile defensiveness, calm-down areas at day care and home, and a decrease in the number of her activities at day care.

The Child Who Craves Movement

Another type of sensory integration problem that may affect sleep is the child who craves vestibular stimulation, but becomes hyperaroused by the movement. Infants with this problem love to be bounced vigorously, wish to be held and carried constantly, like to ride in the infant swing, and may fall asleep only if they ride in the car for long periods of time. Some babies with this need for movement also like vibration. For example, one 9 month old would only fall asleep if he was placed in a laundry basket on the clothes dryer (with the heat turned off, of course). Many parents report how their child is gleeful when father comes home from work and can roughhouse or wrestle with them on the floor after dinner. Although the child needs vestibular stimulation, he becomes overstimulated by the movement and finds the task of settling for sleep very difficult. Many times children who crave movement stimulation also like heavy proprioceptive input (e.g., climbing, pushing heavy objects, wrestling with a sibling). At 7 years, Joshua was a hyperactive boy who constantly moved and sought movement activities. If he wasn't directed to do focused movement activities such as riding his bicycle to get milk from the grocery store after school or playing soccer with his friends, he would become aimless, running up and down the stairs and whirling around the house, and crashing into furniture and people. During the nighttime he was at his worst. After the bedtime routine, his parents would put him to bed, then after a few minutes he would escape from the bedroom, run up and down the hallway, jump on his parents' bed, and laugh loudly. Limit setting at bedtime was unsuccessful until it was coupled with a program of helping Joshua get enough vestibular stimulation in the afternoon, with slow movement and deep pressure activities after dinner.

Problems with Attachment and Separation/Individuation

Some children struggle with falling and staying asleep because of problems related to attachment. Problems separating from the caregiver can occur for several reasons. The child with an insecure or disorganized attachment will become anxious whenever there are separations from the parent during the day or night. The origins of insecure or disorganized attachment need to be explored in order to properly address its impact on sleep. The parent may experience conflicts around leaving the child, projecting fears that relate to their own past. For example, one couple had tried to use the Ferber method with their baby but could not stand the crying and felt compelled to rush in immediately to console the baby. They found the crying so intolerable that soon the child was sleeping in their bed, which lasted for the next 4 years. When I explored this with them, they revealed that each felt they were abandoning their child, but for different reasons. When the mother was 8 years old, she had a sister who died from leukemia. The ghost of the sister seemed to loom over her parenting, affecting how she parented Danielle and her ability to allow her daughter space to leave her side and explore the world. She constantly hovered over Danielle, creating the feeling that there were constant dangers in the world around her. For example, she would not allow her to play at other children's houses or go to birthday parties without her being present and within sight. The father was anxious about being left alone and needed to be surrounded by people and activity all day long. He was less open to exploring what it was about being alone that troubled him. By the time Danielle was 4 years old, she appeared to be a highly anxious, hyperactive child who needed to be occupied by her parents all of the time and was unable to organize even a single play activity by herself. When Danielle was 5 years old and had been in therapy for about 6 months, her parents were finally able to allow her to sleep in her own bedroom. At first, her parents needed to check on her constantly to be sure that she was safe in her bedroom. Mr. P. took to sleeping in a sleeping bag in the hallway for a while until he felt assured that Danielle was secure. Despite their anxieties about leaving her alone, they did not know how to play with Danielle and needed help in allowing Danielle to self-organize her play. It was difficult for Mr. and Mrs. P. not to constantly teach her or provide structured activities all day long. Emphasis in the treatment was placed on helping Mr. and Mrs. P. understand the developmental task of being and sleeping alone, the importance of gaining a sense of self and separateness from others, and of learning how to negotiate normal boundaries of intimacy with others. Addressing the parents' difficulties in engaging with Danielle around developmentally appropriate and pleasurable interactive activities remained a major focus of treatment.

In another family, the mother had set up a video camera, supplemented by an audio monitor, in her year-old child's bedroom to monitor the baby's sleep and wakening patterns. Although it was not readily apparent to the mother why she had done this, she was able to make the connection with a little intervention that this related to her early upbringing. When growing up, her parents often fought at night while Mrs. D. tried to sleep. When Mrs. D. was 6 years old, her father beat her mother in one of these late night fights and broke mother's nose. Her mother gathered up the children during the night and moved them immediately to grandmother's home. All contact with her father was refused by her mother, but after a year he was killed in a car accident. Despite the violence in her home, Mrs. D. loved her father and was traumatized by these events and her loss. Throughout her life, she remained anxious about being alone and often suffered from insomnia. Needless to say, her background influenced mother to feel that bad things might happen to her child if she was not constantly vigilant. Working to make both mother and child feel safe were important to addressing the sleep problem.

Sometimes parents who need to leave their children at a babysitter's or day care during the day feel ambivalent about leaving their child to sleep alone at night, perhaps feeling guilty about leaving them for many hours during the day while they work. Other parents have strong unmet needs for intimacy that are fulfilled by their child. This problem was depicted by Lisa, an 18 month old. The pregnancy was accidental, but mother decided to go through with the pregnancy because she had always wanted children. After she had Lisa, she and her husband adopted the LaLeche League philosophy, allowing Lisa to nurse whenever she wished and to sleep in their bed at night. By 18 months, Lisa was showing no desire to wean from the breast and insisted on nursing every 1½ hours through the night. This problem was the reason that the mother sought help, largely because the constantly interrupted sleep made it difficult for her to work at her job during the day. Because the mother could not tolerate separating from her daughter and enjoyed the physical closeness at night, she encouraged her daughter's sleeping in their bedroom. The bedroom was large, so the parents equipped it with two king-sized beds, placed side by side because Lisa screamed when confined to a crib. Containing Lisa during the day was difficult for the parents. For example, Lisa cried whenever placed in a car seat or playpen. The nanny who took care of her began carrying and rocking Lisa most of the day despite her age. Mother was very anxious about allowing Lisa to separate from her side. She was also resistant to weaning Lisa because she enjoyed the intimacy with her child, even though weaning might help Lisa begin to sleep continuously through the night.

Before mother could consider this, we began to focus on separation games during the daytime to help both mother and child tolerate moving away from one another in play (e.g., hide and seek). We also spent time talking about what being alone meant for both parents. Mrs. B. revealed that it was at nighttime that she felt anxious about being unloved and lonely, something she had felt for many years. She felt that her daughter comforted her at night and made her feel less lonely. Mr. and Mrs. B. explored how they were developing separate lives from one another, rarely doing things together as a couple anymore. Mrs. B. was reluctant to give up breast feeding and sleeping with Lisa but realized the importance of finding better ways to fulfill her own needs for intimacy while providing good boundaries (e.g., this is your space and this is mine), setting limits, and finding appropriate expression of intimacy with her daughter (e.g., through child-centered play and other pleasurable games). Mr. B. welcomed the opportunity to become more involved with his daughter, both in taking charge of some of the child care activities and in finding enjoyable ways to play with Lisa.

Some children use the sleep situation as a means of controlling their parents and getting attention that they may not get during the daytime hours. When exploring sleep problems, it is useful to find out how the parents and child spend their waking hours together and the quality of engagement with one another. In one particular case, a 9 month old, Devon, had learned to control his mother both day and night. When the mother called me to make the first appointment, she described her child as "the devil himself." The problem first began around eating when 6-month-old Devon would refuse to eat for his mother, compressing his lips and turning his face away from his mother. He ate well for the nanny, which caused mother to feel rejected by her baby. By 9 months, Devon began to fight off sleep, sleeping only 20 to 30 minutes at a time for a total of 6 hours per day. When he awakened, he would scream at the top of his lungs until his mother would come and hold him. He would gasp and hyperventilate so badly that his mother would take him out of the crib and hold him. Father could not stand the screaming and would go in and yell at Devon. His attempts to comfort his son made no difference. Devon would shake his head "no," then lunge his body around in the crib, sometimes catapulting over the crib's edge. In the end, the parents concluded that what he wanted was mother to go in to be with him. The parents had tried everything with Devon, including the Ferber technique. They finally resorted to using medications, starting with Benadryl and later Valium, all with a physician's oversight. There was no beneficial effect from any of these medication trials.

In working with Devon and his mother, several things became apparent. Devon was an extremely bright and competent child who was on the verge of walking and talking at 9 months. He was highly vigilant, constantly looking around the room and extremely wary if approached by a stranger. Mrs. P. could play with Devon for short periods of time in a highly engaging way, but after about 10 minutes she would need a break from playing with him, finding the intensity of the interaction overwhelming to her. Mrs. P. revealed that she had several miscarriages before having Devon and was enormously disappointed that she had a baby who was so demanding after trying so hard to conceive a child. Marital issues were an overriding factor, with mother feeling little support from her husband, who tended to work long hours to avoid being around Devon's screaming and controlling behavior. To make any changes in Devon's sleep problems and the family dynamics, it would be important to address issues around attachment, loss and disappointment, and what control serves in this family. Getting attention in positive ways and learning how to engage in pleasurable interactions with one another would be an important direction for the intervention.

The case examples provided in this section demonstrate the wide variety of problems that can occur when sleep is an issue. Although there are some children for whom simple parental guidance is all that is needed, there are many other cases where the problem is highly complex. In such cases, intervention needs to address the child's constitutional or developmental needs, the parent–child relationship, the parent's own past history, and marital issues that may effect sleep.

EVALUATING SLEEP PROBLEMS IN THE CHILD

Evaluating the child's sleep problems should begin with a comprehensive sleep history of the child. Below is a checklist of items that may be included in this history.

1. What time does the child awaken in the morning?
   a. What is the morning routine?
   b. What mood does the child have when he or she awakens?
   c. Do the parents have to do anything special to arouse the child in the morning (e.g., body rub-down, several loud alarm clocks)?
2. What types of activities does the child engage in during the day?
   a. How much time is spent in the following:
      —passive activities such as watching TV
      —movement experiences such as playing on playground equipment or, in the case of the infant, time in a stroller, riding in infant swing, riding in the car, or roughhouse play
      —learning activities and interactive play with the parents

3. What types of demands are placed on the child to separate from the parents during the day?
   a. Are the parents both working?
   b. Is the child in day care or with a babysitter?
   c. How does the child handle separations from the parents in general?
   d. How do the parents feel about leaving their child when they have to go out?
   e. What do the parents do when they leave (e.g., say goodbye versus sneak out the door hoping that the child won't notice)?
4. How does the child handle transitions in activities and limits during the day?
   a. Are there regular routines and certain scheduled activities at home, at day care, etc.?
   b. Does the child like routines and do well with them?
   c. Are the caregivers comfortable keeping routines and an organized life style?
   d. Does the child become overly dependent on routines and refuse to vary from them?
   e. Does the child need extensive warning when a routine will vary or when a new event will be happening?
   f. How does the child respond to limits (e.g., tantrums if not given their own way)? How do the parents set limits on the child (e.g., does the parent warn the child that if they don't behave, the boogie man will come and get them at night)?
5. How much stimulation occurs in the home or day-care setting (e.g., number of persons in household, types of activity going on, noise level, closeness of quarters)?
   a. How does the child respond to everyday stimulation (e.g., retreats to a corner, follows parent around constantly, takes a 3 hour nap when overwhelmed)?
6. Does the child nap, and does it occur at a set time everyday?
   a. How long is the nap?
   b. If the child sleeps too long, does it disrupt the evening sleep pattern?
   c. Where does the child sleep when he or she naps?
   d. Does the child need help to fall asleep for the nap (e.g., bottle, being held)?
7. What is the evening routine like?
   a. What is the bedtime ritual, if there is one? Is it organizing for the child or does it cause the child to become overstimulated (e.g., roughhouse time with dad when he gets home from work, playing a computer game before bed)?

    b. If the child has a nighttime snack, what is it (e.g., sweets, milk products, cola products with caffeine)?

    c. Where does the child fall asleep? If he falls asleep in a place other than his own bed, do the parents take him into his bed later?

    d. What time is the child put into bed and when does he actually fall asleep?

    e. What is the bedroom environment like (e.g., colors, organization, where bed is located in room)?

    f. How does the child fall asleep (e.g., with parent's help or by themselves)? What are the self-soothers that the child uses to fall asleep and which sensory systems do they involve (e.g., auditory—lullabies; vision—reading books; movement sense—rocking; touch-pressure—massage, warm bath, lying next to parent)?

    g. Does the child behave differently for one parent over the other during the bedtime routine?

    h. How does the child's bedtime behavior affect the family?

8. Once the child is asleep, does the child awaken, how often, and what do the parents do when it occurs? For example, do they go into the bedroom and play with child, rock him, feed him?

    a. How do the parents know the child awakens (e.g., use of monitor, parent is in room)?

    b. What does the child do when he or she awakens (e.g., whimper, scream, play loudly with toys in room, shake crib vigorously, dump objects from dresser on floor)?

    c. If the child cries, what does the parent think it means (e.g., the child is being abandoned)?

    d. How does the parent feel when the child awakens (e.g., irritated, enraged)?

    e. What does the parent do when the child awakens (e.g., Ferber method of ignoring for increments of crying)?

    f. Do the parents awaken and find the child in their bed?

9. What are the sleeping arrangements? Do the parents sleep in the child's bed, does the child sleep in the parents' bed, or does the child sleep alone in a room or with other siblings?

    a. How much sleep does the child get in the night (what time does he fall asleep and what time does he awaken in the morning)?

    b. Does the child wet his bed? Does he get up in the night to eat or use the bathroom?

    c. Do the parents feed the child a bottle in the middle of the night while the child is sleeping?

10. Does the child's nighttime behavior disturb others in the family, neighborhood?

    a. What restrictions need to be kept in mind in working on the child's sleep problem (e.g., one parent has medical problem and needs child to be absolutely quiet, neighbors complain in apartment next door, other child awakens and then screams)?

    b. Does the child's sleep problems affect social situations such as sleep-overs with friends?

11. Does the child have bad dreams or nightmares? What about night terrors or sleep walking?

    a. Has the child ever done anything unsafe at night (e.g., get up and watch X-rated TV shows without parents knowing, leave the house at night to go in back yard, cooks something on the stove)?

    b. Does the child usually watch TV before going to sleep? Do the TV programs cause the child to become fearful or overly agitated?

    c. Has the child seen scary movies that cause the child to be more fearful at night?

12. What is the parents' own sleep history? Did they sleep with their parents?

    a. What is their belief about children learning to sleep through the night (e.g., LaLeche League philosophy of family bed)?

13. Did either or both parents suffer any significant losses in their life (e.g., death of parent as a child)?

    a. What was the parents' first memory of being separated from their own parents? How did they handle it?

    b. Do they have any sleep problems of their own and what are they related to (e.g., anxieties about work, depression, snoring, sleep apnea)?

    c. If the parents have sleep problems, what do they do to help themselves sleep?

14. Are the parents comfortable being alone and what do they do with their time when they have an opportunity for aloneness?

    a. Is the child ever left alone to play while the parents are nearby? Can the child play alone or is the child constantly by the parents' side?

    b. Has the child ever been left with a babysitter or in day care? How does the child handle it?

15. Have the sleep problems changed over time? When were they at their worst?

    a. What has worked in the past to help the child's sleep problems? What has not worked?

    b. What do the parents think will help now and what are they willing to try?

MANAGEMENT OF SLEEP PROBLEMS

The best way to approach sleep problems is to provide a program that addresses the sensory, emotional, and biological needs that help organize a child for sleep. Below is an outline of a comprehensive program for sleep management that encompasses these components. Marital problems and psychodynamic issues that the parents bring to the process should also be explored when these affect the process. Suggestions for managing other sleep-related problems such as enuresis and nightmares have been discussed in detail in the *Clinical Handbook of Sleep Disorders in Children* (Schaefer, 1995). Schmitt (1986) and Daws (1989) have also provided many helpful suggestions in addressing sleep problems.

1. *Develop an appropriate sleep–wake schedule for the child and a bedtime routine that is predictable.* Discourage daytime sleeping for more than 3 consecutive hours for a newborn and for more than 1½ to 2 hours for toddlers or preschool-aged children.

2. *Address sensory problems associated with high arousal* (e.g., vestibular underreactivity, noise sensitivity, and tactile defensiveness). A sensory diet should be provided in a scheduled way. Intense vestibular input is useful when provided in the afternoon, avoiding roughhouse and intense movement experiences after dinner. Remember that movement activities help burn off energy and satisfy a need for movement stimulation, but that they also increase arousal. Deep pressure activities are especially useful in the evening.

3. *Evaluate if milk intolerance affects sleep.* If the child is breast fed, the mother needs to be sure that she is not drinking or eating milk products that might affect the child's sleep.

4. *The child should be put in bed awake rather than drowsy or asleep.* This should follow a predictable bedtime routine that both parent and child enjoy. A warm bath, stories, songs, hugs, massage, and holding a transitional object are some of the things that most children and parents enjoy in this ritual. The parents should limit the length of the bedtime routine and not let the child snare them into "just one more story" or "just one more game." Bedtime is not playtime and should be differentiated as such.

5. *Give the child a security object at bedtime to provide the child with comfort in the middle of the night should they awaken.* Most children like a transitional object that they also use during the daytime hours as well, such as a stuffed animal. Some children like having an object that "smells" like the parents (e.g., mother's perfume). It is often helpful for the mother or father to carry the object with them and the child for a few days wherever they go to acquire importance as a transitional object and to get some of the scents of the parents. Some parents will sleep with the object for a few nights to give it their scent. Parents should avoid giving burp rags as transitional objects because they will signal the baby to want to eat.

Child holding transitional object.

6. *Once the child reaches 6 to 7 months of age, use the Ferber method* (Ferber, 1985) *to address night wakings with increments of waiting before going into the bedroom to reassure the child.* The program involves instituting a schedule of visiting the child when he wakes and begins a full-blown cry. The first night, the parents should go into the child's bedroom after 5 minutes of crying. They may pat the child and reassure him but should not pick him up, rock him, or play with him. After he is settled, they should leave. The next night, they wait until 10 minutes of crying before they go in. Each night the length of time is increased by 5 minutes. This interval may be modified to smaller increments for some children who need a more gradual approach.

7. *It is important to talk with the caregivers about how to cope with the child's crying when it occurs at night and to demystify what the crying is about.* Many parents feel they are abandoning their child or the child is insecure and fearful. The child needs to sleep but may be overtired or wants to play. By letting the child cry, the parents help the child learn that this is a time to rest and that sleep will come naturally. It is useful to tell parents that they can't sleep or eat for their child and that these are tasks that the child must learn for themselves. Discourage the parents from projecting their own feelings onto the situation: "Oh, you're afraid of the dark, aren't you?"

8. *Discourage allowing the child to have a bottle to fall asleep or to have a middle-of-the-night feeding* (after 4 months of age). If the parents must feed their infant during the night, they should give 1 to 2 ounces less of formula than they would during the day, or the mother should nurse on only one side. When children are fed in the middle of the night, it becomes increasingly

more difficult to eliminate this as the child grows older. In addition, it is also important that the caregivers try to avoid giving the child cereal before bedtime in an attempt to induce sleep. There appears to be no relationship between feeding the child bedtime solids and induction of sleep (Beal, 1969; Deisher, 1954).

9. *For children over 6 or 7 months, it is a good idea not to play or hold the child when they awaken unless the child is ill.* It is a good idea to leave the door to the child's room open to help reduce nighttime fears. If the child awakens and is fearful, the parents may check in on the child and reassure him. If the child should become so upset that he vomits, it is best to throw a large towel over the vomit rather than taking the child out of the crib or bed to clean the sheets. This way, the parent avoids lifting the child out of the crib and giving more attention to the distressed behavior. It is usually a good idea to remain in the room until the child calms down or has gone back to sleep if they have become extremely upset and are very fearful. If the child is old enough to understand the concept, the parent may encourage the child to "spray" out monsters in the room using a water or perfume spray bottle.

10. *Assure that the bedroom environment supports sleep* (e.g., oscillating fan, white noise, stuffed toy that "smells" of parent, lullabies). When the child is put in bed or the crib, turn on some soft music, a rotating fan, or white noise audiotapes. The room should be reasonably dark and quiet, and the television should be turned off during the bedtime ritual and after the child has gone to sleep.

11. *When a child has motor issues that prevent him or her from positioning comfortably in the bed, a waterbed mattress, crib cradle (similar to a suspended hammock), or vibrating crib attachment sometimes offer help.* These positional devices should not be tried unless the child is completely healthy and there is no risk of the neck compressing to cut off airflow.

12. *Address separation issues during the daytime with games such as peek-a-boo and hide and seek.* Look to see if the child can move away from the parent on his own. Also watch the parent's face for any signs of anxiety on reunion with their child.

13. *Provide opportunities to play about sleep, nesting into pillows or cubbies during the child-centered play.* Older children often like to play with toy animals or dolls using doll houses, beds, stables, wagons, or other symbols of containment. Preschoolers often enjoy role playing putting their parents to sleep and developing a system of rules for the parents' bedtime.

14. *The time between dinner through the bedtime ritual should be organized and presented to the child in a relaxed and enjoyable manner.* If the parents feel rushed or irritable because they feel pressured, the child will also feel this way.

Mother and child playing game of peek-a-boo.

15. *Encourage the parents to get adequate rest and relaxation so they are available for caretaking activities and feel they have the reserves to carry out the bedtime program.* One parent may need to be "on" for certain nights while the other one sleeps in a quiet area. In cases when there is a single parent, obtaining respite services through community or local school agencies may be needed.

16. *Provide emotional support to the caregivers to address feelings of anger or guilt that may arise in carrying out the program.* It is very important that when there are two or more caregivers there is agreement on the philosophy of the bedtime program. This avoids the possibility that one caregiver might sabotage the program (e.g., hold child when they cry, invite child into parents' bed, provide middle of night feeding). If parents insist on sleeping with the child, it is important to address their issues around separation and marital issues that are likely to be present. Parents need to feel secure that they are doing a good job in putting their child to sleep. Reassuring the parents that some children are more difficult and need more attention and emotional security at bedtime is important. It is useful to explain to the parents that they can't help their children feel secure at nighttime if they feel anxious, depressed, angry, resentful, or stressed. Many children develop anticipatory anxiety at bedtime when parents express these emotions. It is often helpful if parents can empathize with how their child feels while providing emotional security to help the child at this difficult time of day.

17. *It is often helpful to maintain a daily sleep log noting activities that were done during the daytime* (e.g., high-intensity movement activities in afternoon,

nap), the child's mood, and the nighttime sleep schedule to help understand the child's sleep rhythms and what has helped or not helped in the process.

18. *Use sedatives at night if other methods described above have not worked.* These should be prescribed by the child's pediatrician. Melatonin has been used successfully under physician guidance as a means of treating serious and chronic sleep disorders (Jan *et al.*, 1994; Jan & O'Donnell, 1996).

Separation Games that Help Support Sleep: Suggestions for Parents

Because sleep is a separation issue, playing separation games during the daytime help both parents and child become comfortable with the process. Below are suggested some activities that can be modified by a parent depending on the age of the child.

1. *Playing disappearing games with objects is easier than having a favorite person disappear.* Start with what is not so emotionally charged for the child. Hide favorite toys under sofa cushions, under tables, around the room threshold, and so on. Then encourage the child to find her "Big Bird." You can hide and retrieve objects or make the game more elaborate by hiding the toy, then take the baoy outside the room for a few seconds with you, then run back to find the toy.

2. *Play peek-a-boo around corners of rooms, from under blankets, and behind furniture.* Play games that move from one room to another, like rolling a ball and chasing it into the next room. Or play a "magic carpet" ride, pulling the child on a beach towel from one place to another in the house. Create spaces to crawl through, like a big box.

3. *Make a "goodbye" book with pictures of mom, dad, and baby, including mom waving "goodbye," coming home, and the like.* Use the book to read to the child. The parents can give it to him when they leave him at the babysitter's or at day care.

4. *Many parents slip out the door to avoid goodbyes.* Let the child see parents get ready to leave. Ritualize the goodbye so that the child can predict the routine. When leaving him or her with the babysitter, take some extra time so that it's not a rushed time. The parents should be sure to have a reunion when they return, offering a hug and a kiss. The parents may practice saying goodbye and leaving for short periods of time while they do a brief chore (e.g., 5 minutes), gradually increasing the time that they are away.

5. *Leave a "transitional object" (stuffed animal, keys, blanket) with him when the parents leave.* The parents should carry this object with them and their baby when going places to attach special meaning to it. It becomes a symbol that they will come back.

In the next section, two cases are presented that demonstrate different types of sleep problems and how they were treated using different approaches.

Case Example of a Long-Standing Sleep Problem: When "Nothing Works"

Ms. T., Madison's mother, came in for the initial intake interview to discuss her 4-year-old child's sleep difficulties. I had met Madison and her mother the first time when she was 18 months, also because of sleep problems. Ms. T. was a 36-year-old single woman who had wanted a child desperately and chose to become pregnant through artificial insemination. At the time I evaluated Madison at 18 months, I found her to be a very competent toddler who was experiencing difficulties around learning to self-soothe and separate from her mother. We worked with mother and child in a short-term treatment model. Although Madison improved temporarily in her sleep problems using approaches described in this chapter, it seemed that Ms. T. had difficulty following through on the treatment program. The Ferber method was one of the things that had been recommended, but Ms. T. found Madison's screaming intolerable.

According to Ms. T., nothing seemed to work, but when I asked how long she tried any one technique it seemed that consistency was a problem. In fact, over the intervening 3 years, Ms. T. tried numerous different approaches to address Madison's sleep problems. When she called me, Madison was 4 years old. She was desperate, feeling that she needed to solve Madison's sleep problems because she was exhausted and unable to function in her job as a schoolteacher. I wondered what Madison's sleep problem served for both mother and child.

During the interview, Ms. T. described Madison as a very sweet and loving 4½-year-old child who could be very demanding. She attended nursery school during the day and seemed to be doing quite well. Madison had a long daytime nap as soon as she got home from school in the afternoon. Because of the long nap, Madison would not be ready to fall asleep until around 10:30 or 11:00 p.m. Up until the past 6 months, Madison would sleep alone in her bedroom as long as mom would lie down beside her until she fell asleep. Because Madison would call out throughout the night for her mother, Ms. T. decided to sleep on a trundle bed beside Madison's own bed so that she wouldn't have to get up and go into Madison's bedroom in the middle of the night.

Once Ms. T. had begun to sleep in Madison's bedroom, she could not break Madison of the habit. When I saw her, Madison would not sleep anywhere else except beside her mother. Not only that, she needed a constant supply of bottles throughout the night, sucking on a bottle while she slept. As soon as a bottle was emptied, she would awaken and want another bottle. Sometimes Madison would awaken and want something to eat, and, because Madison was a poor eater, Ms. T. would give her something, usually a sandwich or yogurt. To avoid getting up to get more bottles, Ms. T. would set out several bottles of juice beside Madison's bed. During the night, Madison would call out because she couldn't find a bottle, she couldn't find her stuffed lamb doll, or she was so wet that she couldn't stand it. Ms. T. felt that she was getting about 4 to 5 hours of sleep a night.

In the morning, the bedroom was filled with empty bottles. The sheets were soaking wet even though Madison wore diapers to bed. Ms. T. felt cranky and tired all day long and was having difficulty working at her job.

During the day, Madison would soothe herself by drinking from a bottle while watching television, which she would do after her day at preschool. Ms. T. stated that the bottle was the only thing that would calm her down and help her feel less cranky and fall asleep. She tried getting rid of the bottle by using rewards and stickers, cutting down gradually, substituting plain water in the bottle and talking about the problem. Ms. T. was also concerned about the serious decay that was found on Madison's teeth. Madison agreed that she needed to give up the bottle but found she couldn't do it.

Ms. T. elaborated further on the importance of the afternoon nap. She stated that, if Madison did not get her nap, she would become overwrought and have a huge tantrum. Apparently, other children had stopped coming over to play with her because she would need a nap and couldn't play after school. Ms. T. felt that Madison had no social life because the nap prevented Madison from having play dates after school.

Ms. T. found Madison to be extremely demanding of her time and attention. She found it hard to find time to do food shopping, laundry, and clean the apartment. She resented fixing the bottles, and washing diapers and wet sheets. The whole apartment smelled of urine.

Ms. T. felt that she, too, had difficulty separating from Madison and hated leaving her when she went to work. Mother appeared exhausted and depressed when I met her and was on antidepressants to help her cope. As a young adult, she had a history of drug and alcohol abuse but claimed that she drank only occasionally in social situations. Her mother was an alcoholic, and during mother's teen years she would yell at Ms. T. to vacuum, cook, and clean to her satisfaction while she drank, then force Ms. T. to lie to her father that her mother was not drinking. It was clear that Ms. T. suffered from issues around codependency.

Evaluation Findings

When I met Madison for the evaluation, I was struck by her waif-like appearance. She appeared anxious about seeing me, but with urging she was able to pick something that she liked to play with. The evaluation began with a play observation with her mother, followed by a clinical interview. At first she chose to play with the doll house. The whole time she played with the dolls, she rarely spoke, sometimes whispering in her mother's ear. She seemed to want her mother to watch her play rather than playing in a more active way. She looked at her mother occasionally but seemed content to engage in solitary play. Madison set up the dolls to eat at the table, doing so in a slow-paced manner, setting the table over and over again but never serving any food to the doll family. I was struck by her expression of a need for fulfillment, but the lack of meeting dependency needs.

Madison did not talk about what the dolls were doing, nor did she make the dolls talk. After this, she put the dolls to sleep. At this point, I joined her play to see how she would engage with me, hoping to draw her out a bit more. Madison allowed me to take on the role of some of the dolls. She put dolls to sleep in the house in a "sleep-over." Soon every room in the house was filled with dolls piled high and sleeping on top of one another. When I brought dolls to the house to ask what was going on, Madison smiled meekly, but still preferred playing alone. When I asked her a few questions about her play, she told me that the dolls liked sleeping on top of one another.

Madison's play seemed to center around play themes related to bodily functions of eating and sleep, dependency, and a lack of separation or differentiation between persons. Although she could organize some simple pretend play, it seemed that she was not comfortable engaging in a range of interactions with others (e.g., back-and-forth interchanges). She could respond to cues from me but only on her own terms. Her play had a highly repetitive quality, and there was little elaboration of play ideas of what was happening. She appeared constricted in expressing herself on both gestural and verbal levels. Even with prompting, Madison could only express basic thoughts about what was happening in her play. She did not ascribe any feelings to the dolls, and she could not take her play to a more elaborate level where more than one event was happening.

These play observations suggested that Madison had difficulties in her ability to organize representational thinking and express emotional ideas. She was limited in her social skills in using eye contact, a range of facial expressions or gestures, in social referencing of others, and in sharing her attention during play with others. She could organize simple sequences of interactions but could not chain together more than two or three interactions in a row without being structured to do so.

After the free play, I invited Madison to the table for the clinical interview and drawings. At this point, I asked Ms. T. to leave the room for about 5 minutes to see how Madison could tolerate separating from her. As mother said goodbye, Madison did not look up and became immersed in drawing at the table with me. When her mother returned and asked if she should stay, Madison told her that she was fine being alone with me. It seemed that when Madison felt that she was in a safe environment she could separate from her mother, at least during her waking hours.

Madison's draw-a-person was a picture of herself. Although there was a general solidarity of form in the trunk, the arms, legs, and trunk consisted of scribbles, lacking form. In addition, the picture lacked hands or feet, something that might suggest feelings of inadequacy. When I asked her some questions about herself, the only thing she would tell me was that she liked to eat cookies and cake. When children of this age have problems describing basic feelings or attributes of people, it can suggest that they have weak ego development and a poor sense of self.

was having difficulties sharing toys with her friends. She attributed this to the new baby's upcoming arrival.

I noticed a change in Rachel's play this week. This was the first week that she didn't lug the heavy chairs around the room, seeming to need less tactile–proprioceptive input in her play. She also did not go inside any structures such as the inner tube or nest of pillows. Instead, Rachel played out a theme of needing to nurture herself. She would put out play food and eat it, then say to her mother, "It's all mine!" At the end of the session, she pretended to blow up her own belly and pretended that she had a baby, too. As I talked about the play with Mrs. D., she expressed that she was upset that Rachel did not want to share the pretend food with her. We discussed how Rachel was becoming very independent in many ways (e.g., riding a tricycle), yet needing to be held and nurtured. She also needed to control events in her life and was not able to prevent or change the upcoming arrival of the baby.

The next sequence of sessions occurred 2 months later, after Mrs. D. had had her baby. During this time, Rachel had begun attending a Montessori school three mornings a week in a classroom with 26 children. In the next six sessions, Mrs. D. came only twice with the baby, arranging for a babysitter whenever she could so that she could give Rachel her undivided attention during the sessions.

Week 6

Mr. and Mrs. D. came to the session and described how Rachel was showing a lot of distress whenever the new baby cried, becoming agitated and angry at him. Mrs. D. sometimes felt frantic that she couldn't calm the baby and Rachel at the same time. She reported that bedtime was still a problem. Rachel was waking several times every night and needing a hug. Her father was lying down and resting with Rachel in the middle of the night on occasions to help settle her. When he wasn't with her, Rachel would get out of her bed, scream, and go to her parents' room. They had begun to lock their bedroom door to keep her out of their bed. Rachel had a lot of trouble being alone and needed much reassurance. Mom complained that she couldn't even go the bathroom without Rachel following her. In addition, the parents were finding that Rachel would scream that she didn't need a nap in the afternoon, screaming up to half an hour, then she would get into her bed and sleep for 1 to 2 hours. It seemed that Rachel had difficulty transitioning from a fully aroused wake state to sleep and didn't know how to help herself fall asleep. I suggested setting up a routine for naps and bedtime that involved stories and songs.

Mr. and Mrs. D. reported that Rachel's tactile hypersensitivities seemed to have diminished somewhat but that she still sought heavy deep pressure activities from time to time. Mrs. D. stated that one night her husband played a game of running back and forth, then landing in a nest of pillows with Rachel. After this game, Rachel let mother read to her for the first time sitting on mom's lap and rocking in a chair. I talked with Mr. and Mrs. D. about Rachel's need for both vestibular and tactile stimulation and the organizing effect that movement and deep pressure activities had for her. She seemed to have a high need for intense stimulation before she could settle from a high state of arousal. I suggested that the parents try using a Sit-'n-Spin, a hippity hop, a hammock swing tied to a tree outside, and a scooter board as pieces of equipment that she could move on. High-intensity movement and high-contact games were suggested for the late afternoon or after dinner, followed by calming activities such as rocking and reading.

Week 7

This week Rachel was taking a nap and getting to bed around 11:00 p.m. Her parents were already in bed with their doors locked while Rachel was still in the hallway at that hour. Mr. and Mrs. D. were very worried about what she was doing in the hallway but felt that they needed to put a limit on the endless bedtime routine with her. She would awaken early in the morning between 4:00 and 6:00 a.m. but could go back to sleep if led back to her room.

Rachel was articulating that she was angry at the baby. Mom made up a game with the inflatable Bop-Man where they hit it back and forth between Rachel and mom, and called the Bop-Man either the "good" or "bad" witch. After the game, Rachel would want to sit in her mother's lap. Mom felt that these types of physical expressions helped Rachel in expressing her anger at the new baby. Mr. and Mrs. D. continued to play with Rachel using the child-centered activity, feeling strongly that this was helping her.

Week 8

Rachel had given up her nap time and was sleeping better. The vigorous vestibular stimulation and deep pressure games that they had been doing for the past 2 weeks seemed to be helping her fall asleep. As long as Rachel received a lot of tactile, proprioceptive, and vestibular types of activities, she slept. Rachel was sleeping through the night more of the time and would awaken and remain in a more consistently good mood. Mrs. D. stated that Rachel was playing with other children one at a time. This change stayed and seemed to be related to her receiving the tactile deep pressure activities. During the next few weeks, the types of activities that she sought were hanging from things such as a chin-up bar assembled in a door jamb or spinning on an inner tube suspended from a tree. She seemed to need deep pressure activities such as burying herself in a refrigerator box filled with uncooked macaroni or bouncing on the edge of a low trampoline.

Week 9

In the last session, both parents came with Rachel. They seemed to need to talk about their relationship with Rachel and what they had learned about her over the course of working with me. Mr. D. expressed how he was feeling overwhelmed with the demands of his job and fathering two children. He felt that he should play with Rachel even when he didn't feel like it. Mrs. D. encouraged him to be more honest with his feelings about Rachel. She shared that she found Rachel to be an interesting and challenging child, but there were times when she had thought of "giving her away." She asked her own mother if she ever thought that about her when she was growing up (mother was oldest of five children). Mrs. D. said that her mother was too nice to tell her if she had negative thoughts about her. I was aware how Mrs. D. seemed to relate strongly to Rachel as the oldest child and what it felt like to have younger siblings. I asked her how she was similar and different to Rachel. It seemed that Mrs. D. had difficulty seeing how she was different from her daughter but could easily identify with Rachel on many levels, including how Rachel had difficulty tolerating touch and her strong need to retreat after being near other children or when engaged in a stimulating activity or noisy environment.

I talked with father about his desire to disengage from Rachel because he was bored and tired when he spent time with her. He shared that he didn't enjoy playing baby games or the kinds of things that she liked to do except for the roughhouse play that they did together. I urged him to do more of what he liked to do with her (e.g., chase games, crashing into pillows, playing on the swing outside) because Rachel would sense when he was having fun with her. I stressed the importance of them both having pleasure when they played together. I brought up how it was important for Mr. and Mrs. D. to find time to take breaks from the children, to have time for themselves as a couple and alone time to restore themselves.

Although our sessions together ended because Rachel was seen as part of a research project, Mr. and Mrs. D. continued to come in periodically to discuss Rachel's progress and their concerns as she grew older. Her sensory hypersensitivities remained a problem over the next few years to the point that it interfered with her ability to cope with school. She would often come home from school and wish to retreat to a corner by herself. Mrs. D. was very creative and suggested that they spend quiet time together doing craft projects, which seemed to help settle Rachel. At 4 years of age, Rachel received occupational therapy, using a sensory integration approach to help her with these needs.

Rachel is an example of a child who was able to solve some of her own problems through the child-centered therapy when materials were provided that helped her to address her sensory needs. Mr. and Mrs. D. could support Rachel's needs through the child-centered play and by providing structure and limits to help Rachel become more organized. They were nonjudgmental and allowed Rachel to express herself in whatever ways she needed. Although the child-centered play was very beneficial in helping Rachel express her emotional needs related to her sleep problem, parent guidance was useful in helping Mr. and Mrs. D. establish bedtime routines and develop a sensory "diet" that helped Rachel modulate her arousal levels. The therapy program was also helpful in providing support to the parents in coping with a challenging child.

SUMMARY

This chapter provides an overview of common sleep problems in children with regulatory disorders, their evaluation, and treatment. The suggestions provided in the chapter should be useful for young children but could easily be modified for school-aged children as well. Problems in sleeping often reflect a difficulty within the relationship between the child and caregivers related to attachment, the capacity to tolerate aloneness and separateness, and the ability to accept limits. They may also relate to constitutional problems that affect the child's ability to self-calm and to modulate levels of arousal and sensory stimulation. Treatment programs addressing sleep should incorporate a blend of child-centered therapy to address the dynamics in the parent–child relationship, parent guidance to provide structure around the bedtime ritual and nighttime awakenings, and sensory organization activities for the child.

REFERENCES

Adams, K. (1980). Sleep as a restorative process and theory to explain why. *Progress in Brain Research*, *53*, 289–325.

Anders, T. F. (1979). Night waking in infants during the first year of life. *Pediatrics*, *63*, 860–864.

Anders, T. F. (1994). Infant sleep, nighttime relationships, and attachment. *Psychiatry*, *57*, 11–21.

Anders, T. F. (1997). Sleep disorders: Infancy through adolescence. In J. M. Wiener (Ed.), *Textbook of child and adolescent psychiatry* (pp. 405–415). Washington, DC: American Psychiatric Press.

Anders, T. F., Keener, M., Bowe, T. R., & Shioff, B. A. (1983). A longitudinal study of nighttime sleep–wake patterns in infants from birth to one year. In J. D. Call & E. Galenson (Eds.), *Frontiers of infant psychiatry* (Vol. 1, pp. 150–166). New York: Basic Books.

Armstrong, K. L., O'Donnell, H., McCallum, R., & Dadds, M. (1998). Childhood sleep problems: Association with prenatal factors and maternal distress/depression. *Journal of Paediatric Child Health*, *34*(3), 263–6.

Beal, V. A. (1969). Termination of night feeding in infancy. *Journal of Pediatrics*, *75*, 690–692.

Chervin, R. D., Dillon, J. E., Bassetti, C., Ganoczy, D. A., & Pituch, K. J. (1997). Symptoms of sleep disorders, inattention, and hyperactivity in children. *Sleep*, *20*(1), 1185–1192.

TABLE 6.1   Food Rules for mealtimes

1. Establish a schedule for mealtimes. If your child doesn't eat a meal, avoid the temptation to try again in another hour. Stay with the schedule. There should be three main meals and two scheduled snacks (in the middle of the morning and afternoon). No extra snacks should be served, even if your child did not eat at one of the meals or snacks. This way your child will start to feel hunger and satiety and understand that when he eats, it satisfies his hunger. When it's time for the next meal, talk about feeling hungry. After eating, talk about being full.

2. Don't worry about how much he eats at mealtime. When it's clear that your child is finished, take away the food and, if your child cannot play unsupervised on the floor, try giving him some measuring cups, Tupperware, and wooden spoons while he's in the high chair. This way you might be able to finish your own meal.

3. Begin with food that your child can eat on his own, such as pieces of banana or bread.

4. Instead of using a spoon, which is often rejected when a child has experienced reflux, use something else—like a Nuk toothbrush, or a bread stick for dipping in yogurt, pureed fruit, pudding, or ground meats. Be sure to use foods that are motivating for your child, yet will stick to the utensil. Let your baby hold the bread stick and try dipping while you hold another one to help. Always let him be in control of the "utensil." You may want to reintroduce the spoon after the bread stick or Nuk toothbrush begins to work.

5. Always eat something with your child. This socializes the mealtime and keeps him interested in eating too. Be careful not to diet when your child is in this program. The child will get the message that you are avoiding foods to lose weight and will model your behavior.

6. All meals are in the high chair or other appropriate seating. No eating should occur while your child roams the house or is in other places (e.g., bathtub, car seat).

7. Take plates, food, cups, etc. away if they get thrown. Give one warning, saying clearly, "No throw!" If the throwing continues, take your child out of the high chair and end the meal.

8. Let your child self-feed whenever possible. For younger children who cannot spoon feed because they have not yet developed competence at managing the spoon, you can put out a small dish for baby to use while you feed him. Focus on foods that let your child self-feed and that are easy to manage in the hands or by spoon. For example, sticky foods such as applesauce or pureed bananas are easier than more liquid foods. Finger foods should be julienne strips of steamed vegetables or pieces of fruit or cheese that can be easily managed in the hand and mouth.

9. Limit mealtime to 30 minutes. Terminate the meal sooner if your child refuses to eat, throws food, plays with food, or engages in other disruptive behavior. If your child is not eating, remove the food after 10 to 15 minutes.

10. Separate mealtime from playtime. Do not allow toys to be available at the high chair or dinner table. Do not entertain or play games during mealtimes. Don't use games to feed and don't use food to play with.

11. Don't praise for eating and chewing. Deal with eating in neutral manner. It is unnatural to praise someone for chewing and swallowing food.

12. Don't play games with food or sneak food into your child's mouth.

13. Withhold expression of disapproval and frustration if your child doesn't eat.

14. Offer solid foods first, then follow this with liquids. Drinking liquids will fill the stomach so that the child will not be hungry for solids.

15. Hunger is your ally and will motivate your child to eat. Do not offer anything between meals, including bottles of milk or juice. The child may drink water if thirsty.

16. Do the "special play time" (child-centered activity) before or after mealtime to give your child attention in positive ways.

17. Emphasize mealtimes as a social, family gathering time. In this way, the focus is on socialization rather than worrying about how much your child is eating. Be sure the TV is turned off.

18. All caregivers need to agree to the program or it won't work!

She spoke in short sentences to convey her needs but did not use language spontaneously when playing with toys. She showed sensory defensiveness to novel touch experiences and would sometimes claw at objects as if the contact on her palms was aversive. She would only take liquids from a covered cup or bottle, drinking formula and sometimes juice. She would not indicate when she was hungry or satiated; therefore, her intake had to be regulated by a schedule. She also seemed to have difficulty with the mechanics of eating. When she took food into her mouth, she used a suckling motion to swallow. Before I began seeing her, Katarina had just begun to munch on crackers and crunchy cereal. Katarina had oral–tactile hypersensitivities, particularly in the mouth. She tolerated toothbrushing and allowed her face to be wiped, but she gagged or threw up when she put solid foods in her mouth.

To evaluate emotional needs, I observed Katarina's play with her parents. Her play was characterized by inattentiveness and an inability to play interactively with toys for more than a short time. She was animated in her social approach, but remaining engaged in interactions was difficult for her. Much of her play tended to involve banging toys, filling and dumping objects out of containers, and hiding toys under furniture. Occasionally she was able to construct simple symbolic play such as putting the doll to sleep in bed. Katarina would sometimes socially reference her mother while playing and would occasionally anticipate with curiosity or excitement the presentation of an interesting object or interaction by her mother. She seemed to have difficulty initiating intentional interactions with the toys, but once organized by her mother about what to do with the toys, she was able to be purposeful with the objects. In the session, she appeared to show a preference for her parents, but was reported to approach strangers indiscriminately and would climb in people's laps and expect a hug.

Katarina seemed to have a high need to control objects and people in the environment. She liked to hold small objects in her hands, keeping them there for long periods of time. She had hoards of small toys that she stashed under her bed. The older brothers sometimes found food that Katarina had hidden in places like behind the sofa. Katarina sometimes indicated that she wanted objects to be in the same place or to use the same objects over and over again (e.g., drink only from the small blue plastic cup). It seemed that she had a high need for sameness in the environment, which probably served both a sensory and emotional need.

When it was time for the feeding observation, Katarina became very excited, but once at the table her interest waned. She did not bring anything to her mouth and began getting in and out of her chair. Her out-of-seat behavior seemed related to difficulties organizing what to do at the table. She ate a few bites of fruit and a graham cracker after much cajoling from her parents or brothers, after which she showed no interest in eating. Her parents agreed that this was typical of what normally happened at mealtimes. Usually one parent or a sibling would entertain her with games while a parent or brother would try to sneak food into her mouth.

Katarina's problems with self-feeding seemed to be rooted in several underlying problems. She was tactually defensive in the mouth and on the palms of her hands. She had difficulties coordinating the suck–swallow pattern. She had problems tolerating change and a high need to control persons and objects in the environment. She also had difficulty organizing interactions with others and in sustaining her attention during play.

We began the treatment using the model described in this chapter, but after several months there was little change in Katarina's feeding. There seemed to be a problem in how her parents viewed the treatment process. At first they came to the therapy sessions, but they soon began to come sporadically, canceling sessions because of their busy work lives. Even when I offered them alternative and more convenient times to come, attendance was inconsistent. I discussed the importance of their involvement if they wished to work on Katarina's feeding, but also stressed the importance of addressing the family's overall needs. During this time, Katarina began to express her protest of their withdrawing from the treatment process by hitting her parents when they played with her in our sessions. She also engaged in self-stimulatory behaviors (rocking and hand flapping) and became increasingly more controlling about which toys could be used. When I stressed to Mr. and Mrs. C. how Katarina fell apart when they were not consistent with the sessions, they were able to commit to coming. Although they reported that they were following through on the treatment at home, in fact, they were not. Mr. and Mrs. C. continued to force feed Katarina and to distract her from the eating process by one parent or sibling entertaining her while another snuck food into her mouth. I learned this indirectly when one of them allowed it slip that the only reason Katarina was growing was because they managed to get food into her.

Despite this resistance, the parents began to develop some trust over the first few months of treatment and were able to disclose some important pieces of information that helped to further explain some of Katarina's eating problem and their difficulties in committing to the treatment. The mother revealed that she had grown up in poverty as a child and had never had enough to eat. She felt shamed by this and often stole other children's lunches to get enough food. Katarina's rejection of food distressed the mother because she was finally able to have and provide enough food. As an adult, Mrs. C. tended to eat for comfort and was quite overweight. She reported that she had been battling weight for many years and had gained and lost over 100 pounds several times. In addition, I further explored what happened in the early months that Katarina was with her American family. Katarina had been eating when they first brought her home. At the time Mrs. C. had recurrence of a gallbladder problem and felt nauseated most of the time. Mrs. C. had lost 50 pounds in the first 4 months they had Katarina and was pleased not to be quite so heavy. Katarina had apparently observed Mrs. C. vomiting, particularly after eating a meal, and skipping meals. Although it was not easy for Mrs. C. to explore her own issues, it seemed to help that she could draw some connections between her own history of deprivation, feeling shame around not having enough food and her own eating problems, and Katarina's history of deprivation and being overly controlled at the orphanage.

Issues related to attachment were addressed in concrete ways with the family, largely because Mr. and Mrs. C. were not psychologically minded and resisted insights into their own behavior. They were attuned to Katarina's developmental progress and often wanted to know if she was catching up in her language and emotional development. To address attachment needs and issues around deprivation and nurturance, I used the child-centered play as a forum to discuss Katarina's development while emphasizing how Mr. and Mrs. C. were central to fostering her skills because of the attachment she had to them. I emphasized how developing mastery in skills could only occur in the presence of an admiring parent who facilitates and elaborates on the child's development while allowing the child time to initiate and organize interactions with persons and toys. A technique that was especially successful was when I talked through Katarina to help Mr. and Mrs. C. learn ways to respond to her (e.g., "When you watch me and smile, I really feel like throwing this ball high in the air.").

Gradually, Katarina's play became more reciprocal in nature, although she would sometimes revert to self-stimulatory behaviors. She developed healthier ways of asserting her autonomy in wanting to do things by herself (e.g., riding a tricycle, putting on her shoes). She continued to need to hold small toys while eating but became adept at managing a fork and spoon and self-feeding thick soups, macaroni and cheese, and chicken nuggets. Remaining in the chair for feeding and the family's tendency to entertain Katarina remained problems, largely because Mr. and Mrs. C. could not enforce these rules and because they were delighted that Katarina was eating by herself. Although not all of my goals for Katarina and her family were accomplished, some nice progress occurred, and the attachment between Katarina and her family continued to strengthen.

CASE EXAMPLE 2: REFUSAL TO EAT IN AN 18-MONTH-OLD BOY

History

Michael was born full term at 7 pounds. As soon as Michael was born, he wanted to breast feed. This pleased his mother because she worried that she would not have enough breast milk. Suck and swallow were good, and growth was reported within normal limits until about 11 months of age, when his weight was only 20 pounds. Solid foods were introduced at 6 months but were rejected. Michael would swallow foods but showed displeasure on his face and gradually began to turn away from the spoon. He continued to breast feed as his sole source of nutrition.

At 17 months, he had a good appetite for breast milk but would not indicate when he was full. Michael had no interest in self-feeding and never mouthed

Chatoor, I., Hirsch, R., & Persinger, M. (1997). Facilitating internal regulation of eating: A treatment model for infantile anorexia. *Infants and Young Children, 9*(4), 12–22.

Dahl, M., Rydell, A. M., & Sundelin, C. (1994). Children with early refusal to eat: Follow-up during primary school. *Acta Paediatrica, 83*(1), 54–58.

Daws, D. (1994). Family relationships and infant feeding problems. *Health Visit 67*(5), 162–164.

Evans, S. L., Reinhart, J. B., & Succop, R. A. (1972). Failure to thrive: A study of 45 children and their families. *Journal of American Academy of Child Psychiatry, 11*, 440–457.

Fraiberg, S, Anderson, E., & Shapiro, V. (1975). Ghosts in the nursery. *Journal of the American Academy of Child Psychiatry, 14*, 387–421.

Goldbloom, R. B. (1982). Failure to thrive. *Pediatric Clinics of North America, 29*, 1.

Gordon, A. H., & Jamieson, J. C. (1979). Infant–mother attachment in patients in non-organic failure to thrive syndrome. *Journal of American Academy of Child Psychiatry, 18*, 251–259.

Greenspan, S. I., & DeGangi, G. A. (in press). *Functional Emotional Assessment Scale.* Madison, CT: International Universities Press.

Greenspan, S. I., & Lourie, R. S. (1981). Developmental structuralist approach to classification of adaptive and pathologic personality organizations: Infancy and early childhood. *American Journal of Psychiatry 138*, 725–735.

Harris, J. C. (1982). Nonorganic failure to thrive syndromes. In P. Y. Accardo (Ed.), *Failure to thrive in infancy and early childhood.* Baltimore: University Park Press.

Homer, C., & Ludwig, S. (1981). Categorization of etiology of failure to thrive. *American Journal of Disabled Children, 135*(9), 848–851.

Jelm, J. M. (1990). *Oral–Motor/Feeding Rating Scale.* San Antonio, TX: Therapy Skill Builders.

Johnson, F. K., Dowling, J., & Wesner, D. (1980). Notes on infant psychotherapy. *Infant Mental Health Journal, 1*, 19–33.

Main, M., & Goldwyn, R. (1984). Predicting rejection of her infant from mother's representation of her own experiences: Implications for the abused abusing interactional cycle. *Child Abuse and Neglect, 8*, 203–217.

Mullen, M. K., Garcia Coll, C., Vohr, B. R., Muriel, A. C., & Oh, W. (1988). Mother–infant feeding interaction in full-term small-for-gestational-age infants. *Journal of Pediatrics, 112*, 143–148.

Robin, A. L., Gilroy, M., & Dennis, A. B. (1998). Treatment of eating disorders in children and adolescents. *Clinical Psychology Review, 18*(4), 421–446.

Spitz, R. (1945). Hospitalism: An inquiry into the psychiatric conditions of early childhood. *The Psychoanalytic Study of the Child, 1*, 53–74.

Wesner, D., Dowling, J., & Johnson, F. (1982). What is maternal–infant intervention? The role of infant psychotherapy. *Psychiatry, 45*, 307–315.

Woolston, J. L. (1983). Eating disorders in infancy and early childhood. *Journal of the American Academy of Child Psychiatry, 22*, 114–121.

Treatment of
Attentional Problems

Treatment of attentional problems is complex because there are many ways that attentional problems are manifested. In addition to inattention, hyperactivity, and impulsivity, the child may show a range of developmental, emotional, and learning challenges, such as poor motor planning, low motivation, poor emotional regulation, and problems with sensory integration, language processing, and perceptual organization. Interventions need to address not only the core attentional deficit, but the accompanying problems that interfere with behavior and learning and how the attentional problem impacts social interactions. It is also important that different treatment approaches be modified or blended together depending on the child's age, developmental level, and overall needs. This chapter provides guidelines to assist clinicians in developing a comprehensive model for treating attentional problems that integrate cognitive–behavioral, sensory integration, and dynamic interactional approaches.

A variety of treatment approaches has been used in treating children with attention deficits. Those that are more widely used because of their proven effectiveness include behavior modification techniques to address problems of impulsivity and behavioral control (Braswell & Bloomquist, 1991; Bloomquist *et al.*, 1991; Cocciarella *et al.*, 1995; Goldstein & Goldstein, 1990), and cognitive training that emphasizes problem solving, organization, and self-monitoring skills (Barkley, 1997). Use of medication to treat symptoms of ADHD is often helpful in reducing hyperactivity, impulsivity, and inattention, particularly when it is combined with parent training and therapy directed at improving the child's self-control (Horn *et al.*, 1991). Other approaches that have been used include the following:

- Special education and tutoring to address learning needs

- Language therapy to improve auditory processing

- Sensory integration to address sensory problems that affect attention and activity level

- Visual training and eye desensitization to improve eye focus

- Auditory training (e.g., Tomatis, Berard) to decrease auditory hypersensitivities and improve auditory discrimination

- EMG biofeedback to inhibit excessive body movement

- Relaxation techniques for self-calming and body inhibition

- Homeopathic medicine

- Dietary supplements and dietary control of sugar intake

Some of these approaches, such as relaxation techniques, have limited success, while others have not been fully researched to prove their effectiveness. Whatever approaches are used, it is generally accepted that most children with ADHD need a multidisciplinary approach that combines more than one type of treatment (Blackman *et al.*, 1991; Maag & Reid, 1996; Whalen & Henker, 1991).

What is striking about this list of treatment approaches is how they are focused primarily on working directly with the child on his or her attentional problems. Although it is important to address the core deficits that underlie attention in the child, the treatment must also include working with the child within the context of the parent–child relationship. It is through this relationship that the child learns to self-modulate activity level, to integrate attention to both objects and persons, and to gain a sense of mastery and control.

This chapter will provide background information about the different types of attentional problems commonly observed in young children. The attentional problems of individuals with autism and attention deficits with hyperactivity, mental retardation, and regulatory disorders will be discussed, along with the process of attention. The foundations of attention—arousal and alerting—are detailed, including their role in sensory registration and orientation and habituation to novel stimuli. Practical information is provided about the impact of different types of stimuli on attention and the importance of selective attention, motivation, and persistence. Different treatment techniques are presented to address the underlying problems that contribute to attention deficit, emphasizing the use of child-centered therapy, described in Chapter 3, with cognitive–behavioral and sensory integration approaches. A case example of a young child illustrates the model.

TYPES OF ATTENTIONAL PROBLEMS

One of the "core" symptoms of behavior disorders such as hyperactivity, learning disorders, and mental retardation is a deficit in attention. Attention deficit disorder has been described as a constellation of symptoms that includes distractibility, poor concentration, lack of persistence, poor self-monitoring, disorganization, and impulsivity (Goldstein & Goldstein, 1990). In addition to problems with impulsivity and disinhibition, many children with ADHD have other associated cognitive problems that impact motor planning, verbal fluency and communication, mood regulation, motivation, and self-control (Barkley, 1997). Prospective studies of attention deficit disorder have confirmed that children in this population are at high risk for academic underachievement and behavioral difficulties (Carey & McDermitt, 1980; Rutter, 1982). Persistent inattention in early childhood has also been associated with poor achievement in reading and mathematics in the second grade (Palfrey *et al.*, 1985). ADHD appears to have a high comorbidity with a variety of psychiatric disorders (e.g., oppositional, affective, anxiety, conduct, and learning disorders) (Pliszka, 1998) that may have different etiologies. When anxiety accompanies ADHD, it appears to increase impulsivity and predict that these children respond less well to stimulants. However, there appears to be a strong genetic predisposition to ADHD; therefore, diagnosing and treating family members as well as the child with ADHD is important in developing the interventions that address the functioning of the child in the family environment and parent–child interactions (Hechtman, 1996).

Epidemiological studies using standardized diagnostic criteria suggest that between 3 and 6% of school-aged children may suffer from ADHD (Goldman *et al.*, 1998). Using teacher-reported measures to examine prevalence, it appears that the rates for attentional problems vary depending on type (Wolraich *et al.*, 1996). Studies have documented prevalence rates for children with attention deficit with hyperactivity (7,3%), ADHD with inattention (5.4%), ADHD with hyperactivity and impulsivity (2.4%), and ADHD combined type (3.6%). This research suggests that children with ADHD are a heterogeneous group; therefore, it is useful to discuss the different types of attention deficit in terms of the symptomatology that underlies the disorder.

Children diagnosed as having an attentional deficit do not always fit into well-defined categories with uniform characteristics. For example, an inability to attend appropriately has been associated with a diagnosis of mental retardation, schizophrenia, autism, hyperactivity, and learning disabilities. The etiologies of attentional disorders are many and often nebulous. Many researchers contend that the etiology is a function of neurologic dysfunction.

Impaired sensory registration is a common problem affecting attentional abilities. A pattern of overarousal is seen when there is difficulty filtering extraneous information. Accompanying this are orienting to irrelevant stimuli, distractibility, excessive motor activity, and a decreased attention span. In contrast, a pattern of underarousal may be manifested by (1) a high activity level associated with stimulus gathering behaviors, or (2) a low activity level with difficulty orienting and acting on novel stimuli. Research suggests that children with ADHD are likely to show somatosensory dysfunction (e.g., tactile defensiveness) (Parush *et al.*, 1997) as well as developmental dyspraxia and problems processing vestibular input (Mulligan, 1996). Some of the symptoms of impaired sensory registration that impact attention include the following:

1. Sensory overload in busy environments (e.g., classroom, malls, playgrounds)
2. Auditory hypersensitivities to certain sounds:
   a. High-pitched sounds such as whistles or children laughing
   b. Low-frequency background noises from heaters or appliances
   c. Loud noises such as vacuum cleaners, toilets flushing, or doorbells
3. Visual distractibility with difficulty screening out relevant from nonrelevant visual stimuli and poor coordination of the eyes for focused work:
   a. Difficulties converging eyes in midline for near-point work
   b. Overwhelmed by too many visual stimuli
   c. Need for clear spatial cues in environment (e.g., boundaries drawn around areas on blackboard)

4. Tactile hypersensitivities to certain types of touch:
   a. Bumps or pushes other children when in close quarters and is bothered by random touch from others (e.g., playground activities or circle time)
   b. Complains about tags in clothing; only want to wear certain types of clothing
   c. May dislike face or hair washing and being hugged or patted by nonfamiliar persons
   d. May become distraught with normal tactile input from the environment such as the feel of the chair when sitting on it

5. High need for proprioceptive input (weight, pressure, traction):
   a. Likes to pull and push on heavy objects (e.g., in play the child may crash trucks together)
   b. Likes to hang from jungle gym bars or bannister
   c. Likes to butt head into things
   d. Prefers roughhousing activities like pillow fights, wrestling
   e. May love deep massage on back
   f. Note that when the child seeks these things, they tend to be more organizing.

6. High need for vestibular movement activities:
   a. May love to swing high for long periods of time
   b. Likes to move about, run, or find opportunities to move on playground equipment
   c. Often leaves desk at school to get something
   d. When a child seeks vestibular activities, it is important to evaluate whether the child is benefiting from the movement or becoming more active by doing it.

7. Motor planning problems:
   a. Difficulty initiating and planning new movement activities
   b. Prefers sameness in movement games
   c. Needs physical assistance and verbal prompts to learn a new motor activity like shoe tying or skipping

Impaired information processing may be associated with attentional deficits. Difficulties in accurately identifying stimuli or detecting sensory information may be the result of an inability to sustain attention. The attentional deficit may result in the individual not orienting appropriately to novel stimuli, having difficulty with understanding meanings of things, and not organizing adaptive responses for efficient performance. This inability to redirect attention to salient stimuli may result in an apparent behavioral perseveration. Concurrent with these problems may be deficits in information storage and retrieval necessary for learning. In addition, dyspraxia (i.e., disorder in planning and organizing adaptive motor responses) is often observed.

Inattention is commonly seen in children with ADD. Problems arise in the their ability to finish activities and follow through on directions, to give close attention to details, and to listen when spoken to. A child may avoid tasks that require sustained mental effort and lose things or forget to do daily activities. Difficulties organizing tasks and activities are evident. Children who show ADD without hyperactivity are less apt to have problems with conduct and impulsivity, but they are more likely to be withdrawn and anxious (Quinn, 1997). Gender differences have been reported with some girls showing ADD but lacking the typical symptoms of hyperactivity and impulsivity.

A deficiency in behavioral inhibition is a component of the attentional disorder (Schachar *et al.*, 1995). Behavioral inhibition is necessary for optimal sustained attention and appears to have a parallel in the autonomic nervous system (e.g., the lowering and stabilizing of autonomic activity) (Porges, 1984). Problems with disinhibition or impulsivity are manifested by a number of different behaviors including the following:

1. Increased activity level:
    a. Fidgetiness, difficulties remaining seated, and restlessness
    b. High need for movement such as running and climbing
2. Poor impulse control:
    a. Excessive talking
    b. Interrupting others
    c. Demandingness
    d. Inability to wait turn or for events to occur
    e. Need for immediate gratification
    f. Responds too often and too quickly during tasks that require vigilance, waiting, or careful work
    g. High need to touch things before thinking what the context or task demands are
3. Difficulties making transitions in activities:
    a. Resistance to changing from one activity to another
    b. Tendency to rush into next activity without thinking about the sequence
4. High need for novelty coupled with a short attention span:
    a. Gets bored easily with toys
    b. Plays only briefly, then wants to do something else
5. Problems organizing and sustaining play:

a. Once focused and on-task with game, often cannot think of more than one thing to do with toy or game

b. Needs help to elaborate on what they are doing

c. Difficulty taking in other people's ideas of what else to do in play

d. Difficulty processing another person's cues while trying to figure out what to do with the toy. Video games and TV are often favorite activities because the child doesn't need to integrate information from others while playing.

Difficulties with executive functioning, including problems in modifying actions and adapting to environmental demands, are present when an attentional deficit is present. Behavioral responses are often stereotypical and perseverative in nature. Often the child is bound by previously learned and explicitly taught behaviors. The ultimate impact of the attentional disorder is on development of communication, perception, learning, and social–emotional skills. Many children with ADHD have problems with motor planning and sequencing, verbal fluency, use of self-directed speech, and other executive functions that affect planning and organization of cognitive resources. Barkley (1997) describes a model that suggests that the core deficit underlying ADHD is a lack of behavioral inhibition, poor self-control, and poor executive functioning. His model is very useful in understanding how executive functions are compromised when the child has ADHD. He stresses the importance of the child with ADHD learning how to self-direct actions and to self-regulate.

In the following sections, hyperactivity, mental retardation, autism, and regulatory disorders are discussed in terms of their symptomatology related to attention.

Hyperactivity

Hyperactivity is a generalized symptom that has been used to categorize a population of individuals who exhibit a lack of control of spontaneous activity. A diagnosis of hyperactivity is often associated with abnormally high levels of motor activity, short attention span, low frustration tolerance, hyperexcitability, and an inability to control impulses.

Several physiological models have been proposed to explain hyperactivity. The high activity level has been interpreted as a parallel of an overaroused or highly aroused central nervous system (Freibergs & Douglas, 1969) as a compensatory behavior to raise the arousal of a suboptimally aroused individual via an increase in proprioceptive sensory input (Satterfield & Dawson, 1971), or a correlate of defective cortical inhibitory mechanisms (Dykman *et al.*, 1971).

Hyperactive children with attentional deficits have also been hypothesized to have deficiencies in the cholinergic systems (Porges 1976, 1980). Studies have indexed cholinergic activity via the parasympathetically mediated heart-rate responses. There have been reports of heart-rate responses that are incompatible with sustained attention (Porges *et al.*, 1975). Heart-rate responses theoretically associated with sustained attention are mediated by the vagus nerve and include slowing and stabilization of heart rate. The hyperactive child may have problems modulating the cholinergic systems and regulating parasympathetic activity. Thus, rather than observing a sympathetic dominance, the hyperactive child may have deficits in regulation of autonomic function via the parasympathetic nervous system.

Autism

Autism, a psychopathology associated with abnormal attention, has been characterized by an enduring failure to recognize and respond with affection to others (Kanner, 1943). The symptoms of autism have been grouped into five categories of disturbances: perception, motility, developmental rate, relationships to persons and objects, and language (Ritvo *et al.*, 1970). Rutter (1966) has described an absence of response both to sound, which has often resulted in the autistic child being diagnosed as deaf, and to pain. The autistic child's response deficit is generally manifested in a lack of responsiveness, but at times the child may exhibit excessive or erratic responses (Ornitz & Ritvo, 1968; Rimland, 1964; Rutter & Garmezy, 1983). Situations exist in which an autistic child who may appear deaf to loud sounds may suddenly overrespond, behaviorally and emotionally, to a soft distant sound with the appearance of extreme distress. Autistic children may also manifest abnormal stimulus selectivity where one stimulus is attended to while others are completely ignored.

Autistic children suffer a deficit along the dimension of reactivity. There is either a hypo- or hyperreactiveness to the environment. Research dealing with physiological correlates of autism has been inconsistent. However, certain relationships have been observed that are of theoretical importance in building the link between the physiological mechanisms mediating attention and autism. Autism may have a correlate in central levels of serotonin (Boullin *et al.*, 1971). Serotonin is involved in reactivity to the environment. Since autistic children characteristically exhibit a hyporeactivity to environmental events, it might be predicted that autistic children have higher levels of serotonin than normal children.

Regulatory Disorders

A common problem of children with regulatory disorders is an inability to develop self-regulatory mechanisms and a strong reliance on structure from the caregiver. The infant may be able to remain organized and focused as long as the mother or caregiver provide structure. One often observes a very limited range of adaptable behaviors and a tendency to go from one toy to the next. Play behaviors tend to be repetitive, with little diversity (e.g., banging, mouthing, or filling and dumping objects, rather than more purposeful play, symbolic actions, or interactive play). When presented with a challenging situation, the child may lack the problem solving to develop strategies to act effectively on the object. The child has a high need for predictability and structure in the environment and resists changes in routine or new challenges.

THE PROCESSES THAT UNDERLIE ATTENTION

In young children, attentional processes operate on a continuum with basic arousal and alerting at one end and focused attention at the other end. Before one can be attentive, one needs to be aroused and alert, but too much arousal or alertness can hamper the capacity to attend. Arousal and alerting have evolutionary consequences, apparently evolving to mobilize the organism in response to survival challenges. Without the ability to attend, we would not be able to filter out irrelevant information, tune into important elements in the environment, process new information for learning, or engage in purposeful activity.

Attention can mean many things, including the following:

- Basic arousal and alerting

- Habituation when a stimulus is no longer novel or relevant

- Interest in novel stimuli

- Screening and selection of information from the environment

- Motivation, persistence in remaining on-task, or sustained processing of information

- Self-monitoring and control of behaviors

Persons can alert to stimuli in a variety of ways. For example, the alerting response may occur at a reflexive level, such as turning the head to a loud noise. This occurs in many everyday settings when there is a sudden change in background noise (e.g., something is dropped, a doorbell or phone rings, a car or truck makes a loud noise).

Knowledge that the alerting response may be reactive to a critical sensory threshold can be useful in therapy for an individual with hyporeactive sensory systems who underrespond to stimulation. This is used in therapy when a new sensory challenge is introduced. For example, a child swinging slowly forward and back in a hammock may experience a decrease in arousal level. But if the therapist introduces irregular and quick movements in a pretend "storm," the child's arousal level increases and he is forced to respond. In contrast, a child who is easily overstimulated by environmental noise (e.g., refrigerator hum, children playing), unexpected touch from others, or visual stimulation may become so overwhelmed by certain everyday experiences that he or she cannot function unless provided with regular calming activities.

At the other end of the continuum of attentive processes there is selective sustained attention. This is related to what we seek to learn and the stimulation that we screen out because it is unimportant to us. Developing good selective sustained attention is something that can be learned, but it is certainly supported by a well-functioning nervous system. For example, some people have an unusual capacity to concentrate on difficult tasks even when they are in a very chaotic and noisy environment. We sometimes see this in young children who give us a "deaf" ear when watching cartoons because they choose to screen our demands out.

Arousal and alerting responses are often regarded as passive and involuntary. However, manipulating the importance of specific stimuli may result in changing the alerting capacity of a given stimulus. For instance, a new mother who was once a heavy sleeper may find that she awakes easily when her young infant whimpers. The infant's cries no long elicit startle or defensive images; rather, they serve to orient the mother to the needs of her infant.

In order to actively attend and learn new information from the external environment, an individual must be awake and alert. When an individual experiences sleep deprivation, both mental and motor functions decrease in their efficiency. Some individuals need to use external stimulation to alert themselves and to raise their arousal levels in order to attend to new and difficult tasks. We see this in everyday situations when people need their coffee before they sit down to work. But what happens when the person is over- or underaroused and cannot modulate arousal for efficient attention and learning? This is one of the problems addressed in this chapter.

Since there is a limited capacity for attention, it becomes necessary to screen out irrelevant information. We have all experienced the need to close the door, tell everyone to be quiet, and clear our desk of debris before we can concentrate. This ability to screen out information and select what is important for attention is crucial for efficient information processing.

Another component of attention that affects learning is the amount of effort expended while sustaining attention. Motivation or persistence will vary considerably based on prior learning and specific task demands. A person with an aptitude for math may be motivated to read technical books about abstract algebra but may have little patience for reading a mystery novel. Likewise, when task demands are high and the individual must learn a great deal of information in a short period of time, such as in a lecture on a complicated topic, the person becomes mentally fatigued after a short while and may begin doodling instead of taking notes to try to raise their arousal level.

WHAT IS ATTENTION? SOME HISTORICAL PERSPECTIVES

The term "attention" is used commonly in education, psychiatry, and psychology; however, it is frequently vague and poorly defined. It often implies some type of internal or cognitive process and is used either to describe the active selection of information from the environment or the processing of information from internal sources. Selective attention may be observed when a person is looking for an approaching friend in a crowd of people. Internal attention can be anything from attention to one's own thoughts to attention to visceral cues (e.g., feeling thirsty).

The notion that there are different psychological processes associated with the process of attention is not new. Even William James, the first American psychologist, emphasized this point:

> Everyone knows what attention is. It is the taking possession by the mind, in clear and vivid form, of one out of what seem several simultaneously possible objects or trains of thought. [...] It implies withdrawal from some things in order to deal effectively with others, and is a condition which has a real opposite in the confused, dazed, scatterbrained state. (James, 1890, p. 203).

In his writings, James (1890) distinguished between two broad categories of attention: passive–involuntary and active–voluntary. Passive–involuntary attention was defined as immediate or reflexive and related only to objects that directly affect the sensory systems. For example, touching a hot stove would elicit passive–involuntary attention. Active–voluntary attention was associated with the concept of interest and was assumed to be directed toward objects perceived via the senses or toward ideational or symbolic objects. Active–voluntary attention may involve purposeful activity that is either observable (e.g., engaging in a task), or a thought process (e.g., planning what to do next).

In order for an individual to attain functional competence, it becomes crucial that attention to ongoing, routine sensory stimulation be passive and involuntary. When an individual is constantly attending to things like the feel of clothing on his body or the constant drone of a fan, there is little reserve for active–voluntary attention to more meaningful environmental events or internal thoughts. When a person is actively engaged in voluntary attention, functional purposeful activity and learning can occur.

AROUSAL, ALERTING, AND SENSORY REGISTRATION

Arousal may be viewed as behavioral or physiological activity that is dependent on changes in the central nervous system. Levels of arousal operate on a continuum from extreme alertness, to drowsiness, to deep sleep. Depending on the person's level of arousal, they will respond differently to sensory stimuli. Thus, we may be more reactive to a given stimulus while in an alert state than in a sleep state. Alerting, on the other hand, is the process of increasing arousal level. For example, a person who feels drowsy would be alerted by a loud noise. In classroom settings, optimal attentive behavior may be maintained by appropriate alerting stimuli (Meldman, 1970). These will be discussed in detail in the treatment application section of this chapter.

Arousal. Arousal level parallels the behavioral states that we experience. For most of us, arousal tracks a 24-hour day–night cycle (i.e., a circadian rhythm). During a night's sleep, a person normally alternates between periods of slow-wave sleep without rapid eye movements (NREM) and desynchronized fast-activity REM sleep. Slow-wave sleep reflects a lower arousal level than REM sleep. Spontaneous awakening occurs usually after the individual has cycled through all stages of sleep but may also occur when a sensory stimulus that is intense or cognitively meaningful is introduced. For instance, a phone or alarm clock ringing are intense stimuli that awaken most people. However, a barely audible stimulus such as the floor creaking may awaken a person in heavy sleep who is suddenly wary of a possible intruder.

Alerting and Sensory Registration. Alerting is the process of shifting arousal states when presented with more intense or novel stimuli. The transition from waking to an attentive and alert state is dependent on sensory registration. This basic central nervous system process prepares the individual to respond to incoming sensory stimuli. In sensory registration, the initial response to the sensory stimulus may be unconscious or conscious. For example, our bodies register basic sensory characteristics about the environment (e.g., temperature, light) on an unconscious level. When incoming sensory inputs become conscious, we become alert and attend to them. In order for perception of a stimulus to occur, there is an internal process of scanning memory for a sensory match or mismatch. Sensory registration of stimuli plays an important role in degree of alertness or wakefulness and an individual's capacity to respond. One major aspect of sensory registration that relates to the attentional process is the orienting reflex.

The Orienting Reflex or the "What-Is-It?" Reaction

The orienting reflex is essential for survival. It is an important mechanism for attention to novelty. In other words, it alerts us to changes in our sensory environment. Once the orienting reflex is elicited, we may decide whether we need to act on the stimulus. Orienting reflexes are elicited by mild and low-intensity stimuli. However, when a very intense stimulus is presented, a defensive reflex is elicited. The primary difference is that an orienting reflex will disappear after repeated presentation (i.e., habituation). In contrast, a defensive reflex is very resistant to habituation. For example, we might rapidly habituate to the noise of young children in our homes, while we would never habituate to the sound of gunshots.

Early discussions of sensory registration and arousal mechanisms may be traced to Pavlov (1927). He described the orienting reflex as the "what-is-it?" reflex that brings the organism closer to the source of stimulation:

> As another example of a reflex which is very much neglected we may refer to what may be called the investigatory reflex. I call it the "What-is-it?" reflex. It is this reflex which brings about the immediate response in man and animals to the slightest changes in the world around them, so that they immediately orientate their appropriate receptor organ in accordance with the perceptible quality in the agent bringing about the change, making full investigation of it. The biological significance of this reflex is obvious. If the animal were not provided with such a reflex, its life would hang at every moment by a thread. In man this reflex has been greatly developed with far-reaching results, being represented in its highest form by inquisitiveness—the parent of that scientific method through which we may hope one day to come to a true orientation in knowledge of the world around us.

The orienting reflex is not always associated with investigatory behavior, but may be related to reactive involuntary attention to changes in stimulation (Sokolov, 1963, 1969). This may range from a reaction to a change in room temperature to the dimming of light in the room. The orienting reflex, according to Sokolov, is the first response of the body to any type of stimulus. It functionally "tunes" the appropriate receptor system to ensure optimal conditions for perception of the stimulus. For example, a person's ears may prick up in order to hear another person whispering an important message.

When the orienting reflex is elicited, all activity is halted, allowing the individual to prepare for necessary action. Increased sensitivity to stimulation results. If the stimulation is intense, the nervous system seeks to dampen stimulus intensity.

duration, or presented in quick succession. This is true for any type of sensory stimulus—tactile, vestibular, auditory, visual, smell, or taste.

The process of selective attention is intimately related to lower brain structures (e.g., reticular activating system), which filter sensory input and modulate arousal states. Processing of inputs at the cortical or conscious level can only occur if there is widespread inhibition of unrelated cortical and subcortical activity. Thus, we can learn new information from the environment more efficiently when we can effectively screen out irrelevant stimuli.

The Neuronal Model

Sokolov (1963, 1969) proposed a "neuronal model" that addressed how stimulus characteristics were stored in memory during attention. Sokolov proposed that the orienting reflex was not merely a response to current stimulation. Rather, he proposed that repeated presentations of a stimulus produced a neuronal representation. Typically, we need to experience a novel stimulus several times before we can understand and remember it. Information regarding stimulus intensity, duration, quality, and order of presentation are transmitted in a neuronal chain. Since incoming information is neuronally encoded on many different dimensions, it is possible to evaluate the characteristics of a stimulus to determine whether it has been previously experienced and stored in memory or is novel.

When a novel stimulus is introduced, the nervous system searches for a match or mismatch between the current stimuli and those already in the individual's memory stores. If there is a discrepancy between what is currently experienced and prior memories (e.g., neuronal representation), the orienting reflex is elicited. The individual experiences a "this is new, what is it?" phenomenon. The orienting reflex will also occur if the stimulus is meaningful or important. In this case, the individual thinks, "I know this. It is important, and I need to respond."

SUSTAINED ATTENTION: ATTENTION GETTING AND ATTENTION HOLDING

In this section, the process of sustained attention will be described in detail. Sustained attention is the ability to direct and focus cognitive activity on specific stimuli. Focusing of attention occurs in many ways in everyday life. For example, we sustain our attention to complete planned and sequenced actions and thoughts such as following a recipe, reading a map, organizing a social event, interacting socially, or writing a report. We know how difficult it is to conduct these activities when there are continuous interruptions such as the phone ringing or a demanding child at your side. Each time we are interrupted, we must redirect our attention and think, "Now, where was I?" sometimes retracing our actions to be sure that we resume our attention and behavior in the proper place in the sequence. Often after an interruption we need to rely on contextual cues to redirect our attention properly. For example, baking soda sitting on the counter may trigger the memory of whether we had already put it in the muffin batter.

Imagine the life experiences of a child who continually experiences interruptions or distractions from internal and external stimuli. This child will have great difficulty in maintaining a state of sustained attention. For example, the child with low thresholds to tactile stimuli may be constantly orienting his attention toward the sensations associated with clothing touching his skin.

The ability to sustain attention is a necessary requirement for information processing. Without this basic ability, the child will have enormous interference in developing cognition. Although there have been numerous theories and definitions of attention, the process of sustained attention can be categorized into three sequential operations. These involve attention getting, attention holding, and attention releasing (Cohen, 1969, 1972).

Attention Getting. Attention getting is considered the initial orientation or alerting to a stimulus. In a young infant, it can be observed in head-turning toward a large, bright object presented in the periphery. In young infants, the types of objects that get their attention are the human face, bold patterns, motion, large objects, or loud sounds. Although the characteristics of objects or faces help elicit attention, the young infant is very active in responding to these stimuli. The attention-getting process is very similar to the earlier discussion of the orienting reflex. However, unlike the orienting reflex, attention getting involves an active–voluntary dimension. Similar to the orienting reflex, the attention-getting response is related to the qualitative nature of the stimulus. The dimensions of stimuli that are attention getting vary according to past experiences. We know our individual reactivity to sensory stimulation and the dimensions of both external and internal stimulation that are important to us. For example, a person who is hungry will orient to the smell of food cooking. An individual with heart disease will be more sensitive to chest pains. A child who learns better through the auditory channel will orient better to a song about body parts than a picture of a body.

Attention Holding. Attention holding is the maintenance of attention when a stimulus is intricate or novel. It is reflected by how long we engage in cognitive activity involving the stimulus. The infant engaged in attention holding will inspect the object visually and manipulate it with his fingers. In an older child, attention holding may be maintained via internal thought processes such as inventing rules to a new game or through attempts to extract principles from observing complex behavior. Novelty and complexity are the most potent mediators of attention holding. Objects or events that are both novel and complex for a young infant may involve interesting patterns, bright colors, unique spatial orientations, surprised looking faces, and meaningful events such as feeding time. If an object, activity, or event is not complex and the demand to process information is low, the duration of attention holding will be very short.

SELECTIVE ATTE

MOTIVATION, PEI

al., 1983). Interestingly, it is not related to compliance. The stubborn, strong-willed child who wants to do it his own way has persistence in attentional tasks. Language competence also helps the child develop self-control. When the child uses verbal mediation, describing his actions as he enacts them, it helps not only to organize the behaviors but to regulation actions.

Kopp's theory of self-regulation is unique as a model of attention because it accounts for the interaction between individual and environment over development and considers the importance of motivation, impulse control, and capacity in attention. The basic process underlying self-regulation is described as the child's ability to initiate, maintain, and cease activity. This process seems to parallel Cohen's attention-getting, attention-holding, and attention-releasing stages. Kopp integrates many of the components of attention into her developmental model. In the first phase of self-regulation, Kopp describes the infant as developing selective attention and the capacity to attend to inputs in the environment. Unlike other models of attention, Kopp stresses the role of the caregiver in facilitating the young infant's attention to salient stimuli and to increasing numbers of relevant inputs. Over the course of development, the infant's attentional capacity shifts from external to internal control. This is a departure from the view of attentional capacity as solely a function of information processing and mental effort. Kopp describes self-regulation as the ability to modify actions in relation to situational and task demands. The organization of the social and nonsocial world, together with an awareness of one's own actions and their results, are considered the basis for generating strategies for self-initiated behavior.

Components of this model have been integrated into the model of executive functions that Barkley (1997) proposes. In his model, it is the interaction of these functions that permits normal self-regulation. At its most basic level is behavioral inhibition, which is the foundation for the other executive functions. Behavioral inhibition has three functions: (1) to prevent a prepotent response from occurring, such as the child's impulse to touch a toy before it is his turn; (2) to interrupt an ongoing response that is not effective or adaptive, such as a child knocking over a tower of blocks before he has completed the tower; and (3) to delay responding and prevent internal thoughts or external distractions from interfering with emitting an appropriate response. In the next level, there are four functions that contribute to self-directed behavior. These are listed here, with some examples of how these functions are manifested in the child:

1. Nonverbal working memory
   a. Memory of events and everyday sequences
   b. Imitation of behavioral sequences
   c. Anticipation of events and preparation to act
   d. Self-awareness of own behaviors (past, present, and future)
   e. Concept of time

2. Internalization of speech
   a. Internal narrative describing external events, actions, and sequences
   b. Verbal reflection of actions and ideas
   c. Self-questioning and problem solving
   d. Internalization of structure and rules from others
   e. Generating rules related to consequences of behaviors
3. Self-regulation of affect, motivation, and arousal
   a. Self-regulation of affect (e.g., inhibiting or delaying affective or behavioral responses)
   b. Reading social cues accurately and social perspective taking
   c. Modulating arousal states for goal-directed actions
   d. Self-regulation of drive and motivation to respond
4. Reconstitution
   a. Analysis and synthesis of behavior (e.g., breaking behavior into sequence or component parts)
   b. Creating a diverse range of verbal responses during social interactions
   c. Generating a range of adaptive motor responses to newly learned situations or behavioral challenges
   d. Generating a range of goal-directed behaviors
   e. Evaluating behaviors and their consequences and modifying actions (if–then)

Nonverbal working memory, internalization of speech, self-regulation of affect, motivation, and arousal, and reconstitution contribute to the child's developing the capacity to

- Inhibit irrelevant responses

- Form goal-directed behaviors

- Persist during activities

- Respond to external feedback and to modify responses accordingly

- Execute new or complex motor plans or sequences

- Respond flexibly in relation to task or situational demands

- Self-control one's own actions via internal or external information

The models proposed by Kopp and Barkley are useful in understanding how self-control, persistence, and motivation develop in the young child and provide the clinician with a template for generating a developmentally based treatment approach.

TREATMENT APPLICATIONS

In this section, a variety of suggestions are offered to improve arousal and alerting for focused attention and to develop better self-control, sustained attention, and self-monitoring. Treatment approaches integrate principles from the child-centered therapy, sensory integration, and cognitive–behavioral treatment models.

Techniques to Improve Arousal and Alerting for Focused Attention

A. Environmental Modifications
  1. Organize toys and work objects in clearly defined bins.
  2. Limit number of toys available at any one time.
  3. Put toys away, recycling them every few weeks to help maintain novelty.
  4. Use enclosed spaces such as a pup tent filled with soft pillows or a refrigerator box lined with soft carpet (taking care about dust allergies with materials used).
  5. Encourage seating along a wall or in a corner of the room in both classroom and home.
  6. A portable fold-up cardboard "cubicle" can be constructed and placed on the child's desk for quiet, focused work.
  7. Allow the child to sit in a bean bag chair for reading activities.
  8. At school, use a soft inflatable cushion for him or her to use when sitting at circle time or at the desk.
  9. Seat the child next to a quiet, organized child who can provide positive cues.

B. Recreational activities:
  1. Suggest enrolling the child in karate, gymnastics, horseback riding, wrestling, or other high contact sports.
  2. Encourage movement on swings and playground equipment in the afternoon.
  3. Avoid high-intensity movement activities after dinner, instead encouraging slow rhythmic movement such as rocking.

Child sitting in bean bag chair while focusing on bubble column.

C. Auditory inputs:
   1. Play Gregorian chants, Mozart, and music with female vocalists as background music.
   2. Some children respond well to New Age music or relaxing music tapes with environmental sounds on them (waterfalls, bird sounds).
   3. Some children need to wear headsets that muffle noise.
   4. Carpeting on all or part of the room may help to minimize extraneous noise.

D. Visual Inputs
   1. Highlight important visual information with bold colors or place boundaries around content that you want the child to focus on.
   2. Keep objects in organized locations.
   3. At school, encourage homework assignments to be listed in a box on the blackboard.

This activity helps to organize the child's tactile system for better attention.

This father is helping organize his child's attention by containing her on his lap while providing a textured toy to organize her tactile and visual systems.

E. Arousal versus calming activities:

1. Find out what time of day is the child's best alert period (most people are morning or evening persons). Try to do things that involve quiet concentration during those times.

2. Some children need to move around frequently at day care or school. Giving the child a "job" such as carrying a heavy box down to another teacher's room or the task of helping move furniture between activities can be very organizing. Instead of random, purposeless movement, the child engages in a goal-directed movement activity.

3. Before a focused cognitive activity, do activities emphasizing body organization for five minutes. Here are some ideas:

   a. Squeeze resistive toys like rubbery toy with eyes and nose that pop out, pulling heavy resistive doll's arms and legs (Stretch Armstrong), playing with therapy putty

   b. Bury hands and feet in bin of dried beans

   c. Have small snack of crunchy hard foods (hard pretzels, rice cakes, ice chips, carrot sticks, apples)

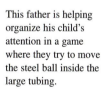

This father is helping organize his child's attention in a game where they try to move the steel ball inside the large tubing.

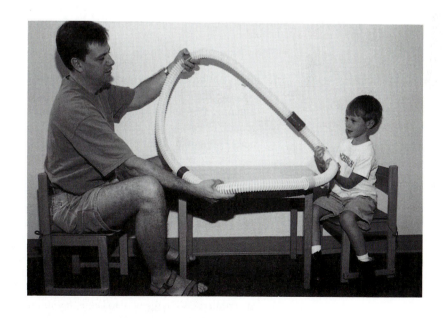

4. Before bedtime, do relaxing calming routine to include:

    a. Warm bath

    b. Back massage and pressure to palms, especially web space of thumb

    c. Linear, forward–back rocking while doing a visual focusing activity (reading, looking at pictures) and listening to rhythmic soft music

    d. Some children like to lie under a heavy quilt or wrap inside a sleeping bag

5. Make a calm-down corner in the home for the child to go to that is a dimly lit, semienclosed place (behind sofa, card table with blanket draped over top, pup tent or refrigerator box filled with pillows).

6. Talk to the child about how his "engine is running"—high, medium, or low—and what he needs to do to get engine in the right place for homework, sleep, or playtime.

7. Label when the child is calm and focused—"your engine is running at the right speed for …"

Some children do very well with occupational therapy using a sensory integrative approach to address arousal needs related to attention.

Things to Do to Help Develop Motivation, Self-Control, and Sustained Attention

Floor Time Activities to do with the Child

1. Many children with attentional problems are often structured most of their day because they function better, but then have little time when they have to organize themselves on their own. As a result, when they go on the playground or have a play date, they are totally lost about what to do because no one is organizing their play for them. Parents should try to set aside 20 to 30 minutes a day to play with their child in "Special Time." The child should be encouraged to pick something that he likes to do and then the parent joins in. For example, if the child picks hide-and-seek, playing ball, action figures, trucks, or craft projects, then that is what the special time should be about. The parents may need to set a limit that this is not TV watching or computer game time. Details about this approach are presented in Chapter 3 on treatment approaches.

2. The play should be fun and interactive. The parent should avoid directing or structuring their child unless he or she needs this kind of help to get started or at certain points in the play to keep playing. If both parent and child are having

fun, then this will be something that both of them look forward to doing. Pleasure is one of the key things that motivates behavior.

3. Board games should be avoided if at all possible. They are highly structured and prescribe what will happen. If this is what the child chooses, the parent may tell them that he can do one board game before or after doing something else.

4. If the child disengages and gets up and leaves what he was doing, the parent should follow him, see where he is going, and what he will do next. It is important to keep the connection between parent and child going. Some children leave and then return to the play materials, so the parent may want to leave out the toys for the duration of special time because the child may come back to playing with those toys. The parent should try to elaborate on what the child's play idea is without taking over the play. They may ask questions about what is happening ("What's going to happen now?" "Why did Batman take the magic rocks from the princess?" "Does Jasmine like being way up high on that mountain over there?"). What, why, how come, and where questions are good to introduce to incorporate use of language into the play. If the child starts a play idea and leaves it hanging, the parent should follow up by asking questions to keep the sequence going. For example, the parent might say, "But what happened to the gorilla over there? He was just waiting for you to deliver him some macaroni?" If the child is totally lost about what to do and how to play, the parent may try taking turns to help the child build a play repertoire.

Social Skills

It is very important that the child have regular play dates with peers to work on organizing attention and play in a child-centered (versus adult-directed) setting. For high success, play dates should be kept short and highly structured at first. The parent may want to ask the child ahead of time what toys he is willing to share with the other child and what he might like to do with his friend. Hands-on play activities where there are plenty of materials for each child are better for play dates (e.g., arts-and-crafts projects, building with Legos or other construction toy, trains). The children may also prepare simple foods together, such as pudding or cookies from prepared dough, then have a snack together while listening to a story. Competitive games should be avoided on play dates.

Social skills groups are often very helpful in working on social skills for children with ADHD. They learn problem-resolution skills, how to play with other children in socially appropriate ways, and develop a play repertoire for use outside of the groups.

These two boys are learning how to share joint attention during a construction game of marble run.

Hold Problem-Solving Family Meetings At Least Two or Three Times per Week

In these meetings, a family member may talk about something that happened to them that day and what they did. They may ask whether what they did to solve the problem was a good idea and ask what else they might have tried. Doing it in this forum teaches the child with ADHD that problem solving is something that everyone needs to work on rather than just the child. Problems that might be discussed are things like a child being picked last on a team sport at school that day, how a child didn't want to share toys with a friend on a play date, or how dad got frustrated in a traffic jam on his way home from work.

Cognitive Activities that Help Children with ADHD

1. Teach self-talk skills. There is a little "voice in the head" that most of us use to guide our actions. Many children with ADHD don't use self-talking to help them. Start by narrating what the child is doing, then ask him to talk through the steps of the task.

2. Discover the child's personal learning style and try to amplify on his/her best way of learning. Some children do well when activities are multisensory, others are more auditory or visually oriented. Use these channels to strengthen the learning approach.

3. Teach the child to visualize. This can be done in motor activities very easily ("Picture the ball flying over and landing in the basket. Now do it."). Try to

show the child what the final product of something will look like first to begin working on visualizing skills: "This is what we are going to make; now I will show you how it is done."

4. Give instructions in attention-grabbing ways (e.g., short commands).

5. Teach focusing and organizational skills.

   a. Use pictures or photographs of the sequence that will happen

   b. Draw out what should happen as instructions are described

   c. Use "check-ins" with parent or teacher at certain points in the task to reinforce completion of steps. This may be accomplished by using a chart of the various steps in a task.

6. Provide immediate feedback when things are going right. Too often we only say things when things are going wrong.

7. Teach the child sequences in everyday activities.

   a. Give the child simple chores to complete and reinforce him with praise, checkmarks on a chart, or the like for completing them.

   b. Use a picture board of activities for the day. The child can check things off as they happen or refer to the board about what will happen next.

   c. Provide the child with toys that have a distinct beginning and end (e.g., build marble chute, then put marble in at the top and watch it roll to the bottom).

8. Use consistent rules, routines, and transitions. This is very important for all children, but especially for children with ADHD. The more organized and predictable their life, the better for the child. Parents can work on flexibility and spontaneity in play interactions, or subtle variations within routines.

   a. Give the child advance notice of things verbally and in picture form if possible.

   b. Use calendars, timers, and other markers that help the child anticipate the beginning and end of things.

There are many good cognitive problem-solving strategies that can be used. Persons with training in special education and clinical psychology can help provide specific suggestions.

CASE EXAMPLE OF CHILD WITH ATTENTIONAL PROBLEMS

Noah was referred at 4½ years of age because of attentional problems. A birth history revealed that Noah did not feed well, could not self-calm, cried for protracted periods of time, and needed to be held constantly. As Noah developed, his parents observed him to be very active in comparison to other children his age.

All of Noah's developmental milestones were age appropriate, although he had a mild lag in language skills.

Mrs. S. described Noah as a very creative and playful child with a good sense of humor. His favorite activities were reading books, listening to music, swimming, and hiking. Mrs. S. was concerned about Noah's ability to stay focused, his high activity level, and impulsivity in touching objects. He often ran in the house, and when they tried activities at the table he was active, squirming in his chair, and leaving the table after 5 minutes. He was clumsy, sometimes falling and bruising himself. He had friends but sometimes had difficulty interacting with them, playing well only as long as it was his own agenda. Transitions such as coming to dinner or getting dressed were difficult for Noah. Adhering to safety rules had been an issue because Noah fidgeted and would not hold his parent's hand when walking outdoors. When outside, Noah often ran and did things like climb trees or get under the car. Mrs. S. speculated that Noah did this to be independent and control the situation. He sometimes tantrummed and could not be consoled, but his parents found that reading him a story while he sat on their lap, watching TV, or playing on the computer soothed him. Noah displayed a range of regulatory and behavioral problems. He was a very picky eater and preferred sweets. He would not sit in a chair for meals for more than a few minutes and typically ate anywhere in the house. His parents tended to eat separately because Noah's behaviors were so unmanageable. Except for reading books, Noah could only attend for a brief period of time for quiet activities such as manipulating small objects. He would squirm when being dressed and hated to be confined. Noah needed constant supervision and could not be left alone even for a moment. He did not understand dangers and was constantly doing things that were harmful to himself or others, such as throwing large objects down a flight of stairs. The parents reported that Noah became easily frustrated and often screamed and threw toys. Sometimes he would get into trouble such as taking his mother's lipstick and smearing it on the wall. When he would become upset, he had been known to open the window and throw his toys and clothes out into the yard. He was not sleeping through the night, tending to wake three or four times and having difficulty falling asleep on his own. Usually, Noah needed to be in the same room as his parents to fall asleep. When he was younger, he used to wake in the night and trash his bedroom. There was a family history of learning disabilities on both parents' sides.

The Assessment

Noah was extremely difficult to test using structured activities because of his short attention span. Within a very short period of time, he pulled toys out of cabinets and off shelves. Throughout the assessment hour, he noticed many environmental sounds not normally noticed by others. When attempting tabletop activities, Noah was constantly out of his seat. Except for preferred activities, he usually handled each toy briefly, then wanted another one immediately. The only time he attended for more than a few seconds was when cars, trains, or toy animals were used—toys that he enjoyed. Oftentimes, Noah would hold toy cars and carry them from one activity to another as a transitional object.

Noah was highly sensitive to touch—pulling away when touched by others, except his mother, and he avoided handling textured toys. He hated having food or dirt touch his hands and wanted to wipe his hands immediately. Noah avoided crunchy or chewy textures. He could not tolerate being restrained in any situation, such as wearing a seatbelt in the car. He would unsnap the seatbelt a few blocks after his mother had started the car, then would begin to move about the car despite firm limits placed on him by his mother. She would stop the car and insist on him wearing the seatbelt. Often Mrs. S. found herself stopping the car every 5 minutes. Noah tended to withdraw from groups at school. Occasionally he would hit or pinch another child as he passed by them. One of the most notable things about Noah was his strong craving for movement activities—including swings, rocking horses, and roughhousing. He also enjoyed carrying and moving heavy things such as chairs and bean bags.

Noah appeared comfortable interacting with me and could easily be engaged in a variety of play activities. He played longest with trains and cars and mechanical things that he could manipulate, playing up to five minutes or so with these materials. Sometimes he talked to his mother or me, but with his back turned toward us.

Play Observations

Noah was interested and motivated to play with some of the toys, showing a distinct preference for cars, trains, and animals. He had definite play ideas but often became distracted by other objects in the room and would abandon what he had started doing to try something else within a short period of time. He often resisted allowing his parents or me to enter his play or to introduce play ideas, appearing to have a high need to control what happened. For example, he placed some cars on a mat with roadways but didn't want his mother to join him in pushing her car on the road. His attention seemed best during activities that were more visually oriented or allowed him to touch toys and move them in space (e.g., constructing a bridge for the trains). He sustained his attention for activities that involved manipulation of toys up to about 5 minutes at a time before losing interest. It seemed that Noah was vulnerable to visual distractions and had difficulty attending when required to listen. He also showed a high need to control persons and objects in the environment.

Noah would only sometimes look at his mother or me while playing, often turning his back toward us or giving only fleeting eye contact. This may have been a function of his difficulties organizing attention to more than one stimulus at a time. He would often anticipate with curiosity or excitement the presentation of an interesting object or interaction by me but tended to lose interest unless it was one of his favorite activities such as trains or animals. He could social reference his parents, a skill that is important for children to gain social feedback about situations and tasks.

Noah could initiate intentional interactions through gestures, verbalizations, and actions. He could sometimes put together two ideas in play—for example, a train moving over the bridge, then riding on the road to another location. In terms of closing circles of communication, Noah was able to respond to his mother's or my cues some of the time. However, if the play context required symbolic action, he had difficulty responding in a contingent manner. His high need to control the environment and the actions of other persons seemed to interfere with his capacity to be flexible in responding to another person's ideas. He also had difficulty elaborating on play ideas and could not sustain the sequence of interaction. Problems with organizational capacities seemed related to motor planning and attention.

Noah's play interests tended to be more sensorimotor or visual–motor in nature (e.g., pushing trains, looking at books, outdoor games). As a result of his difficulties in sustaining reciprocal interactions, in sustaining his attention, and in sharing control of the play topic with others, Noah was only just beginning to organize emotional themes in play such as playing out nurturing, closeness and dependency, or aggression and assertion. His play themes seemed more related to separation and autonomy (e.g., trains going places).

Observations strongly suggested that Noah had difficulties organizing his attention, particularly when listening was required. He had fleeting eye contact, was impulsive and easily distracted, and became overstimulated by busy environments. Noah preferred activities that he could control and resisted structure that was imposed on him. As a result, transitions and listening to safety rules were difficult for him. This high need for control seemed related to emotional issues as well as difficulties being flexible when change was required. He also seemed to struggle with planning the sequencing of new actions.

Noah had difficulty sitting still and concentrating, particularly when presented with auditory information. Noah was socially related and had a warm attachment to his parents. However, he had difficulty with eye contact during play, and his play was immature, with difficulties organizing attention, sustaining reciprocal interactions, and organizing symbolic play. Motor-planning problems, coupled with inattention and a high need for control, seemed to affect Noah's ability to organize sequenced play interactions and generate age-appropriate play. It was likely that problems in organizing play caused him to have difficulties in playing with peers. Despite these needs in the area of play interactions, Noah was creative, had a good sense of humor, and was a very playful and enjoyable child.

The Treatment Process

Treatment was directed toward helping Noah lengthen his attention span, to tolerate different types of touch during play and feeding, and to address the parents' concerns about behavior. A combination of child-centered activity, parent guidance, and sensory integrative therapy was employed.

The Child-Centered Therapy

During the first therapy session, Mrs. S. expressed feelings that she was uncomfortable doing the child-centered activity, in part because Noah was so active and it was difficult to settle on any one toy for more than a few minutes. She could follow Noah's lead for a brief time before she wanted to structure what he was doing. She felt that if she didn't structure Noah he would continue to go from one toy to the next and might become frustrated and tantrum. However, she saw that Noah loved the child-centered activity and he did not, in fact, become out of control. He chose heavy toys to push and throw, thus helping him desensitize himself to new tactile experiences. He particularly liked doing things like pulling the arms and legs on a heavy stretch doll or punching over an inflatable Bop-Man. Noah showed frustration when things did not fit or work for him (e.g., putting together a train track). His mother tended to rush in and solve the problem for him because she felt that if she didn't he would melt down and cry. I urged her to help Noah figure things out on his own, to wait and allow him to problem solve. Mrs. S. was surprised to see that Noah didn't get overly frustrated and that he seemed to take great pleasure in being able to master things by himself in her presence.

Noah had difficulty tolerating his mother playing near him in his space and in sharing toys with her. He would frequently turn his back to her or tell her that she was not allowed to touch the toys. I urged Mrs. S. to simply engage with Noah on a verbal level (e.g., "Look at the cars riding down the road. I wonder where they're going."). Sometimes I provided Mrs. S. with props such as a toy telephone or a walkie-talkie that she could use in calling Noah to find out what he was doing in his play. Noah liked this and began initiating phone calls back to his mother to tell her about his play. I encouraged Mrs. S. to use other props such as binoculars, periscopes, or long tubes to watch Noah, thus highlighting the connection between them. We also incorporated dress-up props such as a colorful clown wig, fireman or policeman hats, and construction worker tools for both mother and child to wear. Noah loved playing with these props and would elaborate on their use in his play. At times Noah sought being inside enclosed spaces, such as retreating to the pup tent filled with pillows or climbing into a bin of plastic balls. It appeared that he did this to regroup when the stimulation of the interaction became too much for him. At other times, he wanted his mother to join him in the pup tent. Mrs. S. was sensitive to Noah's cues and seemed to understand that he might need some time and space to himself after playing in close proximity to her. When he wanted to retreat, it was never for more than a few minutes and, almost always, he would call to his mother and ask her questions that incorporated a play idea (e.g., "Are there any bad guys out there?").

As we looked for ways to help Noah remain engaged and attentive during the play, we found that he did best when the play materials were highly visual and provided proprioceptive input. Noah loved being a fireman, but enacting this play idea was short-lived unless we made the "fire" be shiny red paper shakers and gave him a vibrating tubing for the hose. He also loved taking trains to different places but would usually become self-absorbed in this task, resisting his mother joining him as he pushed the trains. To help him vary his play and encourage him to interact with his mother, we tried setting up obstacles such as a dump truck stuck on the train tracks, or a toy giraffe who persistently asked for a ride on the train to get to his friend the dinosaur's house. Because Noah loved animals and trucks, he was intrigued with these play ideas and eventually allowed Mrs. S. to enter his play.

Noah's play was often more interactive when it involved the idea of constructing an enclosed space, such as building a fort with large foam blocks. Gradually, Noah began wanting to play out stories like the "Three Little Pigs," asking his mother to be the Big Bad Wolf. Noah would take little pig puppets into the house and gleefully enact the story with his mother. I urged Mrs. S. to vary the story and make mistakes on purpose so that he would be forced to elaborate on his play ideas. When she did this, Noah would say, "No, that's not right! It's not a big bad crocodile, it's a wolf," or "No, he doesn't break down the house with a hammer, he blows it down."

As the therapy sessions entered the third month of treatment, Noah's play changed in content and process. His behaviors at home had improved dramatically. He was sitting for meals, listening to his parents and complying with most daily routines, and transitions from one activity to the next were going smoothly. During this month of therapy, Noah began to play in the doll house, playing out how the house was all messed up. He would knock furniture around, saying that it was getting hit by a hurricane. This idea of chaos versus order was played out in other play scenarios. He often constructed play that involved the dolls going to sleep, waking up, and then going to school. While the children were at school, animals came to the house to play with the family dog. When the parents and children came home, they found that the animals playing in the house had messed up the furniture, jumped on the beds, and put food all over the place. Mrs. S. felt that Noah's play reflected his continuing difficulties with impulse control, but she was encouraged that he could express it through play rather than becoming disruptive or impulsive in everyday routines.

Because Noah loved stories, we spent a part of the session focusing on problem solving around impulse control using story telling. For example, one story he particularly liked was about a boy who swam in a pond every day, but one day after a big storm a dolphin got into the pond from the ocean. The dolphin kept taking up the whole pond, jumping and splashing so hard that the boy couldn't swim in the pond. Noah came up with several ideas to help solve the problem. He decided that we should first teach the dolphin tricks. When the boy could ride on the dolphin's back, he lured the dolphin back to the ocean and put a pen between the ocean and pond so that the dolphin wouldn't get confused and come back to the pond. We also played games that required him and his mother to work slowly and carefully; otherwise, the game would be ruined. Building with magnets to make a circus, constructing houses with Legos, and games such as "Don't Spill the Beans" helped him learn how to do this.

Feeding

Since feeding was an issue for Noah, a snack time was practiced near the latter part of the therapy session in the first month. His mother set limits with him regarding out-of-seat behavior and other disruptive behaviors. When Noah wanted to get out of the chair, the snack was terminated. This program was reinforced at home by his parents. It was strongly suggested that mealtimes become a social event for Noah, eating alongside his parents. By the fourth week of treatment, Noah was accepting limits at home around mealtimes and the out-of-seat behaviors had diminished considerably.

Parent Guidance and Home Program

During the therapy program, it was apparent that, the more Noah's parents could reinforce activities that were organizing for him at home, the fewer behavioral outbursts occurred. When Mrs. S. could not practice the child-centered activity with Noah because of time constraints, he was more apt to come to therapy seeking withdrawal in the pup tent filled with pillows, or he would want to do high-intensity activities such as vigorous jumping on the small trampoline.

By the second month of therapy, Mrs. S. was able to talk about her need to control Noah. For instance, if he wanted to brush his teeth himself, she felt she had to finish it for him. Mr. and Mrs. S. were asked to pick a few things that mattered most to them at home where rules counted; for example, if Noah wants to eat, he must sit in his chair. Positive reinforcement was used as much as possible. For example, wearing the seatbelt in the car either yielded a ride to the park or a lollipop. It was stressed that in other activities Mr. and Mrs. S. should let Noah take the initiative and do it his way. Practice setting consistent and firm limits was part of the parent guidance. For instance, Mr. and Mrs. S. practiced how to be firm with Noah, saying "No throwing" while looking stern. They often gave Noah elaborate reasons why he should not throw toys instead of instituting a simple rule. We also implemented a behavioral chart that reinforced sitting for meals, using "walking feet" in the house, and sitting in his bean bag chair for quiet play. If Noah could do these things, he got a reward of going to the library to get a new book, TV time, or a visit to the "mommy treat store." Within a few weeks, considerable improvement was noted in Noah's attention span and behavioral difficulties, in large part because his parents were diligent in following through on the program.

Noah's treatment seemed to be successful for several reasons. Working through the parent–child relationship using child-centered activity helped him organize his attention while engaged in interactions with his parents. Noah was able to make use of environmental modifications (e.g., sitting in enclosed spaces) as well as sensory media (e.g., heavy objects) to organize himself. He was able to learn how to tolerate frustration, make transitions in activities, accept structure and limits, modulate his activity level, and contain his impulses during interactions with persons and objects. The child-centered activity helped Noah to better express emotional themes related to separation, autonomy, and power and control. His ability to express these needs to his mother through play and her sensitivity in responding to him were important in promoting his sense of mastery and control.

SUMMARY

The construct of attention is multifaceted and involves components of arousal and alerting, habituation and interest in novelty, capacity to sustain effort, selection and screening of stimuli, and motivation and persistence in attention. This process operates within the context of what the individual already knows about the world and the types of stimuli, tasks, and events that are encountered.

Because the attentional process is highly complex, attentional deficits may be manifested in many different ways. The discussion of attentional problems associated with autism, attention deficit disorders with hyperactivity, mental retardation, and regulatory disorders revealed differences in symptomatology. It is likely that differences exist in the neurophysiological processes underlying these different disorders.

Continued research is needed to delineate the different types of attention deficits and the most effective ways to assess and treat individuals with attentional deficits. There is a need to develop valid and reliable instruments to measure the different types of attention in varying populations. In addition, research is needed to determine the effects of therapeutic techniques on improving arousal and attention in different populations.

A multimodal approach to treating attentional problems is needed because attentional problems can be manifested in many different ways. In addition, children with problems of inattention, hyperactivity, and impulsivity often experience other developmental, emotional, and learning challenges that impact the way in which they make use of the intervention strategies. Therefore, interventions need to help the child learn to modulate arousal and sensory registration, sustain attention, and develop self-control and mastery in a variety of social, learning, and everyday activities.

REFERENCES

Barkley, R. A. (1997). *ADHD and the nature of self-control*. New York: Guilford.

Berlyne, D. B. (1960). *Conflict, arousal, and curiosity*. New York: McGraw-Hill.

Berlyne, D. B. (1965). *Structure and direction in thinking*. New York: Wiley.

Blackman, J. A., Westervelt, V. D., & Stevenson, R. (1991). Management of preschool children with attention deficit-hyperactivity disorder. *Topics in Early Childhood Special Education, 11*(2), 91–104.

Bloomquist, M. L., August, G. J., & Ostrander, R. (1991). Effects of a school-based cognitive-behavioral intervention for ADHD children. *Journal of Abnormal Child Psychology, 19*(5), 591–605.

Boullin, D. J., Coleman, M., O'Brien, R. A., & Rimland, B. (1971). Laboratory predictions of infantile autism based on 5-hydroxytryptamine efflux from blood platelets and their correlation with the Rimland E-2 score. *Journal of Autism and Childhood Schizophrenia, 1*, 63–71.

Braswell, L., & Bloomquist, M. L. (1991). *Cognitive-behavioral therapy with ADHD children*. New York: Guilford.

Broadbent, D. E. (1958). *Perception and communication*. London: Pergamon.

Carey, W. B., & McDermitt, S. C. (1980). Minimal brain dysfunction and hyperkinesis. *American Journal of Disabled Children, 134*, 926–929.

Cocciarella, A., Wood., R., & Low, K. G. (1995). Brief behavioral treatment of attention-deficit hyperactivity disorder. *Perceptual Motor Skills, 81*(1), 225–226.

Cohen, L. B. (1969). Observing responses, visual preferences, and habituation to visual stimuli in infants. *Journal of Experimental Child Psychology, 7*, 419–433.

Cohen, L. B. (1972). Attention-getting and attention holding processes of infant visual preferences. *Child Development, 43*, 869–879.

Dykman, R. A., Ackerman, P. R., Clements, S. D., & Peters, J. E. (1971). Specific learning disabilities: An attentional deficit syndrome. In H. R. Mylebust (Ed.), *Progress in learning disabilities* (pp. 56–93). New York: Grune & Stratton.

Freibergs, V., & Douglas, V. I. (1969). Concept learning in hyperactive and normal children. *Journal of Abnormal Psychology, 74*, 388–395.

Goldman, L. S., Genel, M., Bezman, R. J., & Slanetz, P. J. (1998). Diagnosis and treatment of attention-deficit/hyperactivity disorder in children and adolescents. *Journal of the American Medical Association, 279*(14), 1100–1107.

Goldstein, S., & Goldstein, M. (1990). *Managing attention disorders in children*. New York: Wiley.

Hechtman, L. (1996). Families of children with attention deficit hyperactivity disorder: A review. *Canadian Journal of Psychiatry, 41*(6), 350–360.

Horn, W. F., Ialongo, N. S., Pascoe, J. M., Greenberg, G., Packard, T., Lopez, M., Wagner, A., & Puttler, L. (1991). Additive effects of psychostimulants, parent training, and self-control therapy with ADHD children. *Journal of the American Academy of Child and Adolescent Psychiatry, 30*(2), 233–240.

James, W. (1890). *Principles of Psychology*. New York: Holt.

Kanner, L. (1943). Autistic disturbances of affective contact. *Nervous Child, 2*, 217–250.

Kopp, C. B. (1982). Antecedents of self-regulation: A developmental perspective. *Developmental Psychology, 18*, 199–214.

Kopp, C. B., Krakow, J. B., & Vaughn, B. (1983). Patterns of self-control in young handicapped children. *Minnesota Symposium on Child Development, 16*, 93–128.

Maag, J. W., & Reid, R. (1996). Treatment of attention deficit hyperactivity disorder: A multi-modal model for schools. *Seminars in Speech and Language, 17*(1), 37–58.

Meldman, M. J. (1970). *Diseases of attention and perception.* Oxford: Pergamon.

Mulligan, S. (1996). An analysis of score patterns of children with attention disorders on the Sensory Integration and Praxis Tests. *American Journal of Occupational Therapy, 50*(8), 647–654.

Ornitz, E. M., & Ritvo, E. R. (1968). Perceptual inconstancy in early infantile autism. *Archives of General Psychiatry, 18*, 76–98.

Palfrey, J. S., Levine, M. D., Walker, D. K., & Sullivan, M. (1985). The emergence of attention deficits in early childhood: A prospective study. *Developmental and Behavioral Pediatrics, 6*, 339–348.

Parush, S., Sohmer, H., Steinberg, A., & Kaitz, M. (1997). Somatosensory functioning in children with attention deficit hyperactivity disorder. *Developmental Medicine and Child Neurology, 39*(7), 464–468.

Pavlov, I. P. (1927). *Conditioned reflexes* (G. V. Annep, Trans.). Oxford: Oxford University Press.

Pliszka, S. R. (1998). Comorbidity of attention-deficit/hyperactivity disorder with psychiatric disorder: an overview. *Journal of Clinical Psychiatry, 59*(7), 50–58.

Porges, S. W. (1976). Peripheral and neurochemical parallels of psychopathology: A psychophysiological model relating autonomic imbalance in hyperactivity, psychopathy, and autism. In H. W. Reese (Ed.), *Advances in child development and behavior* (Vol. 2). New York: Academic Press.

Porges, S. W. (1984). Physiologic correlates of attention: A core process underlying learning disorders. *Pediatric Clinics of North America, 31*, 31–45.

Porges, S. W., Walter, G. F., Korb, R. J., & Sprague, R. L. (1975). The influences of methylphenidate on heart rate and behavioral measures of attention in hyperactive children. *Child Development, 46*, 727–733.

Quinn, P. O. (1997). *Attention deficit disorder: diagnosis and treatment from infancy to adulthood.* New York: Brunner/Mazel.

Rimland, B. (1964). *Infantile autism.* New York: Meredith.

Ritvo, E. R., Yuwiler, A., Geller, E., Ornitz, E. M., Saeger, K., & Plotkin, S. (1970). *Increased blood serotonin and platelets in early infantile autism. Archives of General Psychiatry, 23*, 566–572.

Ruff, H. A., & Lawson, K. R. (1990). Development of sustained, focused attention in young children during free play. *Developmental Psychology, 26*, 85–93.

Rutter, M. (1982). Syndromes attributes to minimal brain dysfunction in childhood. *American Journal of Psychiatry, 139*, 21–33.

Rutter, M., & Garmezy, N. (1983). Childhood psychopathology. In M. Hetherington (Ed.), *Socialization, personality, and social development*, Vol. 4 of P. H. Mussen (Ed.), *Handbook of child psychology* (pp. 775–911). New York: Wiley.

Satterfield, J. R., & Dawson, M. E. (1971). Electrodermal correlates of hyperactivity in children. *Psychophysiology*, *9*, 191–197.

Schachar, R., Tannock, R., Marriott, M., & Logan, G. (1995). Deficient inhibitory control in attention deficit hyperactivity disorder. *Journal of Abnormal Child Psychology*, *23*(4), 411–437.

Sokolov, E. N. (1960). Neuronal models and the orienting reflex. In M. A. B. Brazier (Ed.), *The central nervous system and behavior*. New York: Josiah Macy Jr. Foundation.

Sokolov, E. N. (1963). *Perception and the conditioned reflex*. New York: Macmillan.

Sokolov, E. N. (1969). The modeling properties of the nervous system. In M. Coles & I. Maltzman (Eds.), *A handbook of contemporary soviet psychology* (pp. 671–704). New York: Basic Books.

Whalen, C. K., & Henker, B. (1991). Therapies for hyperactive children: Comparisons, combinations, and compromises. *Journal of Consulting and Clinical Psychology*, *59*(1), 126–137.

Wolraich, M. L., Hannah, J. N., Pinnock, T. Y., Baumgaertel, A., & Brown, J. (1996). Comparison of diagnostic criteria for attention-deficit hyperactivity disorder in a county-wide sample. *Journal of the American Academy of Child and Adolescent Psychiatry*, *35*(3), 319–324.

Treatment of Sensory-Processing Problems

All of us have an inner drive for sensory integration. It is the capacity of the central nervous system to integrate information from the various senses to enable the person to interact with the world. It allows the person to tolerate a range of sensory experiences and to integrate information from the various senses for self-calming, attention and learning, coordinated movement, and purposeful interactions with the world of things and people.

An important aspect of sensory integration is a process called *modulation*. This is when the nervous system balances the person's level of arousal with the intensity of stimulation being experienced. It is the body's own internal thermostat that cues us when to rouse or calm oneself. For instance, a person who feels sluggish may exercise, chew gum, or listen to rock-and-roll music to increase his arousal level. When a child has sensory-integrative problems, he or she does not have this internal capacity to modulate level of arousal. For example, after a stimulating day with many activities, the child may come home and begin to jump on the bed and run up and down the stairs, not feeling in the least bit ready to fall asleep at bedtime.

The wide range of skills that encompasses the area of sensory integration changes as the child develops. During the first 2 years of life, the infant learns to detect and interpret information from the senses. The most important sensory channels at this stage of development are the basic senses, that is, tactile or touch, vestibular or movement, proprioception or position in space of the limbs, vision, and hearing. The infant uses information from these senses to develop coordination of the two body sides, basic posture and balance, fine and gross motor skills, such as walking and using a refined pinch, and basic body scheme.

For the infant, sensory integration occurs in the context of everyday routines and experiences. For instance, when babies are touched, dressed, or bathed, they are learning about their body and that touch can be a pleasurable experience with a loving caregiver. Some infants learn that different sensory experiences are coupled with each parent. For example, when the baby sees her father, she may squeal gleefully in hopes of roughhousing time, yet she likes the holding and cuddling that her mother gives her as she nurses or look at picture books. Parents provide different experiences based on their own knowledge, experience of the world, and their own sensory preferences.

The basic skills learned in infancy become more refined in the preschool years. The child learns how to coordinate both hands in skilled activities such as scissor cutting and buttoning, and to coordinate both sides of the body in activities such as jumping or riding a tricycle. Motor planning develops so that the child can imitate and organize sophisticated sequences of movement, such as climbing up a jungle gym, swinging on the trapeze bar, then sliding down the slide. The preschool child also learns to combine sensory and motor skills for learning. For example, vision and movement are integrated for tasks such as puzzle completion, sorting and stacking cups, and tracing shapes.

By the school-age years, there is continual refinement of sensory discrimination, integrating information from two or more senses. For example, the child can identify shapes by feel (stereognosis) or replicate shapes drawn on the back of his hand (graphesthesia). These skills help in the development of more complex perceptual skills such as learning to read and write.

The earliest descriptions of sensory integration dysfunction were provided by A. Jean Ayres (1972). Through her ground-breaking research, Dr. Ayres identified specific types of sensory-integrative dysfunction (Ayres, 1985; Ayres *et al.*, 1987). She has helped clinicians and researchers to understand the manifestation of sensory-integrative disorders and their treatment. Much of what will be described in this chapter is based on Dr. Ayres's original work and the work of those who have followed in her footsteps. Emphasis, however, is placed on the impact of sensory-processing disorders on the parent–child relationship and the child's social and emotional functioning.

This chapter will describe sensory-integrative disorders in infants and children and their treatment. The first section focuses on the various types of sensory-integrative dysfunction. The following sections highlight common sensory-integrative problems in children and how they are treated. Case examples are presented to illustrate key points, and an in-depth case is described that demonstrates how sensory-integrative therapy is blended with both structured and child-centered therapy approaches for a child with pervasive developmental disorder (PDD). A child with PDD was selected because many children with this disorder show significant sensory-integrative dysfunction while struggling with the process of social engagement.

SENSORY-INTEGRATIVE DYSFUNCTION

Sensory-integrative disorders have been documented among children and adults with learning disabilities, autism, and schizophrenia. It has been estimated that approximately 70% of learning-disabled children have sensory-integrative disorders (Carte *et al.*, 1984). Developmental dyspraxia, a disorder involving the sequencing of motor actions, is the most common type of sensory-integrative disorder, occurring in about 35% of these children (Schaffer *et al.*, 1989). Deficits in the processing of vestibular and tactile information are common among children with learning disorders and motor incoordination (Ayres, 1972; Chu, 1996; DeQuiros, 1976; Fisher *et al.*, 1986; Horak *et al.*, 1988) and in autistic children and schizophrenic adults (Maurer & Damasio, 1979; Ornitz, 1970, 1974; Ottenbacher, 1978). In addition, sensory-processing dysfunction has been identified in postinstitutionalized children—for example, those in Rumanian orphanages (Cermak & Daunhauer, 1997).

The early symptoms of sensory-processing disorders in infancy are often related to regulatory problems such as sleep difficulties, poor self-calming, very low or high activity level, atypical muscle tone with slowness in attaining motor milestones, and under- or overresponsiveness to sensory stimulation (DeGangi & Greenspan, 1988; DeGangi, 1991). Among infants with regulatory problems, hypersensitivities to touch, movement, visual, or auditory stimulation are prevalent (DeGangi & Greenspan, 1988). Infants with poor sensory processing often continue to persist in these problems, developing more serious developmental disorders by the preschool years if left untreated (DeGangi *et al.*, 1993).

Infants experiencing distress from sensory input show their discomfort by grimacing, yawning, hiccupping, sneezing, and averting their gaze. The infant may become drowsy and sleep most of the time in an effort to "shut down" the level of stimulation. Or the infant may become hyperaroused and sleep fewer hours than expected for the infant's age. Many infants with sensory-processing dysfunction are highly irritable, cry excessively, and have difficulties self-calming. For example, the child may be delayed in bringing his hand to mouth for sucking or in holding his hands in midline to self-calm. Some babies require intense vestibular stimulation (e.g., swinging, bouncing vigorously) to calm while others need more soothing types of movement experiences (e.g., slow rocking, riding in a car). Some infants can quiet if they suck on a pacifier or are swaddled tightly in a blanket, thus using the tactile sense to organize themselves.

Infants and children with developmental, learning, and emotional problems often experience constitutional problems related to the processing and integration of basic sensory information. When there is an underlying deficit in the capacity to synthesize the range of sensory experiences (e.g., tactile, proprioceptive, vestibular, visual, or auditory inputs), the child may be unable to organize purposeful actions in areas including communication, movement, and play. Often perceptual thinking and the regulation of affects are impaired as well.

The symptoms of toddlers with sensory-integrative dysfunction occur in relation to how the child is developing autonomy, independence, and mastery of language and motor skills. The toddler with hypersensitivities usually displays discomfort by actively fleeing from the stimulus, retreating to a safe space, or by lashing out at the person or object that imposed the perceived "aversive" stimulus. Hitting, biting, and throwing are behaviors that may be related to hypersensitivities. Toddlers who display the range of sensory hyper- and hyposensitivities (e.g., sensory-modulation problems) often show mood-regulation problems. The toddler may quickly escalate from a content, happy mood to a full-blown temper tantrum, sometimes without warning or an attributable stimulus or event. Frustration tolerance is low, and often the toddler with sensory-integrative problems will become extremely upset when unable to problem solve how to manipulate or handle a particular toy.

The ability to self-calm often remains a problem for toddlers with sensory-integrative dysfunction. Parents find that they must constantly give the child warning about changes in activity (e.g., going to a place, changing clothes, changing task). The toddler with these difficulties relies on the parents to help them find ways to self-calm (e.g., holding a special toy in situations where impulse control is needed; constant verbal monitoring from parents). At the crux of the problem is the toddler's difficulties problem solving and organizing a planned motor action in response to task or situational requirements.

Growing difficulties with separation often become apparent, particularly when the parent is the only person to provide a predictable sensory world for the child. Often the toddler with sensory-integrative problems does not function well in play groups, in a day-care situation, or in other environments where the child is expected to play with peers and/or separate from a parent. Parents may find that they avoid busy environments such as supermarkets, play groups, or shopping malls because their child becomes overwhelmed by the stimulation. Playing with peers is a challenge for the toddler with sensory-integrative problems who may find the unpredictable touch and movement of other children very threatening. Some children react by becoming aggressive, whereas others become avoidant and withdraw to safe places (e.g., under a table).

By the preschool years, delays often become apparent in fine and gross motor skills, balance, planning and sequencing of motor actions, and coordination (De-Gangi *et al.*, 1980). Distractibility, sensitivities to touch and movement stimulation, language delays, and visual–spatial problems may be present (Ayres, 1979; Fisher *et al.*, 1991). By the school-aged years, handwriting problems, dyslexia, attention deficits, and reading disabilities often emerge (DeQuiros & Schrager, 1979).

THE CONCEPTS OF SENSORY DEFENSIVENESS AND SENSORY DORMANCY

When children have sensory-integrative dysfunction, they are apt to show fluctuations in their responses to sensory stimulation. They may withdraw from the stimulation or may not even seem to perceive the sensory input, regardless of how intense or salient it may be. The two concepts of sensory defensiveness and sensory dormancy are important in understanding how children may respond to sensory input.

At one end of the continuum are children who show something called "sensory defensiveness." These children are hypersensitive to sensory stimulation (e.g., olfactory, visual, tactile, auditory, movement) and are usually overly responsive to more than one sensory channel. At the other end of the continuum is the child who is an underresponder, a condition described as "sensory dormancy" (Knicker-bocker, 1980; Kimball, 1993). When this occurs, there is too much inhibition of incoming sensory inputs; this results in a lack of sensory arousal. Typically, the child with this problem will be passive and inactive, with a failure to orient to important sensory stimuli. Figure 8.1 depicts the continuum from sensory dormancy to sensory defensiveness.

FIGURE 8.1

Sensory dormancy ⟶ Modulation ⟶ Sensory defensiveness

        Underrespond   Overrespond

Most individuals with sensory-integrative dysfunction will either be hyperresponsive (e.g., sensory defensive) or hyporesponsive (e.g., sensory dormancy). Some children, however, have such severe sensory-modulation problems that they fluctuate from one extreme to the other within a short period of time. Normal variation is experienced over the course of the day as the individual responds to state of arousal, activity level, and the sensory, cognitive, or motor demands of the task or situation. It has been speculated that sensory-modulation problems underlie both sensory defensiveness and dormancy (Cermak, 1988; Kimball, 1993; Royeen, 1989). The concept of sensory defensiveness and dormancy is useful in considering the various types of sensory-integrative dysfunction that are described in this chapter.

Some children with ADHD, hyperactivity, and sensory-integrative problems are overstimulated not only by the environment, but by their own behavior—squirming in the chair, running, and moving. It becomes very difficult for them to organize purposeful tasks because they are struggling with overstimulation. However, some children who appear to be overly active are seeking stimulation to increase their level of arousal. Because they do not have well-organized ways of doing this, they may appear hyperactive, aimless, or unfocused. It is important to determine what the child's activity serves for him—to stimulate or calm.

THE TACTILE SYSTEM

The somatosensory system is a primal sensory system that responds to various touch stimuli on the surface of the skin. It is a predominantly sensory system at birth and remains critical throughout life as a major source of information for the central nervous system. An infant's first movements are in response to tactile input; for example, when the baby is touched on the cheek, he will root toward the touch, trying to seek contact for sucking. Early learning depends on making contact with the external world and is important in guiding experiences and interactions with the environment (Collier, 1985; Gottfried, 1984; Reite, 1984; Satz *et al.*, 1984; Suomi, 1984).

The sense of touch involves the ability to receive and interpret sensation and stimuli through contact with the skin. Since exploration through the sense of touch is typically combined with limb movement, the tactile and proprioceptive systems have overlapping neural mapping (Kandel & Schwartz, 1981). Tactile receptors are activated by touch, pressure, pain, and temperature. The most sensitive parts of the body are the face, palms, soles of the feet, and the genitals. The least sensitive area of the body is the back. For example, if a person has an itch on their back, it may be hard to tell someone exactly where to scratch, but if the itch were on their hand, they could be very specific about it.

The tactile system has both a protective and a discriminative system. The tactile protective system is activated by skin temperature changes, a light touch, and general contact with the skin. Light touch, such as a tickle on the face or a light stroke on the shoulder, might cause someone to react with alarm if the touch occurred without them seeing it. Light touch acts as a protective mechanism for the central nervous system by giving warning if an outward stimulus is too close for safety.

In the newborn child, this protective reaction predominates until the baby becomes accustomed to being touched and learns to discriminate which tactile experiences are dangerous versus enjoyable. Through holding and cuddling, infants learn to become less sensitive to touching experiences. Swaddling an infant—that is, wrapping the baby tightly in a blanket—is often necessary to help the infant remain calm and organized. Learning to tolerate these early touch experiences is one aspect of developing early self-regulation or homeostasis—the ability to take in sensory stimulation from the world and take pleasure from it.

The tactile protective system matures quickly, and by the time the child has reached the preschool years it no longer is a predominantly sensory system.

A mother provides normalizing touch experiences for her infant by cuddling.

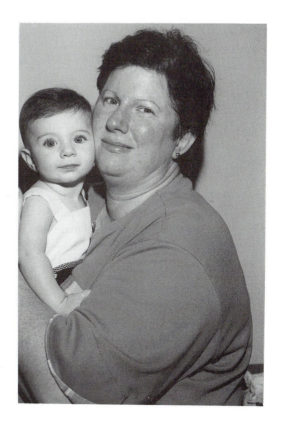

However, if the person is in a dangerous situation, the tactile protective system becomes activated, along with other sensory responses such as pupillary dilation. Children who are unable to tolerate light touch and are highly sensitive to tactile experiences such as standing next to another child, wearing a long sleeved shirt, or even sitting on a chair surface are termed "tactually defensive."

A second important function of the tactile system is discrimination. Tactile discrimination is the ability to differentiate various textures, contours, and forms by feel. It plays an important role in initiation and planning of movement as well as exploration of the environment. Tactile discrimination is important for being able to localize where touch occurs on the body, to decipher if two or more points are being touched at the same time, to recognize shapes by feel, and to organize the body and its parts into an integrated scheme. Since hand skills involve many discrete manipulations of objects, fine motor skills are often compromised in the child with poor tactile discrimination (Haron & Henderson, 1985; Nathan *et al.*, 1986). It is touch combined with movement that allows for tactile discrimination to occur, which is also an important aspect of motor planning.

When the tactile discriminative system is not functioning properly, the child often links a negative emotional meaning to touch. As a result, social interactions and emotion regulation are frequently maladaptive in children with poor tactile discrimination. For example, children learn to interpret different types of touch in social interactions, linking emotions to pleasant or aversive types of touch (e.g., aggression, love). The mother who burrows her face on her baby's tummy in a game of touch should elicit smiling and laughter from her baby. The infant or child with poor tactile discrimination may avert gaze, pull away from contact, or even cry. The toddler or preschooler may not tolerate close proximity with others and will respond by fleeing or engaging in aggressive actions.

In order for normal development to occur, this protective and discriminative system must be balanced. When the central nervous system malfunctions, as seen in learning-disabled and developmentally delayed children, there is a tendency to regress to a developmentally earlier response that has greater survival value. In these children, the protective system is overaroused and they experience normally pleasant tactile stimulation as irritating or threatening. These behaviors have important implications for emotional development.

Tactile Dysfunction

The tactile dysfunctions most commonly observed are tactile defensiveness and tactile hyposensitivities. Reactions to somatosensory stimuli can range from overresponsivity to underresponsivity. Overresponsiveness is more commonly characterized by feelings of discomfort and physical withdrawal from certain types of tactile stimuli. Ayres has described this as tactile defensiveness (1972, 1979, 1985).

Sensitivities to touch may be environmental (e.g., fleeing from contact with furniture, discomfort from clothing touching child), other-initiated (e.g., withdrawal from mother hugging child; avoidance of being in groups of children), or self-initiated (e.g., avoidance of touching textured objects). The child may respond aggressively by hitting or kicking, or by physically retreating (e.g., hiding under furniture). Emotional responses including hostility are not uncommon.

Tactile Defensiveness

Tactile defensiveness is a severe sensitivity to being touched and usually involves an adverse reaction to initiating touch with nonnoxious tactile stimulation. It has been suggested that the phenomenon of tactile defensiveness results from a failure of the central nervous system to modulate and inhibit incoming tactile stimuli (Fisher & Dunn, 1983). The child with tactile defensiveness will express feelings of discomfort and a desire to escape from the situation involving touch. The symptoms are much worse in situations where touch is induced on the child rather than when the touch is initiated by the child. The child responds by attempting to remove himself from the situation and will state, "I hate this game; it hurts" or "It tickles." The child may pull away from being touched, run away from the adult, hit or kick aggressively, or hide under furniture. Even if the child is touched slightly, he may exclaim "Don't push me!" or "Watch where you're going!" Anxiety, discomfort, a need to withdraw, and hostility are common behavioral manifestations of tactile defensiveness.

The phenomenon of tactile defensiveness is characteristic of some children with learning disorders and has been correlated with hyperactivity and distractibility (Ayres, 1964; Bauer, 1977). It has also been documented in autistic children (Ayres & Tickle, 1980). Inadequate cortical inhibition of sensory processing and poor regulation in the reticular activating system have been speculated to cause symptoms of increased activity level, sleep–wake disturbances, tactile defensiveness or withdrawal from sensory stimulation (Royeen, 1989). Table 8.1 presents common symptoms of tactile defensiveness.

Case Description of Tactile Defensiveness in an Autistic-Like Child

Andrew was a 5-year-old child with developmental delay and autistic-like tendencies. Developmental skills were developed to the 3-to-4-year level. Andrew's underlying tactile defensiveness was considered to be the most predominant problem affecting his development. Behaviorally, he exhibited a very short attention span and could only sit with a teacher-directed task for a few minutes at a time. When sitting in the chair, he constantly assumed bizarre positions and contortions. Andrew engaged in many self-stimulatory behaviors, including finger flapping, humming, and hanging and swinging on any apparatus that lent itself to this behavior.

TABLE 8.1 Symptoms of Tactile Defensiveness

Infancy

 1. Arches away when held (not high muscle tone)
 2. Makes fist of hands to avoid contact of objects
 3. Curls the toes
 4. Dislikes cuddling
 5. Rejects nipple and food textures (not oral–motor problem)
 6. Strongly prefers no clothing or tight swaddling
 7. Prefers upright or sitting position rather than lying on back or stomach
 8. Dislikes face or hair being washed
 9. Hates car seat and other confining situations

Toddler

 1. Dislikes being touched or cuddled by others: pulls away from being held, cries or whines when touched, or hits back
 2. Distressed when people are near, even when they are not touching (e.g., standing nearby, sitting in a circle)
 3. Avoids touching certain textures. Hates getting hands messy (e.g., fingerpaints, paste, sand)
 4. Likes firm touch best and may enjoy games where there is very intense contact (e.g., jumping into stack of pillows from a height)
 5. Prefers touch from familiar people
 6. Dislikes having face or hair washed. Especially dislikes having a haircut
 7. Prefers long sleeves and pants even in warm weather, or prefers as little clothing as possible, even when it's cool
 8. Touches everything in sight
 9. Bumps hard into other people or object
10. Withdraws from being near others, particularly groups
11. May hit, kick, or bite others and is aggressive in play
12. Has a strong preference for certain food textures (e.g., only firm and crunchy, or only soft)
13. Dislikes being dressed or undressed
14. Bites or hits self
15. Likes to hang by arms or feet off of furniture or people
16. Uses mouth to explore objects

Andrew would not permit others to touch him at all, including his family. If touched by another person, Andrew responded by pinching, biting, or kicking. At school, he was a severe behavior problem and would scream and kick when touched. Once these behaviors had occurred, Andrew could not be calmed for long periods of time. He often withdrew into places where he could avoid being touched, such as under a table or in a corner of the room, after which it would be very difficult to get him out of his hiding place. Andrew did not like other people to be too close to him, and when in groups Andrew would kick, bite, and scream.

Tactile defensiveness was also observed in Andrew's inability to tolerate having his face or hair washed. All of his clothing tags had to be cut out routinely. On one occasion, the tag was left in a new shirt by accident. Andrew began fidgeting with the tag, scratching his whole body. Over the course of the morning, he began to rip his clothing off and could not be controlled.

Andrew's tactile problems are representative of a child with severe tactile defensiveness. Although Andrew's problems were not solely attributable to his tactile disorder, they affected his capacity to develop appropriate interactional skills, attentional behaviors, and self-calming. His severe tactile defensiveness needed to be addressed as a major component of his classroom and home management program.

Using guidance from the occupational therapist at school, Andrew's parents found that his behaviors at home and school were much better when they instituted play times throughout the day that involved pleasurable contact with them. Before school, his mother rubbed lotion on his body using firm touch, emphasizing his palms and the soles of his feet. Sometimes Andrew would use a surgical scrub brush and brush himself on his arms and legs while he and his mother sang songs together. His parents also found that it made a difference if they gave Andrew some focused activity to do before school that involved heavy objects. Some examples of these activities included having Andrew helping them move chairs to the breakfast table or carrying his heavy backpack filled with a thermos, bean bags, and books on his back while he "checked" the house to see if all the lights had been turned off. After school, they instituted a roughhouse playtime with Andrew that involved deep pressure to his body. He particularly liked swinging on the tire swing outside and crashing his body into soft things like a large gymnastic ball that his mother would roll toward him. They thought of many creative interactive games using the concept of giving him heavy pressure to his joints and skin. For example, his mother and Andrew would kneel on opposite sides of a large foam "wall" and try to push the other person over. At the end of the day, Andrew needed time to settle himself down and responded well when his parents did soothing activities involving deep pressure. He loved lying back to back with his father while they sang songs and played with flashlights on the wall in the darkened bedroom. He also enjoyed sitting in a bean bag chair with his feet buried in a bin of dried beans or with a heavy quilt wrapped around his body while they read stories together.

Case Description of Tactile Defensiveness in a Child with Motor and Language Delays

Michael was a 2 year old with a moderate expressive language disorder who was normal in all areas of development except motor coordination. His parents were very concerned that he still had not regulated his sleep cycles. He had difficulty falling asleep and could only nap if driven around in the car. Bedtime was typically a major ordeal, with many ritualized manipulative types of behaviors. The use of timeouts and behavioral procedures had not worked due to Michael's strong fear of separation or being left alone and his adverse reaction to being held. Calming techniques such as swinging in a hammock have not worked.

Michael was evaluated by an occupational therapist to determine if there were any sensory-integrative problems underlying his sleep difficulties and motor incoordination. Throughout the testing, Michael was very fearful of being physically moved and touched by the examiner and, consequently, refused to attempt many tasks. An interview with the mother confirmed Michael's hypersensitivities to touch and movement. He hated having his face washed and avoided messy activities such as fingerpaints. He was very picky about the textures of clothing. In group situations, he tended to withdraw into hiding places (e.g., under a table or inside a tent) and became very irritable when in close quarters. He resisted being hugged and held, but would tolerate cheek-to-cheek contact with his mother on occasion. In addition, Michael avoided movement experiences such as swings or slides and was very cautious about heights and climbing. He preferred to initiate movement activities rather than being moved by others. Sometimes he enjoyed making himself dizzy but became fearful if he moved too fast.

The treatment program was directed toward alleviating his tactile defensiveness and sensitivities to movement through activities that Michael could self-initiate. The tactile activities emphasized firm deep pressure. He particularly enjoyed wedging himself between heavy mats, covering himself with pillows, and jumping into bins of plastic balls. Some of these activities were modified for use before bedtime to help Michael develop self-calming mechanisms.

Tactile Hyposensitivities

Decreased tactile awareness, or hyporeactivity to touch, is less often seen than tactile defensiveness. Children experiencing hyporeactivity to touch have decreased tactile awareness and do not experience touch unless the experience is very intense. They may laugh and actually enjoy a firm pat on the buttocks when being disciplined. It is as if their thresholds for noticing or reacting to tactile stimuli are very high. Oftentimes these children do not seem to experience pain, are slow to initiate movement for tactile exploration, and therefore suffer from a type of sensory deprivation. It is common for these children to seek touch–pressure input. Some self-abusive behaviors may be interpreted as a means to trigger very high thresholds (e.g., biting, head banging). Some children may bite themselves very hard, actually breaking skin without reacting. Another problem seen in children with diminished tactile awareness is that they are very slow in initiating movement and exploring objects by feel.

Very often the child with either tactile defensiveness or tactile hyperactivity will exhibit a lag in motor development because of inefficient use of touch in exploring objects. Frequently, children with tactile dysfunction have low muscle tone, contributing to poor sensory support for movement experiences. For instance, one may see the child sitting half on and half off a chair or sitting with the arm caught under their body with no apparent discomfort. It is important to note that the same child may exhibit both elements of tactile hyper- and hyporeactivity to tactile experiences (e.g., crave deep pressure contact on hands but have an aversion to light touch or certain textures on palms).

An infant who is underreactive to tactile input may appear very passive and content to be left alone. Often the baby does not cry during physically painful medical procedures. There is often a low activity level. When these behaviors are observed, it is important to differentiate the child's responses from other medical problems or a severe cognitive delay that can resemble these behaviors.

How Tactile Problems Evolve Over Time

Because tactile perception is learned within the context of social interactions (e.g., parent–child interactions), it is important to consider not only the infant's tactile functioning, but what the caregiver and environment bring to the experience. Consider the effects of the tactually defensive parent on the infant's emotional development. For example, the parent who is defensive to touch may avoid holding and cuddling their infant. Traumas early in life such as child abuse or poor mother–infant bonding may affect the person's responses throughout life in interactions involving touch. Likewise, the environment may cause a sensory deprivation such as that experienced by the very premature infant who suffers a prolonged hospitalization with invasive medical procedures (e.g., oral intubation, heel sticks) and a minimum of holding and carrying from a loving caregiver. The effects of sensory deprivation are commonly seen in children who have been institutionalized in their early years.

Discomfort at tactile experiences becomes heightened as the child grows older and encounters more challenging and varied tactile experiences. For example, the child must deal with the touch of playmates and adults other than mom and dad's familiar touch. Although the child's own parents may have found ways to approach and touch him in ways that feel acceptable to the child, other children and adults have not made this accommodation. As a result, the child's tactile problems may appear worse.

As the child enters the second year of life, independence and mobility allow the child to flee from uncomfortable tactile experiences, or to approach and touch those that are pleasurable. Some parents begin to notice that their child seems unusually active as they move from one unpleasant tactile experience to another. Some children are observed to mouth or bite toys, seeking hard deep pressure in an area of the body that can more easily adapt to incoming tactile sensations. The child often prefers intense deep pressure activities such as roughhousing with mom or dad.

Preschool and school-aged children with tactile hyper- or hyposensitivities often display fine motor difficulties because they lack the tactile discrimination to handle and manipulate objects within the palm and fingertips for refined use. Tasks such as drawing with a pencil or buttoning are very difficult. The child may always look at his hands when manipulating objects. Mouthing of toys may still occur. There is often an avoidance of touching new textures with a preference for firm, hard toys. The child may have a strong preference for certain types of clothing, complain about clothing tags, and dislike having hair and face washed. More advanced tactile discriminative skills such as stereognosis (e.g., detection of objects by feel alone) and graphesthesia (e.g., identification of letter or number drawn on a body part while vision is occluded) are usually delayed as well.

Play difficulties are common among children with tactile hypersensitivities. Destructive or aggressive play occurs frequently when the child is required to play with other children in close proximity. The child may touch other children with force even when trying to be gentle. If given a choice, some children withdraw from other children or find spaces to play that provide them with tactile security, such as a corner of the room.

Treatment Approaches for Children with Somatosensory Dysfunction

Techniques for the Tactually Defensive Child

1. Provide opportunities in the environment that allow the child to self-initiate touch. Use enclosed areas, heavy objects, objects that vibrate, and materials that provide deep pressure on large body surfaces.

2. Encourage games with high contact with other people that allow the child to withdraw from other people in socially acceptable ways, as shown in the accompanying photos. Children can play a game called "earthquake." When lying under the foam blocks, they must keep their bodies very quiet until signaled by the therapist to start the "earthquake." In another version of this activity, they lie very still on top of the blocks, then wait for the therapist to shake the blocks, causing them to fall into the pile of blocks. Playing inside a large stretchy tube can be a fun way of tolerating contact between children, as is pushing over a large foam block in a game for two children, or making a "people sandwich" while lying on a soft foam "cloud" mattress. All are fun ways to engage children in physical contact while addressing their tactile needs. Group games using a parachute or with a large stretchy tube do not provide direct physical contact between children but allow them safe physical boundaries that help them tolerate being in close proximity with one another without touching.

3. Override the tactile system by using highly visual tasks (e.g., putting stickers on body parts). Going inside an inflatable pup tent filled with plastic balls, playing dress-up, or playing with small toys in a sand table are ways to

These children are learning how to keep their bodies very still under the stack of foam blocks to prevent the "earthquake."

These children need to balance very carefully when the "earth-quake" shakes the stack of foam pillows.

These children are learning how to tolerate contact from one another while playing inside a large stretchy tubing.

These children are providing tactile–proprioceptive input to one another as they try to push over the foam wall.

These children are learning to tolerate touch from one another in this "people sandwich" on a foam mattress.

A game of parachute works on both bilateral coordination and touch in a group activity.

These children are providing tactile–proprioceptive input to one another as they play with a large stretchy tubing.

Playing in an visually interesting contained space helps children with tactile hypersensitivities.

Combining fantasy play with touch in a game of dress-up helps these girls tolerate different tactile sensations.

By creating a story with small objects in sand, these children can work on their ability to tolerate textures in the hands while playing in close proximity with one another.

incorporate the tactile and visual senses. In these activities, the emphasis should be on the visual channel versus the tactile stimulation. This can be done with the auditory system, too. For example, taking a stick and pulling it over a grate to make a noise or holding a vibrating ball that makes humming noise are activities that emphasize the auditory over the tactile channel.

4. Use vestibular input coupled with tactile stimulation for children who enjoy vestibular stimulation. For example, the child can ride prone in a hammock swing while skiing with his hands in crazy foam on a wedge or burying his hands inside an inner tube filled with marbles and other small toys.

5. Scratchy textures such as bristle blocks and sandpaper are often more accepting because they involve multiple points of contact and provide deeper input than smooth textures.

6. The proprioceptive sense is very important in helping children feel more comfortable with their tactile sensitivities. Pulling a resistive medium such as Theraputty, a rubber hoop, or a heavy stretch doll, squeezing the "pop-it" man with the hands so his eyes, nose, and ears pop out, or burying the hands inside a bin of dried beans to find small objects are examples of how one may incorporate the proprioceptive sense into therapy. The adult should use firm,

While suspended in a hammock, this girl explores in a large bin of marbles to help her be less sensitive to touch on her hands.

Playing with resistive putty while sitting in the bean bag chair is very organizing for this child's tactile system.

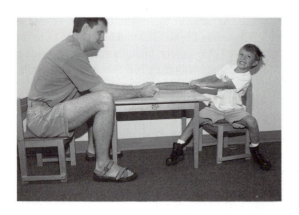

This boy enjoys a resistive activity with his father.

These two boys enjoy stretching a resistive doll by the hands and feet.

This boy is desensitizing his palms by squeezing this "pop-it" man.

Searching for small objects in a bin of dried beans is useful in desensitizing the hands to touch.

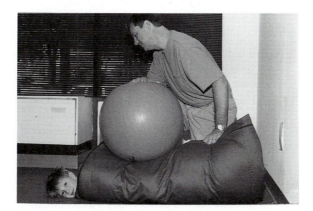

This child is receiving inhibition to the tactile system in this game of "hot dog," where he is wrapped in a comforter "bun," then given various "toppings" by his father.

sustained contact when touching the child, providing input on the child's back, abdomen, and pelvis first. Many children prefer a squeeze–release type of touch rather than a stroke or massage. When it is impossible to touch the child directly, it is often useful to begin with games like the "hot dog," whereby the child is wrapped up in a soft comforter, while the back is massaged with a large ball that rolls up and down the back in different ways (e.g., light tapping, firm rub) to provide "toppings" on the hot dog.

7. Address tactile defensiveness in everyday activities. For example, if the child avoids food textures, begin by using an electric toothbrush and Nuk toothbrushes on the gums and focusing on firm food textures first. Let the child self-initiate and provide touch to himself first if possible.

8. For the severely tactually defensive child, the therapist may need to set up a few things that can be "done to" the child to help overcome the defensiveness (e.g., Pat Wilbarger's brushing technique that involves rubbing the extremities, back, hands, and feet with a surgical brush in a systematic way) (Wilbarger & Wilbarger, 1991). It is very important, however, not to suggest these types of activities to parents if there are significant problems in the parent–child relationship, if there might be potential abuse, or if the parent is already overly intrusive and controlling. In such instances, it is better for a therapist to initiate these adult-directed experiences.

9. Because of the intimate link between touch and emotions, it is critical that all tactile activities be introduced in a nurturing, caring manner. The therapist should address the negative meaning that touch has taken on for both child and parent. The parent who feels rejected by a noncuddly child and the child who interprets other children as hurting him when they are simply coming into his/her physical space are examples of these kinds of problems.

10. Encourage the family to keep a log of behaviors that occur after intervention, including changes in sleep and attending behaviors. Tactile stimulation affects the nervous system at least half an hour after administration. However, there is a loading effect, and touch experiences occur all day long, so the therapist may not know when the peak effect has occurred. Watch for unusual behaviors such as self-abuse, rapid breathing, sweating or flushing, destructiveness, problems sleeping, and extreme restlessness. These behaviors are particularly hard to differentiate if the child has a motor problem and cannot move easily. If the child experiences negative effects from tactile stimulation, use slow rocking, firm pressure on the back and abdomen, and visual focus on a task.

Techniques for the Child with Hyporesponsivity to Touch

1. Registering touch is the central issue for children who are undersensitive to touch. Therefore, the therapist needs to provide tactile experiences that force the child to attend to the fact that they are receiving touch. The stimulation

needs to be done by combining touch with another sensory channel—vestibular, auditory, visual. It is also important to force an adaptive response from the child, thus giving him a motor action that goes with the tactile input. For example, one activity may be wrapping the child's hand up in resistive putty, then waiting for the child to look at his hand and figure out what to do about it. The therapist may wrap the child up in a large piece of paper to be a "hot dog" instead of using a blanket, so that the noise of the paper orients the child to the touch.

2. Vibration and traction are helpful to introduce, thereby using proprioception as the main sensory channel.

3. If the child has self-abusive behaviors, institute a daily regime whereby several times a day the therapist applies light touch and stroking to the areas that are affected (e.g., bit, hit). If the child hits his head, be sure to provide input to both the face and hand. Make it a fun routine that the child can anticipate.

4. REMEMBER! The child who is underreactive to touch almost always has elements of tactile defensiveness!

THE VESTIBULAR AND PROPRIOCEPTIVE SYSTEMS

Like the tactile system, the vestibular system develops early, enabling the fetus and infant to receive and respond to specific movement stimuli. *In utero*, the fetus receives constant vestibular stimulation from movement of the amniotic fluid, as well as the mother's own body movements. Because of its role in assisting the infant in orienting himself in space and in initiating exploratory and adaptive movements, the vestibular system, along with the tactile system, is particularly critical for development of basic functions in the infant. The vestibular system has an impact on the development of body posture, muscle tone, ocular–motor control, reflex integration, and equilibrium reactions (Keshner & Cohen, 1989). These vestibular-based functions have a strong impact on the development of motor skills, visual–spatial and language abilities, hand dominance, and motor planning (Ayres, 1972; Clark, 1985). It is important for coordination and motor planning of the two body sides. In addition, the vestibular system plays a role in arousal and alertness. When moving, visual alertness and attention increase.

Another important function of the vestibular system is to provide gravitational security when moving in space. A secure sense of where the body is in space contributes to the development of emotional stability. A child who lacks adequate vestibular functioning may be insecure in his body movements, fearful of movement in space, particularly when the feet leave the ground, and is likely to exhibit emotional insecurity.

The proprioceptive system develops through weight bearing and movement against gravity. This sense is critical in maturation of reflexes, particularly the equilibrium or balance reactions, in perception of body position and movement in space, and in providing security and stability as the child moves. Visual feedback is important in developing proprioception because it helps a person monitor posture and movement. The proprioceptive sense develops in conjunction with the tactile and vestibular senses.

The primary purposes of the vestibular system are summarized in Table 8.2.

TABLE **8.2**   Primary Purposes of the Vestibular System

1. Detect motion
2. Detect and respond to the earth's gravitational pull
3. Detect motion within the visual field
4. Influence muscle tone and posture
5. Influence motor coordination including bilateral motor control and sequencing
6. Impact body scheme
7. Provide gravitational security during body movement
8. Modulate arousal and alertness for attention and calming

Vestibular-Based Problems

Because the vestibular system is very complex in its anatomy and neurophysiology, there are many types of vestibular-based problems (Fisher *et al.*, 1991; Kimball, 1993). The most common vestibular-based disorders are presented in Table 8.3.

Infants with vestibular hypersensitivities typically show an intolerance for low-to-ground positions (e.g., prone or supine), a strong preference for upright postures, low muscle tone, slowness in developing motor skills, delayed balance, and/or fear of irregular or unexpected movement (DeGangi & Greenspan, 1988). When underresponsive to movement in space, the infant seems to crave movement and may become very fussy and demanding unless the parents provide movement stimulation. Once the baby is more adept at moving about, he or she may rock vigorously while sitting or on hands and knees. The infant may seek swinging for long periods of time and particularly enjoy roughhousing with parents.

Vestibular processing problems in the toddler may take the form of hyper- or hyposensitivities to movement. When the toddler is gravitationally insecure—that is, fearful of movement experiences with a strong preference for movement activities near to the ground—there is often an accompanying separation anxiety disorder. The child relies heavily on the parent to provide safety in new situations,

TABLE **8.3** Common Vestibular-Based Disorders

1. Gravitational insecurity
2. Underresponsiveness to movement in space
3. Intolerance or aversive response to movement
4. Postural-ocular movement disorder
5. Vestibular–postural deficits
6. Bilateral integration and sequencing problems
7. Motor planning problems associated with the underlying vestibular disorder

such as helping them find a place to play where other children won't bump into them, causing them to fall. Since the toddler with gravitational insecurity usually dislikes playing on playground equipment, one usually sees the child with this problem standing close by an adult when outside or preferring to play with small manipulative toys. The child's play in a large space is very constricted, using a small area, even when engaged in play with cars and trucks on the floor.

When a toddler is underreactive to movement stimulation, different issues emerge. Toddlers are notorious for their desire to test limits and attempt activities that allow them to master new motor skills. The child who is underreactive to movement often challenges parents by climbing onto dangerous surfaces, jumping from unsafe heights, or trying a movement activity that exceeds their motor capacity, such as climbing high on a jungle gym. Often the child who is underreactive to movement is fearless and constantly tests limits. They may crave movement activities and become very upset when restrained from continuing to swing, climb, or spin. Parents often report that on days where the child is unable to engage in such movement activities the child becomes very irritable, tantrums frequently, and has difficulty with sleep.

In addition to gravitational insecurity and vestibular hyperactivity, the preschool and school-aged child with vestibular problems often has problems in postural control, balance, and sequencing and coordination of movement. The child may have poor equilibrium reactions in different body positions. When sitting at a desk, the child may be fidgety, with extraneous body movements due to weak trunk stability. When asked to engage in activities such as walking on hands in a wheelbarrow walk or climbing a trapeze bar, the child may show weakness of the trunk and neck. As a result of weakness at the shoulders, the child may have poor distal prehension, holding small objects with the pads of the fingers rather than the fingertips. It is not unusual for the child to have ocular–motor problems as well, such as difficulties looking up from a paper to the chalkboard and back again to the paper.

Vestibular dysfunction is often observed in combination with bilateral integration problems, particularly in children who have postural deficits. Bilateral motor integration involves the ability to coordinate the two body sides and develop lateralization (Magalhaes *et al.*, 1989). Children with problems in this area frequently do not establish a hand dominance by the time they are school aged. Frequently, the child will interchange hands with no consistent preference for one hand. Bilateral assistive skills, where one hand acts as a specialized hand and the other as an effective stabilizer, are difficult. For example, simple tasks such as buttoning and scissor cutting are delayed. Reciprocal bilateral movements such as skipping, jumping, or alternating the hands in a drumming pattern are difficult. Oftentimes the child lacks precision in hand function and cannot sequence hand movements. The child may lack symmetry and control in large body movements. As a result, the child is often very clumsy and stiff in gross motor tasks such as rolling and walking since these movements require coordination of the two body sides. The child lacks flexibility in rotating the trunk, and there is also a strong resistance in crossing the body midline. Consequently, the child may turn the entire body when required to cross the midline rather than rotating the trunk. Table 8.4 presents many of the traits of children with vestibular problems.

Gravitational Insecurity and Intolerance for Movement

Postural or gravitational security seems to play an important role in the development of emotional stability as well as balance, postural mechanisms, and spatial

---

TABLE 8.4 Symptoms of Vestibular Hyper- or Hyposensitivities

Vestibular Hypersensitivities:

1. Easily overwhelmed by movement (e.g., car sick)
2. Strong fear of falling and of heights
3. Does not enjoy playground equipment and avoids roughhousing play
4. Is anxious when feet leave ground
5. Dislikes having head upside down
6. Slow in learning skills such as climbing up stairs or playground equipment and relies on railing longer than other children same age
7. Enjoys movement which she/he initiates but does not like to be moved by others, particularly if the movement is unexpected
8. Dislikes trying new movement activities or has difficulty learning them

Underresponsiveness to movement:

1. Craves movement and does not feel dizziness when other children do
2. Likes to climb to high, precarious places. No sense of limits or controls
3. Is in constant movement, rocking or running about
4. Likes to swing very high and/or for long periods of time
5. Frequently rides on the merry-go-round while others run around to keep the platform turning
6. Enjoys getting into an upside-down position

perception (Fisher & Bundy, 1989; Matthews, 1988). Children who are hypersensitive to movement are usually overwhelmed by intense movement stimuli such as spinning, frequent changes in direction and speed, or unusual body positions (e.g., inverted). Typically, they are fearful about leaving the earth's surface and are thus called gravitationally insecure (Ayres, 1979). Often they display considerable autonomic responses (dizziness, nausea) during and after any type of vestibular stimulation. Increased sensitivity to vestibular stimulation can result in motion sickness (Baloh & Honrubia, 1979).

The gravitationally insecure child demonstrates an extreme fearfulness of moving in space. Children with gravitational insecurity typically have a strong preference for upright positions, avoid rotational movement patterns such as rolling, prefer close-to-ground positions (i.e., a W sitting posture), "lock" the body and neck in rigid postures to avoid movement stimulation, and tend to avoid movement activities. Not only are they fearful of body movement in space, but they resist any change in their body which they may perceive as threatening. Movement that is imposed and/or unexpected is particularly upsetting to the child. The emotional response that accompanies gravitational insecurity is associated with a sudden change of head position, a displacement in the body's center of gravity, or the feet suddenly leaving the ground. As a result of insecurities in moving in space, children with gravitational insecurity tend to be emotionally insecure also. They frequently display fearfulness of new situations, rigidity, and a resistance to change. It has been hypothesized that gravitational insecurity may be due to poor modulation of otolithic inputs (Fisher & Bundy, 1989). In infants one may observe a strong preference for sameness in routines with crying and agitated behavior when routines vary, a strong need to be held and carried constantly, and a fearfulness of certain body positions (e.g., back or stomach).

This child shows fear when confronted by unexpected movement.

Some children experience an intolerance for movement and considerable autonomic discomfort during movement activities. The child may also exhibit gravitational insecurity as well. Typically, the child feels nauseated and dizzy, particularly during rapid movement activities such as spinning. Motion sickness in a car or boat ride is not infrequent. It is hypothesized that the individual with intolerance for movement is hyperresponsive to semicircular canal stimulation (e.g., spinning) (Fisher & Bundy, 1989). Since gastrointestinal symptoms are common, vestibular–vagal connections are also involved. Sometimes a person with intolerance for movement has visual motion sensitivity and feels autonomic responses while watching spinning or swinging objects, or watching motion pictures that simulate movement or flight in space (Fisher *et al.*, 1986).

Hyporeactivity to Movement in Space

When children have a high tolerance for vestibular input (hyperreactivity to movement), the behavioral repertoire is different. These children may seek movement experiences and yet do not seem to profit from them. One may see explosive movement quality, poor judgment in starting and stopping movement activities, or difficulty with transitional movements. Children with vestibular problems typically exhibit low muscle tone and may not be able to move against gravity easily enough to stimulate the vestibular system in a variety of movement planes. As a result, poverty of movement provides fewer opportunities for developing vestibular output for postural control and balance. Children who are hyporeactive to movement usually crave movement and do not display any evidence of autonomic responses such as dizziness associated with spinning.

Vestibular–Postural deficits

Vestibular–postural problems are among the most common type of vestibular-based deficits. Frequently children with minor neurological impairments have difficulty with postural reactions including balance, ocular–motor control, and visual–spatial skills (Steinberg & Rendle-Short, 1977). Children with severe emotional and behavioral problems have also been reported to display deficient equilibrium and postural responses, decreased postrotary nystagmus, and an absence of autonomic responses such as dizziness and nausea following vestibular stimulation (Ottenbacher, 1982).

The primary problem underlying a vestibular–postural problem is inadequate postural control. The neck and trunk muscles provide stability in movement, and their development provides the foundation for postural control. If the proximal musculature is not well developed, the child is often unstable in maintaining body postures, has poor balance, and may have poor fine manipulation and locomotor skills.

Treatment Approaches to Address Vestibular Problems in Children

General Treatment Principles

In treating children with vestibular-based problems, therapy needs to be directed toward normalizing the child's responses to sensory input and in developing more adaptive and functional motor skills. Since many children with vestibular dysfunction also exhibit emotional problems, these need to be addressed in the therapeutic process. The major principle underlying treatment of vestibular problems is improving the child's ability to organize and process vestibular input provided during meaningful events, thus allowing the child to produce an adaptive response to the environment. The child's ability to actively control the sensory stimulation while simultaneously engaging in purposeful motor activity is essential to the intervention process.

Sensory-integrative therapy utilizes vestibular stimulation to influence balance, muscle tone, oculomotor responses, movements against gravity, postural adjustments, and activity level. Linear movement activities (e.g., walking, jumping) assist the child to acclimate in relation to the environment, facilitating the development of an understanding of the body position and body movement in space while rotary and irregular movement activities (e.g., spinning, accelerating and decelerating, playing in unusual positions) provide powerful input to the system for arousal and alerting. A major premise of sensory-integrative therapy is that movement activities should be self-initiated to elicit adaptive responses. Since children with severe tonal disturbances often have considerable difficulty self-initiating adaptive movement, opportunities for active, purposeful movement need to be provided via mobile surfaces (e.g., waterbeds, large foam mattress "clouds").

There is no set prescription for therapy for a child with vestibular dysfunction. Since each child brings with him a unique combination of characteristics, these must be addressed in the therapy process. Therapeutic activity should involve the child's choice of activity guided by his or her own interest and skill. Play is the medium through which therapy is adapted. For example, the child may develop an imaginary game where he is flying through space like "Flight Man." The therapist seeks to structure the environment to facilitate the child's responses. Table 8.5 presents a list of guidelines when providing vestibular stimulation activities.

As with any sensory stimulation, the child's responses should be watched carefully to ensure that it is perceived as pleasurable and useful to the child as they learn new skills. Autonomic responses such as increased respiration, flushing or pallor, sweating, nausea or yawning, or severe dizziness and loss of balance should be observed. They may not always occur immediately during or after the stimulation. Instead, the child may become disorganized or ill later in the day or after additional vestibular stimulation (e.g., ride home) loads the system to its maximum toleration level. Slow rocking with firm pressure on the abdomen, use of firm tactile input, and cognitive games such as counting or singing will help the child regroup if the input has been too intense.

TABLE 8.5 Guidelines for Vestibular Stimulation Activities

1. The child should always be actively involved. (Examples: Pushing himself on equipment, or actively involved by telling the therapist when to stop or start the motion.)
2. Vestibular stimulation should always be provided within the context of what the child needs. (Improved postural control, bilateral integration, or better attention and self-calming.)
3. Without a purpose, vestibular stimulation can be extremely disorganizing.
4. Activities should be selected that provide ocular input since the vestibular system works optimally in conjunction with visual input from the eyes and with proprioceptive input. (Example: The lights may be dimmed while the child navigates through a tunnel on a scooter board with his flashlight.)
5. Proprioceptive input may be enhanced through the use of weighted objects, firm pressure to joints, movement against gravity, traction, or resistive activities.
6. In order for responses to vestibular stimulation to be adaptive, the movement should be provided in all planes and in all directions of movement. (Example: The type of movement should be varied—head-to-toe rocking, side to side, forward–back, or rotary movements (orbital or circular spinning). Vestibular input may vary in terms of speed, direction, regularity and timing, and plane of movement.)

Approaches for Hyperresponsivity to Movement

Very different treatment approaches are used with children who are under- versus overresponsive to movement stimulation. The child with gravitational insecurity needs a slow, gradual approach to introducing movement. This child responds best when movement is linear such as forward–back or side to side, since gravitational insecurity is hypothesized to be the result of poor modulation of otolithic input. The reason that this type of input is so calming and easy to accept is that it does not involve any rotary movements or large movement displacements of the head in space. Orbital spinning (modified spinning with face remaining in one direction) is usually accepted as well. Coupling movement activities with firm deep pressure activities helps the child organize the movement experience through the sense of touch. The child needs a very gradual approach, starting with activities that are close to the ground. For instance, a movable tube can be stabilized with bricks on each side so that the child crawling through the tube learns to tolerate moving inside it in a safe way before we challenge her to move through it when it is mobile.

If vestibular stimulation is imposed or forced on the child, it can be more disorganizing than integrating. Therapy must be carefully graded to challenge the child within the confines of what the child can tolerate and integrate. The child should be moved slowly and in a rhythmical movement. Maintaining close body contact with the child helps him learn to tolerate any movement, thus providing inhibition through the tactile sense. Providing visual or auditory cues also helps the child anticipate where his body is moving in space. Activities should be

By stabilizing a movable piece of equipment, children with gravitational insecurity can start to become more comfortable with movement.

selected that are first close to the ground (e.g., a Sit-'n-Spin or T-stool). The child may need to be enticed to just touch moving equipment or put a favorite toy on the swing in the first weeks of treatment. In this way, the child may gradually learn to tolerate the visual component of watching the movement before he is expected to move in space. If the child is allowed to decide on a movement and then enact the movement, it helps to modulate the vestibular input. The accompanying photo shows two children engaged in a fishing game while sitting in inner tubes, suspended to the ceiling with bunjey cords. The highly visual aspect of the game and the fact that they can control how much movement they will get helps them tolerate the movement experience of this activity. In another photo, a child is wearing a compression vest and braces while sitting on a therapy bench mounted on the suspension swing. By helping her remain in good alignment and by providing her with the security of being able to hold on and to sit with her sister on the swing, she was able to tolerate the movement.

Techniques for Hyporeactive Responses to Movement in Space

The child who is hyporeactive to movement in space often craves spinning and will seek fast moving, rough kinds of games. This type of child may disorganize very rapidly and without warning. Vestibular stimulation needs to be carefully directed and combined with purposeful, goal-directed activities so that the child learns to control the sensory stimulation and modify his responses accordingly. Movement activities that are very intense and stimulating should be coupled with inhibitory or calming ones. Rotary (spinning, rolling down a ramp) and irregular

These boys learn to tolerate movement in suspended inner tubes during a visually enticing fishing game.

By using a compression vest and therapy bench on the platform swing, this child can experience movement that she would not have otherwise because of her poor postural tone in sitting.

fast moving input that requires the eyes to constantly adapt to a new visual focus is typically used in treatment for this type of child. Inverted body positions (upside down) are also highly stimulating because they involve a complete displacement of the head.

Techniques for Vestibular–Postural Problems

Intervention directed toward improving postural mechanisms should focus on improving muscle tone, developing antigravity postural control, improving muscle cocontraction, and developing righting and equilibrium reactions. Intervention should first be directed toward improving muscle tone and developing antigravity postural control. Through the use of basic antigravity postures, combined with vestibular stimulation and functional activities, muscle tone may be improved. Sometimes specialized handling techniques may be required to increase tone in the low-tone child. For example, one may have the child sit on inflatable equipment to work their postural tone and balance as shown. A variety of materials such as stretchy ropes, resistive therapy bands, or heavy weighted toys help to stimulate tone as well.

Approaches for Inattention and Problems with Self-Calming

Vestibular stimulation may be used to help regulate arousal levels to enable self-calming and focused attention. One of the strategies to decrease a hyperaroused state in a child is to use sensory inhibition to diminish arousal prior to bedtime or at other times when the child is overly active and needs to sit quietly for learning or tabletop activities. Linear movement activities (e.g., forward–back and head-to-toe rocking, swinging) are calming and serve to inhibit the reticular activating system via the vestibular system. When the child is unable to fall asleep on his own, movement may be introduced to dampen hyperarousal. Crib cradles (e.g., a hammock swing designed for the crib), a vibrating mattress, or a waterbed mattress help to further soothe the overaroused child. Swinging the child within a

These children are working on postural tone and balance while sitting on this barrel.

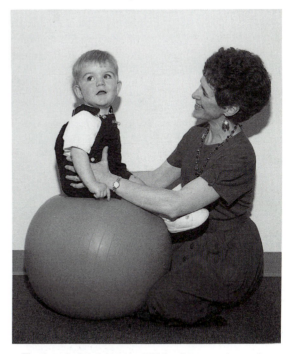

The therapist is helping this child develop postural control in sitting by challenging his equilibrium reactions.

soft blanket filled with pillows or having him lie with his head inverted slightly may also inhibit arousal level.

Motor Planning Disorders

Developmental dyspraxia, also known as a motor planning disorder, is a sensory-processing deficit that is often related to tactile and/or vestibular processing disorders. The problem lies not so much in the processing of sensory input or the ability to produce the movement skill, but in the intermediary process of planning the movement. The child with developmental dyspraxia has significant problems in planning and directing goal-directed movement, skilled, or nonhabitual motor tasks. Because the dyspraxic child lacks internal cognitive organization to focus thoughts and actions, the child is often vulnerable to distraction (Ayres *et al.*, 1987). The distinct types of motor planning problems are presented in Table 8.6. Children with vestibular or tactile dysfunction may exhibit any of these types of dyspraxia (Ayres, 1985; Conrad *et al.*, 1983; Cermak, 1985).

The underlying problem in developmental dyspraxia is the ability to organize a purposeful plan of action. The components that are needed include:

Stage 1: Ideation.   In this first stage of motor planning, the child must develop the conceptual organization of the skill or task. The child needs to link the feeling of enacting the motion or action with the concept of which actions lead to task completion. In treatment, the occupational therapist may move the child through

TABLE 8.6	Types of Motor Planning Problems
Postural dyspraxia	Inability to plan and imitate large body movements and meaningless postures
Sequencing dyspraxia	Difficulty making transitions from one motor action to another and in sequencing movements (e.g., thumb-finger sequencing)
Oral and verbal dyspraxia	Inability to produce oral movements on verbal command or in imitation, a skill that affects speech articulation
Constructional dyspraxia	Inability to create and assemble three-dimensional structures (e.g., block bridge)
Graphic dyspraxia	Inability to plan and execute drawings
Dyspraxia involving symbolic use of objects	Inability to use objects symbolically

the action while describing what is happening. Sometimes children are more interested in trying a difficult task if they have experienced what it feels like to move through the motions. Once the child has engaged in the task successfully a few times, it is important to vary the task demands slightly to present a new challenge. In this way, the child learns to self-correct and to execute new movement patterns.

Stage 2: Planning the action.   Before the child can plan out what he wants to do, he must be prepared to act. He needs to be motivated to do the action; therefore, it is important to find activities that excite the child and solicit his interest and involvement. The first step in learning to plan an action is to be able to experience it and to verbalize or conceptualize what needs to happen. Once the child has conceptualized the action with a model or the therapist's assistance, he needs to understand what the end goal will be and how to get there. Selecting activities that give sensory feedback throughout the sequence helps the child construct a plan. For example, if an obstacle course is used, the child may crawl through an opening in a large foam tunnel, then pull himself on a scooter board by holding a resistive rope, and then swing while pushing over a large sandbag man. Each of these would have distinctly different sensory inputs that would help him mark each event in time and space.

Stage 3: Executing the plan.   This is often the easiest stage of praxis. An important component of plan execution is self-correction and verbal mediation. The therapist may help the child articulate what he is doing to help him link language with motor actions. Verbal commands from the therapist while the child engages in a task help to organize the sequence for the child. Once the child has consolidated his actions with verbal guidance from the therapist, he should be helped to articulate what he is going to do next.

The most common types of motor planning disorders observed in children with somatosensory and vestibular-based problems are related to postural, sequencing, bilateral motor coordination, constructional, and praxis to verbal commands (Ayres, 1985). An emphasis of therapy is on the ability to plan whole body movements in space and to combine the body with objects. Through the use of postural patterns of flexion and extension against gravity, trunk rotation, and diagonal rotary patterns, the child can learn to map simple body movements in space. These postural patterns are combined with functional activities so that the movement pattern has a purpose for the child. Therapy focuses on the use of sensory stimulation in combination with a strong visual component to help the child see what he is doing in space and to visualize the effect his actions have on objects. For example, having the child sit in a hammock and swing to kick over a tower of cardboard blocks will give him vestibular, proprioceptive, and visual feedback to consolidate the motor plan of kicking over the tower. The major emphasis is therefore placed on relating the body in space in relation to objects.

By the second year of life, motor control and motor planning problems begin to become more evident. In the area of motor control, one observes the child having difficulty coordinating use of the two hands in simple bilateral tasks such as putting together pop beads. Muscle tone may be diminished. For instance, the child may sit or stand in a slumped body posture. Balance may also be poor, with problems in learning tasks such as descending steps while holding a railing.

Motor planning problems become evident as the child experiences extreme frustration over tasks that he cannot problem solve. Because of the motor planning disorder, the child often breaks toys easily, then become very upset when he cannot fix them. Often the child relies heavily on the parents to guide him whenever an activity is going to change. Some parents find that they need to prepare their child several days in advance about upcoming events to prevent major emotional upsets. The parents often explain everything that is going to happen and give verbal feedback while the activity is occurring. The child seems to struggle with getting started and carrying out the necessary steps to complete the task. Activities with sequences such as undressing and dressing are struggles for the child.

Some of the common symptoms of the child with dyspraxia are delays in dressing and in fine and gross motor skills involving imitation, sequenced movements (e.g., lacing, skipping), and construction (e.g., building from a block model). Poor accuracy of movement is observed, and skilled hand movements such as handwriting are very difficult for the dyspraxic child. Their movement quality may be explosive with poor judgment of force, speed, and aim. Speech articulation may be poor since this is also a planned, skilled motor activity. Nonhabitual tasks are very difficult for the dyspraxic child, who prefers routines and strongly resists changes. Transitions from one activity to the next may cause behavioral upset.

Initiation of new movement sequences or new organized plans of behavior are difficult. For instance, the child may not be able to tell you what he plans to do because he lacks an internal plan. As a result, one may see the dyspraxic child becoming either very disruptive and aggressive, particularly when there is no external structure to organize the child, or very passive, preferring repetition of certain favorite activities and resisting new and different tasks. One may observe tantrums, aggressive behavior, poor play skills with peers, frustration, and a strong resistance to change. Some children become very controlling and manipulative because of their inability to control and impact their environment. Needless to say, poor self-concept is a major problem of the dyspraxic child. Tables 8.7 and 8.8 list some of the common symptoms of motor control and motor planning problems observed in children.

TABLE **8.7** Motor Control Problems in the Child

1. Frequently breaks toys—cannot seem to judge how hard or soft to press when handling toys
2. Trips over obstacles or bumps into them
3. Falls frequently (after 18 months)
4. Slumped body posture when sitting or standing
5. Leans head on hand or arm
6. Prefers to lie down rather than sit, or to sit rather than stand
7. Has a loose grip on objects such as a pencil, scissors, or spoon, or grip is too tight on objects
8. Fatigues easily during physical activities
9. Is loose jointed and floppy; may sit with legs in a W
10. Has difficulty manipulating small objects, particularly fasteners
11. Eats in a sloppy manner
12. Does not use two hands for tasks that require two hands such as holding down the paper while drawing, holding the cup while pouring

TABLE **8.8** Motor Planning Problems in the Child

1. Fear of trying new motor activities; likes things to be the same and predictable (e.g., routines)
2. Difficulty making transitions from one activity to next
3. Must be prepared in advance several times before change is introduced
4. Cannot plan sequences in activities; needs structure from an adult
5. Easily frustrated
6. Is very controlling of activities
7. Difficulty playing with peers
8. Aggressive or destructive in play
9. Temper tantrum easily
10. Did not crawl before starting to walk
11. Difficulty with dressing and sequenced motor actions

Case Description of the Gravitationally Insecure Child with Developmental Dyspraxia

Emily was a 4½ year old with low muscle tone, fearfulness in new movement activities, and poor balance. She fell frequently at school and avoided any playground activities. Although her fine and gross motor skills were at age level, she had difficulty with dynamic balance. Emily was a very shy and withdrawn child. When presented with motor tasks, Emily tended to cry silently, even during very appealing activities. At tabletop tasks, Emily was very anxious, sitting with her shoulders in a tense, elevated posture. Emily was not sensitive to touch; in contrast, she would seek close proximity with the examiner or her mother whenever she was required to move.

When assessed, Emily demonstrated weakness in postural control (e.g., lifting her body up against gravity in flexed or extended body postures). She would sit in a W sitting posture and preferred close-to-ground activities. Low muscle tone was observed in her winged scapula and rounded trunk posture when standing upright. She often yawned and complained of feeling tired. Her movement quality was stiff, awkward, and lacked fluidity. Emily was very slow and deliberate in her movement patterns. When sitting on the therapy ball, Emily clung to the examiner and was extremely fearful. In addition to definite indicators of gravitational insecurity, Emily showed some evidence of motor planning difficulties. She displayed much fear and anxiety when approached with a new motor challenge, particularly sequenced, unfamiliar movement patterns such as galloping.

Emily received sensory-integrative therapy by an occupational therapist that focused primarily on her gravitational insecurity. Like other children with this problem, she responded best when movement was linear such as forward–back or side to side. Coupling movement activities with firm deep pressure activities helped her to organize movement experiences through the sense of touch. Her parents found that they needed to be very gradual in their approach to Emily, starting with activities that were close to the ground. For instance, they found that Emily could tolerate movement while sitting on their laps and rocking together while they pretended that they were traveling in a spaceship or boat to different places. It was important not to impose vestibular stimulation on her because it could be more disorganizing than integrating. Slow, rhythmical movements were used. Emily liked it when her parents moved with her slowly in creative movement to music with strong drumbeats and nature sounds. Helping Emily anticipate where her body was moving in space by providing visual or auditory cues also helped her to learn where she was about to move. At first, it was necessary to entice Emily just to touch moving equipment or to put a favorite toy on the swing in the first weeks of treatment with the occupational therapist. When her parents took her to the playground, they would bring a favorite stuffed animal and watch it ride on the seesaw or swing before Emily would ride with it. In this way, she gradually learned to tolerate the visual component of watching the movement before she was expected to move in space. After several months of occupational therapy and a home program, she was spontaneously climbing on playground equipment and did not display the fear that she originally experienced. Balance and motor planning skills began to improve through continual occupational therapy intervention.

Treatment of Developmental Dyspraxia

There are three primary processes that must occur in treatment for the child with developmental dyspraxia. These include: (1) developing the conceptual organization of the skill or task; (2) developing a plan or program of action; and (3) executing the plan. It is rare for a child to have a motor planning problem without difficulty in the tactile or vestibular system. Treatment for children with vestibular-based motor planning problems should first focus on vestibular awareness; therefore, vestibular stimulation activities should precede motor planning tasks in a therapy session. Postural and other motor problems associated with the vestibular-based motor planning problem should be addressed in the treatment process as well.

Step 1: Ideation.   In this first stage of motor planning, the child with vestibular-based dyspraxia will have difficulty initiating purposeful movement. The child needs to link the feeling of enacting the motion or action with the concept of what actions lead to task completion. The therapist may move the child through the action while describing what is happening. By using vestibular stimulation in a very specific way, the child can attach meanings to the action. For example, a child may not be able to motor plan how to push himself on a scooter board. The therapist may hold the child's hands and contrast fast and slow movement on a scooter board in a game, then vary other task characteristics, such as holding a hoop versus the therapist's hands, or riding down a ramp or inside a tunnel. Each of these variations of the same action will help the child conceptualize the motor action that is required to propel through space on the scooter board. Motor planning activities should be varied according to sequence, ordering, position, and timing.

The child may not be able to choose a motor task at first because he does not have a concept of what he is able to do with the different toys and materials. The therapist may select a simple planning task, and then model how to do it. For example, the therapist may demonstrate jumping off a platform into a large bin of balls, a task that offers both challenge and success. If the child shows fear or is unable to complete the action required, the task should be modified to ensure that the child can succeed. Sometimes children are more interested in trying a difficult task if they have experienced moving through the motions. Once the child has engaged in the task successfully a few times, it is important to vary the task demands slightly to present a new challenge. In this way, the child must learn to self-correct himself and to execute new movement patterns.

Step 2: Planning the action.   Before the child can plan out what he wants to do, he must be prepared to act. He needs to be motivated to do the action; therefore, it is important to find activities that excite the child and solicit his interest and involvement. The first step in learning to plan an action is to be able to experience it and verbalize or conceptualize what needs to happen. Once the child has enacted the action with a model or the therapist's assistance, he needs to understand what the end goal will be and how to get there. Selecting activities that give sensory feedback throughout the sequence helps the child construct a plan.

Verbal mediation is an important aspect of learning to motor plan. The therapist may help the child articulate what he is doing to help him link language with motor actions. Verbal commands from the therapist while the child engages in a sequenced task help organize the sequence for the child. Once the child has consolidated his actions with verbal guidance from the therapist, he should then be helped to articulate what he is going to do next.

Vestibular-based dyspraxias. The most common types of motor planning disorders observed in children with vestibular-based problems are related to postural, sequencing, bilateral motor coordination, motor planning, constructional, and praxis to verbal commands. Treatment should focus on the ability to plan whole body movements in space and combine the body with objects. Through the use of postural patterns of flexion and extension against gravity, trunk rotation, and diagonal rotary patterns, the child can learn to map simple body movements in space. These postural patterns should always be combined with functional activities so that the movement pattern has a purpose for the child. The body flexors are the mobilizers, while the extensors are the stabilizers. Therefore, flexion is often needed in children who have troubles learning how to initiate movement patterns. These whole body patterns should be used first before small skilled movements are attempted (e.g., cutting a Play Doh snake with scissors). Activities should use vestibular–proprioceptive sensory stimulation in combination with a strong visual component to help the child see what he is doing in space and visualize the effect his actions have on objects. The major emphasis is therefore placed on relating the body in space to objects. Activities involving motor accuracy (e.g., throwing velcro balls at a target), bilateral motor coordination, and sequencing of fine and gross motor movements (e.g., skipping, cutting out a triangle) should follow treatment directed toward basic postural patterns.

CASE EXAMPLE OF TREATMENT APPROACH WITH CHILD WITH PERVASIVE DEVELOPMENTAL DISORDER

This example of the treatment process of a young child with pervasive developmental disorder illustrates how the sensory-integrative therapy and child-centered activity are blended in treatment, with emphasis on developing the child's social relatedness through the parent–child relationship.

Sandra was a 2-year-old child who was diagnosed as having developmental delay with autistic-like symptoms. She had had a medical workup that ruled out genetic and neurological disorders and had not yet had early intervention services. Her parents were hoping to gain a better understanding of Sandra's problems and how they might begin to help her.

Sandra's parents first became concerned about Sandra when she turned 1 year of age. They noticed that she was not making eye contact or pointing to body parts or objects like their older, 4-year-old daughter had done at that age. By 15 months of age, they alerted their pediatrician that Sandra was not talking. By 18 months, they expressed concern again about her talking and were told that if she did not begin talking by 2 years her hearing should be checked. The parents did not want to wait any longer, and at 22 months they began investigating the nature of Sandra's problem.

Presenting Concerns

Mr. and Mrs. T. came to the intake interview to discuss their concerns about Sandra. She had no words but could make sounds, sometimes in a social context. For example, she could make an "aaaaah dadada" sound in greeting. Her sounds tended to be high pitched, with short bursts of screams. Vocalizing occurred the most when she was in front of a mirror. If she wanted to communicate a need, Sandra would cry. Sometimes she would move her mouth with great effort as if she were trying to say something. Sandra could imitate mouth and tongue movements such as sticking her tongue out, and she could make simple sounds. She was not able to follow any commands, although she understood the meaning of "no." If touched by her parents after a command was given, Sandra had an easier time following through although this was inconsistent.

Sandra's favorite play activities were playing pop-up pals, rolling balls, twirling or swinging string, dragging fake pearls on the tile floor, and listening to music. She enjoyed visual stimulation such as looking in mirrors, watching reflections and shadows, creating visual effects with a swinging string, and watching Sesame Street videos. She loved music and would jump up and down or wave her hand while she listened. She appeared interested in making sounds with objects. For example, when she hit the string of pearls on the floor, she created different types of sounds. She carried the pearls about with her, almost as a source of comfort like "worry beads." Sandra would spin dishes, dump objects, or throw toys. She was fixated on strings and would go to great lengths to find them, pulling threads out of a rug to put in her mouth. Mr. and Mrs. T. reported that she had few imitation skills and no symbolic play. There was little turn-taking ability, although her father stated that he could get her involved in a reciprocal game of rolling the ball. Wandering occurred almost constantly. Sandra would mouth toys and try to eat or chew on books. Sandra was most connected with another person during singing activities. She also enjoyed hide-and-seek and peek-a-boo games. Sometimes she would pinch others, especially if she was angry or jealous when her older sister was sitting with her mother.

Sandra was a picky eater, with definite food preferences. She had just begun to use a spoon or fork. When she did not like the food or was finished, she would throw the plate or cup on the floor or against the wall. Usually, Sandra would handle or feel the food with her fingers before eating it. During mealtimes, Sandra was whiny and had a hard time sitting still.

Sandra experienced some hypersensitivities. She would cover her ears when she heard unusual sounds such as an animal noise or the videotape rewinding. Sensitivity to light was noticed when she was in sunlight. Sometimes Sandra enjoyed being held, but she didn't hold onto her parents when they hugged her. Instead, she would bury her hands under her body and act as if she was just putting up with being hugged. She didn't hold onto a person's hand when being led someplace. She loved swings, riding in a stroller, and jumping in the crib. Motor planning problems were noted in certain situations. When coming down stairs, she would scoot on her bottom rather than holding onto the rail and walking.

History

The pregnancy was planned and uneventful, with no complications. Sandra was born full term after 6 hours of labor via vaginal delivery. She had been healthy except for an ear infection. Sandra was big for her age, falling at the 95th percentile for height and the 90th percentile for weight.

Motor development was reported to be on course. Sandra walked at 13 months, although her parents stated that she was more content to sit than move about. She smiled at 4 months and engaged in games like peek-a-boo as a baby. Communication, play, and social–emotional skills were delayed for Sandra. Her parents suspected that she might be bright. For example, she understood where things were in the house and appeared to remember events.

Both parents were unsure about the future for Sandra. They had been told that she would probably need "special education services forever" from various doctors. They had just begun the process of identifying her problems and had been focusing on her medical diagnosis. They felt that Sandra had potential and that she was smart, but did not know how much she would progress.

Clinical Findings

A variety of clinical observations and tests were used to help delineate the nature of Sandra's problems. When observed in play, Sandra engaged in aimless wandering, a behavior that also occurred at home. She seemed most interested when given toys that involved the sense of touch (e.g., Koosh balls, paintbrush). There was no symbolic play, and vocalizations only occurred during play with textured toys. Although Sandra was reported to enjoy movement, she did not want to move on the various pieces of moving equipment that were presented to her in play (e.g., inflatable bolster). No reciprocal interactions were observed, nor did she respond to her mother's attempts to interest her in particular toys or herself. The only time Sandra responded to her mother was when she was told "no" to mouthing toys. Affect was noted to be flat and eye contact was fleeting.

When cognitive and language skills were tested using the Bayley Scales of Infant Development, Sandra attempted to mouth all the objects presented to her. She did stop her mouthing when her mother cautioned her, "Not in your mouth." She manipulated the objects in her hands, rubbed them on her face, and at times waved her arms back and forth across her body or flapped her hands while holding the toys. At times, Sandra seemed angry or frustrated, throwing things on the floor or refusing to cooperate. She especially liked the red ring on the string and anything that was shiny, like the mirror, bell, and spoon. Eye contact was minimal with the examiner or her mother. Most of her sounds were vowels, squeals, or grunts. After about 20 minutes, Sandra tired and refused to cooperate any further. Based on the testing, her functioning was overall at the 8-month level with scatter to 13 months. Her best skills were fine motor and simple problem solving. Language and social skills were the most difficult for her.

When the Test of Attention in Infants was administered, Sandra showed little visual engagement with the toys. She did best with toys that involved movement, such as a toy that had penguins marching up the ladder and sliding down the slide. The auditory and tactile items held no interest for her. There was a great deal of off-task attention. When on task, she had difficulty organizing motor actions to press the switch or reach for the toy. She would look at the toy and only touched the switch to operate the toys occasionally.

Impressions

Two-year-old Sandra was experiencing significant difficulties with social interactions, attention, purposeful activity, language, and cognitive development. The basic stage of social engagement was seriously compromised, making it difficult for her to use gestures or sounds in interactions or read signals from others. Her play was repetitive and immature, with a predominance of manipulating objects in stereotypical ways (e.g., dragging pearls on floor, mouthing, twirling string). What was lacking was the capacity to generate new ways to manipulate toys and to interact with others.

Her attention was poor, with considerable off-task attention during interesting events that normally interest children her age. Aimless wandering also dominated her behavior, which suggested a poor capacity to organize purposeful actions and focus attention.

Hypersensitivities to sounds, light, and touch were present. Her best exploration was with textured toys. She sought out vestibular stimulation (e.g., spinning herself) and enjoyed visually induced vestibular stimulation (e.g., twirling string in front of eyes). She also liked to create unusual sounds. In the area of communication, Sandra had only a few sounds that were used communicatively. Communication involving gestures was limited. She could respond to "no" and a few simple commands, apparently because the verbal commands were delivered in a clear, simple way with more volume and accompanying gestures.

The family functioning was healthy, and her parents were very invested in helping Sandra, doing whatever was needed to help her. In working with the family, we were aware of the need to consider the fact that the parents had just learned about Sandra's diagnosis and had been given a bleak picture of what the future held for her. Grieving for their loss, denial of potential problems, and other normal emotional adaptations were apt to occur during the early stages of treatment. These needed to be respected, allowing the parents to accommodate at their own pace.

The Treatment Plan

The goals for the treatment were as follows:

1. Develop social engagement and basic communication skills:
   a. Facilitate Sandra's toleration of being near other people without the need to escape or wander away. Explore what sensory modalities (e.g., tactile–proprioceptive, vestibular, auditory, or visual) would help Sandra sustain social engagement with others.
   b. Help Sandra give signals about what she wanted by creating play experiences that made it clear to her that her gestures or sounds created an effect on the environment and a reaction from other people.
   c. Develop Sandra's capacity to tolerate face-to-face interactions, exploring what types of activities support eye contact without avoidance or overstimulation (e.g., focusing on tolerating sitting side by side with parent).
   d. Once social engagement and gestures emerged, emphasize reciprocal interactions through turn taking.
   e. Establish social routines in everyday life that Sandra can predict, then facilitate communication around those events.

2. Develop the capacity for more varied and adaptive responses during object and social play, with more elaborated attention to the task or person.
   a. When Sandra was engaged in a stereotypical or repetitive activity, challenge her by introducing a conflict, element of surprise, uncertainty, or complexity to the task or interaction that forces her to engage in a different response.
   b. Find the balance in the level of stimulation in the task, the way the environment is structured, and how the parent interacts with Sandra so that she can tolerate the stimulation and engage in an

adaptive response without becoming disorganized, avoidant, or overstimulated.

c. Employ the use of activities or materials that give an obvious beginning and an end so that it is clear to Sandra when she has successfully completed a task, or engage in simple interactions that are predictable (e.g., game of hiding the ball under mom's shirt). Once Sandra can remain attentive to a simple activity, expand on the steps that need to be taken before the task or game is completed.

The Treatment Program

Sandra was seen for 12 weeks in once-a-week therapy as part of a research project. The therapy program began with 6 weeks of child-centered therapy followed by 6 weeks of structured developmental therapy. Her therapists were a psychologist and a pediatric nurse. Both parents attended the first treatment session, after which the father attended the remaining sessions until the very end of the treatment program, when Mrs. T. returned. Mrs. T. experienced a great deal of sorrow and distress about her daughter's impairment. She adapted by removing herself from the intervention process until Sandra began to show progress. At the time that the therapy program was initiated, Sandra was placed in a local school system's early intervention program. She did not start the school program until the fourth week of treatment.

Session 1

The basic premises of child-centered play were explained and practiced in the first session. In addition to the guidelines presented on child-centered play, several modifications in the approach were necessary because Sandra became overstimulated when in proximal space to her parents. Her parents were more comfortable with a teaching approach; therefore, it was necessary to be explicit about how to do the therapy.

At the first session, Sandra reacted to the child-centered play by running and fleeing from her parents. She was accustomed to playing alone or wandering about the house aimlessly. We suggested to Mr. and Mrs. T. to try to make it a game of chase, saying "gotcha," then catching her with their arms or a hula hoop. Most of the session was spent with her parents running around the room after Sandra. We found that, if they sat in one spot and didn't move, Sandra shut them out completely. Later in the session, she became interested in playing with some plastic balls that were in a wading pool. She would hold the ball, then reach for another. We suggested that Mrs. T. hold out a ball in her palm for Sandra to reach toward. When Sandra tried to grab the ball, Mrs. T. gave the ball a little tug or resistance.

When this happened, Sandra would sometimes look at her mother's face. At other times the slight resistance frustrated her.

In this first session, both parents learned the principles of child-centered play. Mom took a turn first in trying the child-centered activity. Because she was more comfortable with a teaching approach, she often instructed Sandra to do things like putting balls in a cup. When we suggested that she try to get on Sandra's level and figure out what she was getting out of the activity, she found it to be upsetting. We talked later in the session about her sadness for Sandra and the pain of thinking what it might be like for Sandra. Mom had a hard time talking about her emotions, choking back tears. Dad, too, expressed his deep concerns for Sandra but focused his discussion on what they could do to help Sandra. They discussed that they both wanted to come to all the treatment sessions despite the distance to our center. Mom did not return until the end of the intervention program. She apparently became depressed about Sandra and coped by withdrawing from the process.

Session 2

During the second week, Mr. T. asked why Sandra ran away from them when they came near her. He interpreted it as rejection. We discussed how Sandra had difficulty tolerating the sensory stimulation of having another person enter her world. Sandra engaged in play with bean bags and seemed to organize herself when sitting inside of an inner tube with her father. She was able to tolerate her father's proximity for short periods of time. We noticed that Sandra tended to look at father's face through the mirror rather than face to face. Sandra also did well engaging with her father when they sat face to face. There was more eye contact this week and less avoidance or running away. We made several suggestions for child-centered therapy to try at home from the written handout for both parents:

1. Provide things that Sandra can roll on (like the bed or a rug) or objects that she can touch (Legos, Koosh balls, bristle blocks). If she likes something like the bristle blocks, hold the bag so that she has to come to you to get them.

2. Imitate her actions—if she stomps her feet, do the same with her.

3. Since Sandra seemed to like your rubbing her back, try lying down facing her while you do this. Start rubbing her back, then see if she indicates that she wants more.

4. Label her gestures "push," "jump," "give" when she does them.

5. Sandra likes when you create a space for her that she can sit inside of—like facing you with your legs out straight or in an inner tube or wading pool filled with pillows.

Mr. T. reported noticing that Sandra played differently with mom and dad. Dad felt that the play went better with him than with his wife. Although they did not seem to be competitive with one another about the play, we reminded him that children normally play differently with each parent because of their unique meaning for the child. We stressed the importance of avoiding comparisons.

Session 3

Mr. T. reported that Sandra was not avoiding the interaction anymore. She tolerated being face to face more of the time. They played on the bed with pillows, rolling about and roughhousing with each other. She continued to enjoy looking at herself and her parents in mirrors. She played among other children one day, eating a snack with them, which she never had done before. Mr. T. noticed that Sandra was starting to notice her older sister and her friends. This week she smiled at mom and dad several times—a first! In the treatment, we observed that Sandra looked at her father on several occasions. For example, her father walked away from Sandra to take off his jacket, and Sandra looked at him almost insistently, like "Hey, get back over here!" No running or avoidant behavior was observed. Sandra was still mouthing toys, but we saw more purposeful manipulation, in particular, feeling the texture of Koosh balls. Her best play was when she was playing with the plastic balls in the wading pool and sliding down a small slide into the balls. Dad and Sandra played a little tug of war with the plastic balls on several occasions, a game that both enjoyed. To help Sandra tolerate looking directly at father's face, we suggested holding an object up in front of dad's face (e.g., two plastic balls in front of his eyes). This week we also observed that Sandra would gesture and vocalize more when she was frustrated or angry, such as when something was taken away that she wanted.

Dad was encouraged by some of the changes he had seen this week, yet he expressed the worry that Sandra was not showing improvement in language. We assured him that Sandra was making steps in that direction by looking more at him, tolerating the proximity of the interaction, and protesting when she was angry.

Session 4

Dad spent most of the time talking about the alarm his wife and he felt at seeing Sandra in the special school setting with other "autistic" children. They felt that Sandra was very different from the other children and seemed more impaired than them. Sandra was very tired from being at school her first day. Her attention span was short, and she tended to mouth most of the toys. After about 10 minutes of play, she wanted to be cuddled by her father. When we talked about how the play had been going at home, dad stated that Sandra was looking much more at them and drawing them into her play, particularly when they did roughhousing on the

5. Sandra liked a carpet ride on a towel while she laid prone. Dad learned to stop the ride and wait for her to indicate "more."

6. To help Sandra with her attention, we suggested confining her space and limiting distractions by having her sit in an inner tube under a table with a cloth over the top, or in a refrigerator box filled with pillows. When inside these spaces, they tried looking at a book with a flashlight, playing pop-up pals, singing, listening to a tape player, or playing with the vibrating tooth-brush on her hands, face, or feet. She also seemed to like searching for her favorite doll in the box. In all of these games, we encouraged Sandra to initiate the activity, then have her parents respond to her after she took a turn.

7. We expanded on the mirror play to include an activity like smearing crazy foam with hands or a paintbrush, or picking stickers off the mirror.

8. We also suggested keeping fewer toys out at a time at home and working on attending activities for short chunks of time.

During this session we noted that Sandra was not using any gestures or vocal utterances. She would cry or fuss to express distress.

Mr. T. expressed his concerns that Sandra's attention span was very short for activities. Techniques that we discussed such as enclosing her space by having her sit in a refrigerator box were viewed as drastic and "abnormal." He feared that Sandra would always need these things. We noticed that dad seemed to want to observe more when things were tried with Sandra. The therapist invited dad to try activities with Sandra. We wanted to support the notion that Sandra's progress was attributable to what the parents were doing, not some magical techniques that a therapist might try. A few times during the session, dad was visibly upset as he watched Sandra, tears welling in his eyes. He expressed fears that, even when professionals tried things, they were struggling to figure out how to reach Sandra. Could anyone reach her? Mr. T. felt that Sandra was showing a period of regression where she was twirling strings repeatedly, pulling strings out of the carpet and finding them anyplace she could. The parents could not take the strings away fast enough to prevent the behavior.

Session 8

The next week we observed that Sandra was most attentive when there was intensity in sensory stimulation—loud sounds, vigorous movement, or deep touch pressure. By nature, Mr. T. was a quiet person and had trouble expressing exuberant sounds like "wheeee" as Sandra would ride down the sliding board. We encouraged him to try even if it was hard for him because it got such a good response from Sandra. We saw a lot of excitement and pleasure in the sensory activities that we tried, like Sandra kicking a ball with her feet while sitting on a swing. A few times we noticed Sandra initiate interactions or show her wants by pursuing a toy or bag of crackers. Most of her communication was still bound by actions rather than gestures or sounds. Once in a while she would say the word "up" and raise her arms. At home, she had just started greeting her parents at the door when they came home after an errand or from work. In all of the activities, we stressed the importance of two-way communication, refining gestures and signals, and taking turns.

During debriefing after the play activities, we talked about how mom was involving herself in cleaning, shopping, and other household tasks. Dad continued to feel that he had little time for himself to refuel. He wished that he had time to go out to play basketball with a group that he used to play with on Monday nights. We encouraged him to do this, and stressed the importance of each parent taking time for themselves.

Session 9

Dad reported that Sandra was engaging in perseverative behavior again with string twirling. He was worried that Sandra was regressing. We suggested that dad try to enter into the string play by grabbing the other end and tugging, covering the string up with his hand, or trying some other way to get some variety in the play. Apparently, Sandra would look desperately for more strings and would pull them out of the carpet if they were taken away from her. Despite this, her parents had started a game of playing ring around the rosy that Sandra loved. Sandra spent the first part of the session running about the room, after which she was much more interactive and communicative. We needed to dim the lights to help decrease her overstimulated state while running. After the motor discharge, she was able to engage in many circles of communication, looking for an object hidden in dad's hand repeatedly or playing ring around the rosy and asking for it again and again, clapping with delight, then grabbing our hands for more. We felt that Sandra was showing great strides in her social interactions, but that she also needed help with modulating her overarousal. The behaviors that father reported at home were worrisome because Sandra was regressing into a maladaptive pattern to regroup rather than seeking a more purposeful and productive outlet to self-calm.

Session 10

This week we observed that Sandra's gestures were getting better. It was possible to wait for Sandra and ask, "What do you want?" and she would either tug her father and point to what it was or would vocalize a sound for something. We suggested giving Sandra choices at mealtimes, such as, "Do you want the cookie or the juice?" holding each choice up for her to pick from. We brainstormed on games that had obvious beginnings and ends to them like ring around the rosy, or kicking a ball into a can. We also discussed some social interaction games that Sandra would enjoy, such as putting funny sunglasses, hats, and stickers on her face and her parent's faces.

Session 11

We continued similar activities as the previous session. We noticed that Sandra needed movement, firm deep pressure, and vibration to help organize her attention. An electrical vibrating massager, held up to her face, then to her father's, was very intriguing to Sandra. Her attention was getting longer, and she was staying with tasks for up to 5 minutes each. She particularly enjoyed games with the magnetic balls and wand.

This week, Mr. T. talked more about his fears about what the future held for Sandra. Despite his worries, he persisted in trying all of the activities that had been suggested over the course of the intervention. He stated that mom was now getting involved again in the home program and was noticing some changes in Sandra.

Session 12

In the last week of the intervention program, both parents came and talked about how Sandra was responding to them when they gave her choices about toys and food. For example, they were holding up two different toys, two different videos, or two food choices, and Sandra could point or vocalize. They were also able to get her to communicate "more" with a game using bubbles. The mother would recap the lid on the bottle and wait for her to indicate her desire for more bubbles. Sandra now enjoyed interactive games that had bouncing or clapping while the family sang or listened to music. She continued to respond well to tactile activities such as riding on the blanket and rolling up in the mattress like a hot dog. Both parents played with Sandra this session and were able to get her to complete multiple back-and-forth interchanges (e.g., "circles of communication") by hiding toys and getting her to pursue them, chasing games, play with the bubbles, and singing and movement games. Sandra appeared particularly happy having both parents there. She smiled and laughed a great deal.

Mom appeared much more upbeat this session and talked about what a hard time she had had in coping with Sandra's diagnosis. Both parents were very worried about her future but felt that she had made substantial gains. They now believed that Sandra could be reached and that she was related and interested in people. They felt less like Sandra was in her own little world. We acknowledged the hard work that they had put into the therapy process that resulted in these changes. We talked about what Sandra needed so as to continue her progress and what had worked best in the treatment. They felt strongly that the sensory activities helped to support her attention, communication, and interactions. We talked about getting this type of therapy in the school program and how they would need to advocate for this since their program was very behavioral in nature.

Conclusion of Treatment

Sandra showed many traits of pervasive developmental disorder. Those things that challenged her most were in the areas of social interaction, engagement, attention, sensory processing, and basic communication. In the therapy program, we found that the child-centered therapy helped her to become engaged, tolerating the proximity of her parents while playing. She was beginning to initiate purposeful actions and was less repetitive and stereotypical in her play behaviors. There was also the beginning of reciprocal interactions by the time we finished with this part of the therapy. The structured therapy program elaborated on the core principles used in child-centered therapy. The most success was in finding sensory activities that supported her attention, interactions, and communication. Gains were made in gestural and vocal communication, turn taking, attention, and sensory modulation. Sandra was less apt to become overwhelmed by the level of stimulation and, by the end of the treatment, could find adaptive activities to engage in rather than stereotypical, repetitive, or regressed activities.

This case depicts the importance of respecting how the parents feel as they cope with their child's diagnosis and what it means for them and their child. It was important for us to respect the grieving that each parent experienced, allowing them time to adapt while providing opportunities for them to express their concerns and supporting them in ways that helped. Integrating this concern into the treatment was just as important as providing practical guidance, sensory integration techniques, and child-centered activity in helping Sandra become more related to the people and object world.

SUMMARY

Sensory-integrative disorders involve a dysfunction in the child's capacity to modulate incoming sensory input to allow for purposeful adaptation to the environment. These disorders are common among learning-disabled and emotionally disturbed children and may be observed as early as infancy. The tactile system is important for protection and survival and impacts motor and reflex development, tactile perception, motor planning, and emotional stability. The tactile dysfunctions most commonly observed are tactile defensiveness and tactile hyposensitivities. Tactile defensiveness is a severe sensitivity to being touched that may be environmental, other-initiated, or self-initiated. On the other hand, children with tactile hyposensitivities do not experience touch unless it is very intense.

The vestibular system impacts development of body posture, muscle tone, ocular–motor control, reflex integration, and equilibrium reactions. The vestibular system is important in motor planning, arousal and alertness, and security when moving in space. The common vestibular-based problems include gravitational insecurity, underresponsiveness to movement in space, intolerance for movement, postural–ocular movement disorder, vestibular–postural deficits, bilateral integration and sequencing problems, and dyspraxia.

Developmental dyspraxia is a disorder in the planning and direction of goal-directed movements that are skilled or nonhabitual in nature. Motor planning problems are typically based in the somatosensory and vestibular systems and affect postural movements, sequencing movements, language, spatial constructions, drawing, and symbolic use of objects.

In addition to describing the different types of sensory-integrative dysfunction and common symptoms observed during infancy through childhood, this chapter presented treatment strategies for children with sensory-integrative dysfunction in infants and children..

REFERENCES

Ayres, A. J. (1964). Tactile functions: Their relations to hyperactive and perceptual motor behavior. *American Journal of Occupational Therapy, 18,* 6–11.

Ayres, A. J. (1972). *Sensory integration and learning disorders.* Los Angeles: Western Psychological Services.

Ayres, A. J. (1979). *Sensory integration and the child.* Los Angeles: Western Psychological Services.

Ayres, A. J. (1985). *Developmental dyspraxia and adult onset apraxia.* Torrance, CA: Sensory Integration International.

Ayres, A. J., & Tickle, L. S. (1980). Hyper-responsivity to touch and vestibular stimuli as a predictor of positive response to sensory integration procedures by autistic children. *American Journal of Occupational Therapy, 34,* 375–381.

Ayres, A. J., Mailloux, Z. K., & Wendler, C. L. (1987). Developmental dyspraxia: Is it a unitary function? *Journal of Research in Occupational Therapy, 7*(2), 93–110.

Baloh, R. W., & Honrubia, V. (1979). *Clinical neurophysiology of the vestibular system.* Philadelphia: F. A. Davis.

Bauer, B. (1977). Tactile-sensitive behavior in hyperactive and non-hyperactive children. *American Journal of Occupational Therapy, 31,* 447–450.

Carte, E., Morrison, D., Sublett, J., Uemura, A., & Setrakian, W. (1984). Sensory integration therapy: A trial of a specific neurodevelopmental therapy for the remediation of learning disabilities. *Developmental and Behavioral Pediatrics, 5*(4), 189–194.

Cermak, S. (1985). Developmental dyspraxia. In E. A. Roy (Ed.), *Advances in psychology, Vol 23: Neuropsychological studies of apraxia and related disorders* (pp. 225–248). New York: Elsevier.

Cermak, S. (1988). The relationship between attention deficits and sensory integration disorders (Part I). *Sensory Integration Special Interest Section Newsletter, 11*(2), 1–4.

Cermak, S. A., & Daunhauer, L. A. (1997). Sensory processing in the postinstitutionalized child. *American Journal of Occupational Therapy, 51*(7), 500–507.

Chu, S. (1996). Evaluating the sensory integrative functions of mainstream school children with specific developmental disorders. *British Journal of Occupational Therapy, 59*(10), 465–474.

Clark, D. L. (1985). The vestibular system: An overview of structure and function. *Physical and Occupational Therapy in Pediatrics, 5,* 5–32.

Conrad, K., Cermak, S. A., & Drake, C. (1983). Differentiation of praxis among children. *American Journal of Occupational Therapy, 37*(7), 466–473.

Collier, G. (1985). Emotional expression. Hillsdale, NJ: Erlbaum.

DeGangi, G. A. (1991). Assessment of sensory, emotional, and attentional problems in regulatory disordered infants. *Infants and Young Children, 3*(3), 1–8.

DeGangi, G. A., & Greenspan, S. I. (1988). The development of sensory functions in infants. *Physical and Occupational Therapy in Pediatrics, 8*(3), 21–33.

DeGangi, G. A., Berk, R. A., & Larsen, L. A. (1980). The measurement of vestibular-based functions in preschool children. *American Journal of Occupational therapy, 34*(7), 452–459.

DeGangi, G. A., Porges, S. W., Sickle, R., & Greenspan, S. I. (1993). Four-year follow-up of a sample of regulatory disordered infants. *Infant Mental Health Journal, 14,* 330–343.

DeQuiros, J. (1976). Diagnosis of vestibular disorders in the learning disabled. *Journal of Learning Disabilities, 9*(1), 50–58.

DeQuiros, J. B., & Schrager, O. L. (1979). *Neuropsychological fundamentals in learning disabilities* (Rev. ed.). Novato, CA: Academic Therapy Publications.

Fisher, A. G., & Bundy, A. C. (1989). Vestibular stimulation in the treatment of postural and related disorders. In O. D. Payton, R. P. DiFabio, S. V. Paris, E. J. Protas, & A. F. VanSant (Eds.), *Manual of physical therapy techniques* (pp. 239–258). New York: Churchill Livingstone.

Fisher, A. G., & Dunn, W. (1983). Tactile defensiveness: Historical perspectives, new research. A theory grows. *Sensory Integration Special Interest Section Newsletter, 6*(2), 1–2.

Fisher, A. G., Mixon, J., & Herman, R. (1986). The validity of the clinical diagnosis of vestibular dysfunction. *Occupational Therapy Journal of Research, 6,* 3–20.

Fisher, A. G., Murray, E. A., & Bundy, A. C. (1991). *Sensory integration theory and practice.* Philadelphia: F. A. Davis.

Gottfried, A. W. (1984). Touch as an organizer for learning and development. In C. C. Brown (Ed.), *The many facets of touch* (pp. 114–122). Skillman, NJ: Johnson and Johnson.

Haron, M., & Henderson, A. (1985). Active and passive touch in developmentally dyspraxic and normal boys. *Journal of Research in Occupational Therapy, 5,* 102–112.

Horak, F. B., Shumway-Cook, A., Crowe, T. K., & Black, F. O. (1988). Vestibular function and motor proficiency in children with impaired hearing, or with learning disability and motor impairments. *Developmental Medicine and Child Neurology, 30,* 64–79.

Kandel, E. R., & Schwartz, J. H. (1981). *Principles of neural science.* New York: Elsevier.

Keshner, E. A., & Cohen, H. (1989). Current concepts of the vestibular system reviewed, 1: The role of the vestibulospinal system in postural control. *American Journal of Occupational Therapy, 43*(5), 320–330.

Kimball, J. G. (1993). Sensory integrative frame of reference. In P. Kramer & J. Hinojosa (Eds.), *Frames of reference for pediatric occupational therapy* (pp. 87–175). Baltimore: Williams & Wilkins.

Knickerbocker, B. M. (1980). *A holistic approach to learning disabilities.* Thorofare, NJ: C. B. Slack.

Magalhaes, L. C., Koomar, J. A., & Cermak, S. A. (1989). Bilateral motor coordination in 5- to 9-year-old children: A pilot study. *American Journal of Occupational Therapy, 43*(7), 437–443.

Matthews, P. B. C. (1988). Proprioceptors and their contribution to somatosensory mapping: Complex messages require complex processing. *Canadian Journal of Physiology and Pharmacology, 66,* 430–438.

Maurer, R. G., & Damasio, A. R. (1979). Vestibular dysfunction in autistic children. *Developmental Medicine and Child Neurology, 21,* 656–659.

Nathan, P. W., Smith, M. C., & Cook, A. W. (1986). Sensory effects in man with lesions of the posterior columns and of some other afferent pathways. *Brain, 109* (pt. 5), 1003–1041.

Ornitz, E. (1970). Vestibular dysfunction in schizophrenia and childhood autism. *Comparative Psychiatry, 11,* 159–173.

Ornitz, E. M. (1974). The modulation of sensory input and motor output in autistic children. *Journal of Autism and Childhood Schizophrenia, 4,* 197–215.

Ottenbacher, K. (1978). Identifying vestibular processing dysfunction in learning disabled children. *American Journal of Occupational Therapy, 32*(4), 217–221.

Ottenbacher, K. J. (1982). Vestibular processing dysfunction in children with severe emotional and behavioral disorders: A review. *Physical and Occupational Therapy in Pediatrics, 2*(1), 3–12.

Reite, M. L. (1984). Touch, attachment and health: Is there a relationship? In C. C. Brown (Ed.), *The many facets of touch* (pp. 58–65). Skillman, NJ: Johnson and Johnson.

Royeen, C. B. (1989). Commentary on "tactile functions in learning-disabled and normal children: Reliability and validity considerations." *Journal of Research in Occupational Therapy, 9,* 16–23.

Satz, P., Fletcher, J. M., Morris, R., & Taylor, H. G. (1984). Finger localization and reading achievement. In C. C. Brown (Ed.), *The many facets of touch* (pp. 123–130). Skillman, NJ: Johnson and Johnson.

Schaffer, R., Law, M., Polatajko, H., & Miller, J. (1989). A study of children with learning disabilities and sensorimotor problems, or Let's not throw the baby out with the bathwater. *Physical and Occupational Therapy in Pediatrics, 9*(3), 101–117.

Steinberg, M., & Rendle-Short, J. (1977). Vestibular dysfunction in young children with minor neurological impairment. *Developmental Medicine and Child Neurology, 19,* 639–651.

Suomi, S. J. (1984). The role of touch in rhesus monkey social development. In C. C. Brown (Ed.), *The many facets of touch* (pp. 41–50). Skillman, NJ: Johnson and Johnson.

Wilbarger, P., & Wilbarger, J. (1991). *Sensory defensiveness in children 2–12.* Santa Barbara, CA: Avanti Education Programs.

Infant–Toddler
Symptom Checklist:
Long Version

Georgia DeGangi, PhD, OTR
Susan Poisson, MA

Dear Parent:

The symptoms or presenting problems below are common complaints presented by parents when they seek help for their children. In order to help us understand your child/children's development and functioning from birth, we would appreciate your reading this list carefully and responding to each item:

- **no/sometimes** if your child has **never** had this difficulty or infrequently/some of the time

- **yes-current** if this is a difficulty she/he may experience frequently/most of the time at present

- **yes-past** if this was a problem in the past but has since been resolved.

The behaviors in this list will help us understand the nature of early problems and what may be contributing to these difficulties. We appreciate your patience in taking the time to complete this list.

Baby's full name: _____ Sex: ___ M ___ F

Date of birth: __/__/__ Birth order: ____

Parent's Name: _____

Today's date __/__/__

Daytime phone _____ Evening phone _____

Delivery: __ Natural __ Cesarian Full term: __ Yes __ No

Weeks gestation _____

Medical problems:

During pregnancy: __ Yes __ No

After birth: __ Yes __ No

If Yes, please explain:

....

....

Baby is currently: __ Bottle-fed __ Breast-fed

Highest grade or degree completed by mother _____

Highest grade or degree completed by father _____

	NEVER OR SOME-TIMES	YES MOST TIMES	PAST
1. SELF-REGULATION			
A. Frequently irritable and fussy			
B. Easily escalates from whimper to intense cry			
C. Can't calm self effectively by sucking on pacifier, looking at toys, toys, or listening to caregiver			
D. Unable to wait for food or toy without falling apart			
E. Can't change from one activity to another without distress			
F. Must be prepared in advance several times before change is introduced			
G. Demands adult company constantly			
H. Temper tantrums (severe and frequent)			
I. Amount of time spent calming child during day (circle one)			

15–30 min   1–2 hr   3 hr+

	NEVER OR SOME-TIMES	YES MOST TIMES	PAST

2. ATTENTION

   A. Easily distractible, fleeting attention (for infants over 1 year)

   B. Tunes out from activity, difficult to reengage

   C. Can't shift focus easily from one object or activity to another (for infants over 9 months)

3. SLEEP

   A. Wakes up three or more times in the night and is unable to fall back to sleep

   B. Requires extensive help to fall asleep; specify: rocking, long walking, stroking hair, car ride, other _____

4. EATING OR FEEDING

   A. Eats only soft food (for children over 9 months)

   B. Craving for certain foods/drinks (for infants over 1 year)

   C. Excessive drooling beyond teething stage

   D. Gagging or vomiting

   E. Too distracted to stay seated for meals

5. DRESSING, BATHING, TOUCH

   A. Doesn't want to wear clothing (with young infant, is most content when in diaper or naked)

   B. Prefers certain clothing, complains that certain garments are too tight or itchy

   C. Seeks many layers of clothing (for infants under 19 months)

   D. Distressed by having face or hair washed

   E. Resists cuddling, pulls away or arches

   F. Bumps against people or things (for infants over 19 months)

   G. Hates car seat (for infants over 1 year)

   H. Doesn't notice pain when falling, bumping, or when the doctor gives shots

   I. Resists being placed in certain positions, e.g., stomach/back

   J. Avoids touching certain textures, getting hands messy (for infants over 9 months)

   K. Distressed when clothes removed (for infants over 9 months)

	NEVER OR SOME-TIMES	YES MOST TIMES	PAST

6. MOVEMENT

    A. In constant movement, rocking, running about, unable to sit still for an activity

    B. Never crawled before started to walk (for infants over 18 months)

    C. Fear of being swung in air, swings, merry-go-rounds

    D. Craves swinging and moving upside down (for infants over 18 months)

    E. Clumsy, falling, poor balance, bumps into things (for infants over 1 year)

7. LISTENING, LANGUAGE AND SOUND

    A. Startled or distressed by loud sounds, e.g., vacuum, doorbell or barking dog

    B. Distracted by sounds not normally noticed by average person

    C. Doesn't respond to verbal cues (hearing not a problem)

    D. No or very little vocalizing or babbling

    E. Repeats or echoes previously heard words, phrases or sentences (for infants over 18 months)

    F. Extreme repetition of familiar words or phrases (for infants over 2 years)

8. LOOKING AND SIGHT

    A. Sensitive to bright lights—cries or closes eyes

    B. Becomes excited when confronted by crowded bustling settings such as a crowded supermarket, restaurant (for infants over 1 year)

	NEVER OR SOME-TIMES	YES MOST TIMES	PAST

9. ATTACHMENT–EMOTIONAL FUNCTIONING

    A.   Avoids eye contact, turns away from the human face, prefers objects and toys (for infants over 9 months)

    B.   Does not appear joyous and happy (for infants over 9 months)

    C.   Does not initiate interaction with caregiver: parent needs to constantly woo infant/child (for infants over 9 months)

    D.   Does not interact reciprocally (back and forth exchanges with caregiver)

    E.   Does not show age-expected symbolic play/imitation (for infants over 18 months)

    F.   Breaks toys and other things destructively (for infants over 2 years)

    G.   Difficulty separating from parents, school, or babysitter

    H.   Will go to anyone including strangers (for infants over 2 years)

    I.   Does not play with other children, withdraws or is aggressive (for infants over 18 months)

    J.   Does not respond at all to limit setting, discipline

    K.   Appears anxious or fearful of new people, situations (for infants over 1 year)

    L.   Stays preoccupied with fearful/traumatic event (for infants over 18 months)

    M.   Self-abusive (for infants over 2 years)

    N.   Needs total control of the environment—"runs the show"

    O.   Everyone has difficulty understanding the child's cues or emotions

HOW CONCERNED ARE YOU ABOUT THE ABOVE CHECKED SYMPTOMS?

NOT CONCERNED   **SLIGHTLY**   **MODERATELY**   **VERY**

SCORING: 2 points are assigned to all items checked in "most times" column, 1 point for "past," and 0 points for "never or sometimes." Item 1I is scored as follows: 2 points for 3+ hours, 1 point for 1–2 hours, and 0 points for 15–30 minutes.

Tally the points for each category and enter the score. Then look in the table below at the child's age and the cutoff scores. Scores at or above the cutoff denote a potential problem and are indicated as "at-risk" on the scoresheet

SCORESHEET

DOMAIN	TOTAL POINTS PER CATEGORY	INTERPRETIVE RANGE	
		AT RISK	NORMAL
Self-regulation			
Attention			
Sleep			
Eating or feeding			
Dressing, bathing, touch			
Movement			
Listening, language, sound			
Looking and sight			
Attachment, emotional functioning			

CUTOFF SCORES FOR INTERPRETING SYMPTOM CHECKLIST

DOMAIN	AGE (in months)				
	7–9	10–12	13–18	19–24	25–30
Self-regulation	6	4	5	3	4
Attention	–	–	4	3	3
Sleep	3	3	2	2	2
Eating or feeding	–	2	–	4	–
Dressing, bathing, touch	3	3	4	2	2
Movement	2	2	2	3	2
Listening, language, and sound	–	2	2	3	–
Looking and sight	2	3	2	2	3
Attachment, emotional	3	4	4	3	3

Functional Emotional Assessment Scale

Stanley I. Greenspan, MD

Georgia A. DeGangi, PhD

PROTOCOL BOOKLET
Long Version

Child's name: _____ Date of birth: _____

Age: _____ Date: _____

Person playing with child: __ Mother __ Father __ Caregiver __ Examiner

General Scoring:

Scoring is on a two-point scale for most items except where indicated. Scoring is as follows:

    0 = Not at all or very brief

    1 = Present some of time, observed several times

    2 = Consistently present, observed many times

Indicate N/O for behaviors that are not observed.

    Where indicated to convert a score, transform the scoring as follows:

        0 becomes a 2, 1 = 1, 2 becomes 0.

    Scores for symbolic play should be entered in the SYM column and scores for sensory play entered in the SENS column. When the examiner facilitates play with the child, enter scores in the EX (examiner) column. The last column may be used for entering scores for additional caregivers (e.g., mother, father, foster parent, babysitter) observed playing with the child.

    Scores are interpreted for the primary caregiver playing with the child for the symbolic and sensory play situations. If scores do not differ for symbolic and sensory play, then only one score is interpreted. However, if behaviors differ for the different play situations, then two scores are calculated, one for symbolic play, one for sensory play. These are interpreted using the cutoff scores presented in the profile form.

Caregiver Behaviors

	SYM	SENS	EX
REGULATION AND INTEREST IN THE WORLD			
1. Shows interest in toys through facial or verbal expressions of interest or by handling and touching toys, but not so absorbed by toys that the caregiver plays alone with toys, ignoring the child			
2. Shows sustained interest in child, focuses on child's signals (gestures, vocalizations), keeping child involved in play			
3. Interacts calmly with child, able to wait for child's responses			
4. Shows pleasant or animated, happy affect throughout play			

4. Shows pleasant or animated, happy affect throughout play

        Scoring:

                0 = Flat, somber, or depressed affect

                1 = Content, but neutral

                2 = Happy and animated with warm and engaging smiles

	SYM	SENS	EX

5. Is sensitive and responsive to child's need for touch by stroking or touching baby in pleasurable ways and/or encourages child to explore textured toys

6. Provides pleasurable movement experiences to the child or encourages movement exploration

    TOTAL FOR SELF-REGULATION _____

ATTACHMENT

7. Is relaxed during interchange with child, not overly attentive to child's every action

8. Looks at child with affection, showing a warm connection

9. Enjoys being with and playing with the child through smiles or a joyful look and emotes a sense of warmth by providing inviting gestures. Keep in mind cultural differences in how this may be expressed.

10. Is overly anxious in attachment to child, overwhelming child with affectionate touching OR is not comfortable showing feelings and relating warmly and intimately with child, appearing overly vigilant toward child. (Circle one.)

        Scoring:
            0 = Many times
            1 = Sometimes
            2 = Briefly or not at all

11. Maintains a verbal or visual connection with child, showing clear availability and interest in the child. Child may move away from caregiver to explore room, yet the caregiver remains connected to the child across space through gestures, vocalizations, and facial expressions.

    TOTAL FOR ATTACHMENT _____

	SYM	SENS	EX

INTENTIONAL TWO-WAY COMMUNICATION

12. Opening circle of communication: initiates interactions with child through vocalizations or gestures, creating interactive opportunities with child

13. Responds to child's wishes, intentions, and actions in a contingent way, building on how the child wishes to play. For example, child may hand toy to parent, and parent responds by taking it and saying something about the toy, then gives the child an opportunity to respond to what they just did.

> Scoring:
> > 0 = Consistently does opposite to what baby seeks, misreads child's cues, changing activity from what child wants to do
> > 1 = Misreads child's signals about 25 to 50% of time, changing activity or toy while at other times reads child's signals accurately
> > 2 = Responds to child's signals in appropriate way most of the time (up to 75% of time responsive to child), staying on the activity that the child has chosen

14. Predominantly handles toys, engaging in parallel play and removing attention from playing with child. CONVERTED SCORE*

15. Plays with child at developmentally appropriate level. Caregiver may play slightly above child's level of skill, modeling new ways to do things or labeling what child does or describing the functions of objects.

16. Stimulates child at pace that allows child to respond, waits for child's responses. Avoids overstimulating child with language or actions.

17. Allows child to decide on the play topic, to initiate play and explore toys in ways that the child seeks or needs

TOTAL FOR INTENTIONAL TWO-WAY COMMUNICATION _____

STOP HERE FOR PARENTS OF 7 TO 9 MONTH OLDS

	SYM	SENS	EX

COMPLEX SENSE OF SELF: BEHAVIORAL ORGANIZATION AND ELABORATION

18. Responds and initiates reciprocal back-and-forth chains of interactions with child, stringing together connected circles of communication or units of interaction. For example, caregiver introduces baby doll, baby touches doll's face, mother touches doll's hair, baby pats the doll, mother says "baby," and baby glances between mother and doll. The caregiver may imitate child (e.g., pushing car alongside child), then interject her turn by an action or verbalization related to the child's actions (e.g., "Oh, a bump!" and then bumps her car into child's car).

      Scoring:
            0 = 0 to 2 circles
            1 = 3 to 5 circles
            2 = 6 or more circles

19. Uses gestures and facial expressions as a modality to promote circles of communication

20. Uses touch or roughhouse play as a modality to promote circles of communication

21. Shows pleasure and excitement in playing with child in whatever way the child wishes to play

      Scoring:
            0 = Little pleasure and excitement
               shown by caregiver
            1 = Pleasure and excitement sustained
               by parent over the course of several
               (3–5) circles of communication
            2 = Pleasure and excitement sustained
               for many (6 or more) circles of
               communication

Note here whether child is unable to sustain circles of communication if it affects caregiver's score:

      Child can sustain circles ___   Child cannot sustain circles ___

	SYM	SENS	EX
22. Expresses appropriate limits on baby. The caregiver may redirect child not to leave room, not to hit her, or not throw toy. If no need for limits arise during play, mark N/O and give 2 points.			
23. Elaborates on and builds complexity into the child's play behaviors while engaged in interactive sequences between parent and child. The parent expands on what the child does while remaining on the child's play topic (e.g., the parent does not introduce a completely new play idea). The parent provides a small challenge or interesting twist to the play that requires the child to respond slightly differently than before, thus creating a problem-solving opportunity for the child. For example, the parent and child are pushing a car back and forth toward each other. The parent expands on this by creating a wall with her leg to prevent the car from rolling, then waits to see how the child will solve this situation.			
24. Allows child to assert self in play, exploring with confidence what he or she wishes (e.g., child expresses strong wish to play in a certain way such as banging toys, being silly, holding a doll, or running around room). Parent supports the child's needs for dependency and closeness, assertiveness and curiosity, aggression, autonomy, or pleasure and excitement by admiring, showing interest, and/or by joining in to the child's play in whatever way the child seeks. Problems that may interfere with caregiver's capacity to support this area might be intrusiveness, withdrawal, overprotectiveness, or playing at a level far above child's level of competence.			

TOTAL FOR BEHAVIORAL ORGANIZATION AND ELABORATION _____

STOP HERE FOR PARENTS OF 10 TO 24 MONTH OLDS

	SYM	SENS	EX

REPRESENTATIONAL ORGANIZATION AND ELABORATION

25. Encourages child to engage in symbolic play by modeling or combining materials in ways that encourage representational actions (e.g., mother holds spoon near baby doll's mouth and says, "Feed baby?"). Parent appears comfortable in playing makes believe.

26. Elaborates on child's pretend play idea by building on child's ideas and adding some complexity to them (e.g., child puts doll in car and pushes it and caregiver says, "Oh, is daddy going to the store?")

27. Allows child to express pretend play themes involving closeness or dependency (e.g., nurturing doll) without competing for child's attention to be the one nurtured.

28. Sustains pretend play, showing interest, pleasure, and excitement about the child's pretend play idea by asking questions, laughing or smiling, and joining in the child's play with enthusiasm (e.g., caregiver says "Oh, that's a good idea. What happens now? That's so funny!").

29. Allows child to express themes of assertiveness in pretend play (e.g., child pretends he's a policeman and puts caregiver in jail; child pretends to go to work and tells caregiver to stay home).

TOTAL FOR REPRESENTATIONAL
   ORGANIZATION AND ELABORATION _____

STOP HERE FOR PARENTS OF 25 TO 35 MONTH OLDS

SYM	SENS	EX

EMOTIONAL THINKING

30. Elaborates on child's pretend play, creating opportunities to logically connect ideas in play. The caregiver accomplishes this by asking questions to give depth to the drama such as "how," "why," or "when." If the child strays off the topic, the caregiver asks questions to bring the circle of communication back to the pretend play theme (e.g., "But what happened to the crocodile? He was ready to go for a swim and now you're playing with the truck.").

31. Incorporates causality into pretend play by helping child to logically connect three or more ideas into a reality-based story sequence. For example, if the child is playing out how two animals fight, the caregiver might ask, "How come they're fighting?" "Do they know each other?"

32. Helps child to elaborate on a wide range of emotional themes, whatever they might be—assertiveness, pleasure and excitement, fearfulness, anger, or separation and loss. The caregiver is accepting of the child's expressions of different feelings and themes through play and shows no discomfort at the expression of different ideas from the child.

    TOTAL FOR EMOTIONAL THINKING _____

    TOTAL CAREGIVER SCORE FOR SCALE _____

SYM	SENS	EX

Child Behaviors

REGULATION AND INTEREST IN THE WORLD

1. Is interested and attentive to play with toys.

2. Explores objects freely without caution.

3. Remains calm for play period with no signs of distress (crying or whining), showing appropriate frustration.

4. Is comfortable touching textured toys and in being touched by caregiver.

5. Enjoys moving on equipment or engaging in roughhouse play.

6. Is overly visual, looking at toys rather than playing with them. CONVERTED SCORE*

7. Shows happy, content affect.

     Scoring:
          0 = Flat, somber, or depressed affect
          1 = Content but neutral
          2 = happy and content, robust smiles, warm and engaging affect

    NOTE: SCORE ONLY ITEM 8 OR 9, WHICHEVER APPLIES

8. Underreactivity: Appears sluggish or withdrawn.

     Scoring:
          0 = Withdrawn, difficult to engage
          1 = Sluggish or slow-paced in actions but can eventually be aroused or engaged
          2 = Shows a bright, alert state with focused play throughout

	SYM	SENS	EX

9. Overreactivity: Appears overaroused by toys and environment.

> Scoring:
>> 0 = Very active, moves quickly from one toy to the next or constantly wanders away from caregiver and toys
>> 1 = Moderately active, occasional bursts of changing activity quickly or wandering away, then settles into play with one toy for short period
>> 2 = Well-modulated in pace and activity level, focusing on a toy or caregiver for long periods before changing activity

TOTAL FOR REGULATION AND INTEREST _____

FORMING RELATIONSHIPS (ATTACHMENT)

10. Shows emotional interest and connection with caregiver by vocalizing and smiling at her.

11. Anticipates with curiosity or excitement when caregiver presents an interesting object or game.

12. Initiates physical closeness to caregiver but is not clingy; if child is active and moves away from caregiver, child maintains a visual or verbal connection with caregiver.

13. Turns head away, averts gaze, moves away, or sits facing away from caregiver without social referencing caregiver. Appears indifferent, aloof, withdrawn, or avoidant of caregiver.
CONVERTED SCORE*

14. Social references caregiver while playing with toys.

15. Evidences a relaxed sense of security and/or comfort when near caregiver. If child is active and moves away from caregiver, he references her from across space and shows relaxed security in distal space.

	SYM	SENS	EX

16. Displays signs of discomfort, displeasure, or sadness during interactive play if caregiver should become unresponsive or engage in anticontingent behaviors. [If caregiver is responsive or contingent, note that this was not observed with "N/O," then assign 2 points.]

17. Initiates physical closeness to caregiver but is not clingy. If child is active and moves away from caregiver, child maintains a visual or verbal connection with caregiver.

18. After moving away, communicates to caregiver from across space by looking, gestures, or vocalizations.

    TOTAL FOR ATTACHMENT _____

    STOP HERE FOR 7 TO 9 MONTH OLDS

INTENTIONAL TWO-WAY COMMUNICATION

19. Opens circles of communication: initiates intentional actions with objects while also engaged in interactions with caregiver (e.g., manipulates object then looks at mother and smiles or vocalizes).

20. Gives signals: initiates purposeful and intentional actions in play with objects.

    Scoring:
        0 = Needs considerable help to get started in play or to engage in purposeful actions; no clear gestures or organized intent
        1 = Initiates play but engages in stereotypic actions (e.g., lining toys up, mouthing toys for long periods of time, banging toys without engaging in any other actions with the same toy) OR initiates play but actions appear aimless or disorganized
        2 = Play shows intentionality and variety, engaging in two or more different behaviors with a given toy or activity. Gestures are specific and activity is functionally tied to objects.

	SYM	SENS	EX

21. Closes circles: Responds to caregiver's cues in contingent manner (e.g., mother offers toy, baby takes it and puts it in a container).

> Scoring:
> 0 = Does not notice caregiver's response
> 1 = Notices caregiver's response and looks, but does not respond contingently through actions; instead does something that has nothing to do with what caregiver did (e.g., mother holds toy out for child; child looks at mother and toy, then returns to what he was doing before)
> 2 = Notices caregiver's response, then responds contingently by elaborating on what caregiver did by taking toy held by caregiver and examining it, by imitating her, or some other response that is clearly linked to what caregiver did

22. Shows anger, frustration, aggressive behavior (e.g., hitting), or protests repeatedly.
CONVERTED SCORE*

23. Uses language (e.g., sounds, words, and/or gestures) during interactions. Circle which ones were used:
> sounds   words   gestures

TOTAL INTENTIONAL TWO-WAY COMMUNICATION _____

STOP HERE FOR 10 TO 18 MONTH OLDS

COMPLEX SENSE OF SELF: BEHAVIORAL ORGANIZATION AND ELABORATION

24. Engages in complex patterns of communication, stringing together several circles of communication with caregiver (initiated and elaborated on by child) using gestures, vocalizations, and/or words.

> Scoring:
> 0 = 0 to 2 circles
> 1 = 3 to 5 circles
> 2 = 6 or more circles

	SYM	SENS	EX

25. Imitates or copies something new that the caregiver introduces, then incorporates idea into play (e.g., caregiver feeds doll; child copies this).

    TOTAL BEHAVIORAL ORGANIZATION
      AND ELABORATION _____

    STOP HERE FOR 19 TO 24 MONTH OLDS

REPRESENTATIONAL CAPACITY AND ELABORATION

26. Engages in symbolic play with the various toys or equipment (e.g., plays out cars racing), going beyond simple concrete actions (e.g., feeding self with cup).

27. Engages in pretend play patterns of at least one idea in collaboration with caregiver (e.g., one part of a script or scenario played out).

28. Uses language or pretend play (e.g., playing out with doll figures) to communicate needs, wishes, intentions, or feelings.

29. Uses pretend play to express themes around closeness or dependency (e.g., putting dolls to sleep next to one another, feeding caregiver and dolls).

30. Uses pretend play to express themes around pleasure and excitement around humorous theme (e.g., imitating humorous behaviors).

31. Uses pretend play to express themes around assertiveness (e.g., cars racing).

32. Creates pretend drama with two or more ideas that are not related or logically connected.

    TOTAL REPRESENTATIONAL CAPACITY
      AND ELABORATION _____

    STOP HERE FOR 25 TO 35 MONTH OLDS

	SYM	SENS	EX

EMOTIONAL THINKING

33. Pretend play, however unrealistic, involves two or more ideas which are logically tied to one another. Child may build on adult's pretend play idea.

34. Elaborates on pretend play sequence of two or more ideas that are logically connected and grounded in reality. There is a planned quality and child can elaborate on "how," "why," or "when" questions, giving depth to drama.

35. Uses pretend play or language to communicate themes containing two or more ideas dealing with closeness or dependency (e.g., doll gets hurt, then gets kiss from daddy, then both play ball).

36. Uses pretend play or language to communicate themes containing two or more ideas dealing with pleasure and excitement in humorous game (e.g., imitates funny word heard, watches how caregiver reacts, then laughs).

37. Uses pretend play or language to communicate themes containing two or more ideas dealing with assertiveness (e.g., soldiers search for missing person, find her, then battle to save her again).

TOTAL EMOTIONAL THINKING _____

TOTAL CHILD SCORE FOR SCALE _____

Profile Form for 7 to 9 Month Olds

Subtest	Score SYM	SEN	EX	Normal	At risk	Deficient
Caregiver						
Regulation				6–10	5	0–4
Attachment				6	5	0–4
Two–way communication				8–10	7	0–6
Total caregiver				20–26	18–19	0–17
Child						
Regulation				14–16	13	0–12
Attachment				8–10	7	0–6
Total child				22–26	20–21	0–19
Total scale				41–52	38–40	0–37

Profile Form for 10 to 12 Month Olds

Subtest	SYM	SEN	EX	Normal	At risk	Deficient
		Score				
Caregiver						
Regulation				8–10	7	0–6
Attachment				8	7	0–6
Two-way communication				9–10	8	0–7
Behavioral organization				4–6	3	0–2
Total caregiver				27–34	25–26	0–24
Child						
Regulation				14–16	13	0–12
Attachment				10	9	0–8
Two-way communication				7–8	6	0–5
Total child				31–34	29–30	0–28
Total scale				61–68	54–56	0–53

Profile Form for 13 to 18 Month Olds

Subtest	Score			Normal	At risk	Deficient
	SYM	SEN	EX			
Caregiver						
Regulation				6–8	5	0–4
Attachment				7–8	6	0–5
Two-way communication				9–10	8	0–7
Behavioral organization				7–10	6	0–5
Total caregiver				30–36	28–29	0–27
Child						
Regulation				13–14	12	0–11
Attachment				9–10	8	0–7
Two-way communication				7–8	6	0–5
Total child				29–32	27–28	0–26
Total scale				60–68	55–59	0–54

Profile Form for 19 to 24 Month Olds

Subtest	Score			Normal	At risk	Deficient
	SYM	SEN	EX			
Caregiver						
Regulation				3–6	–	0–2
Attachment				6	5	0–4
Two-way communication				9–10	8	0–7
Behavioral organization				11–14	10	0–9
Total caregiver				28–36	26–27	0–25
Child						
Regulation				13–16	12	0–11
Attachment				12–14	11	0–10
Two-way communication				9–10	8	0–7
Behavioral organization				3–4	–	0–2
Total child				36–44	34–35	0–33
Total scale				64–80	60–63	0–59

Profile Form for 25 to 35 Month Olds

	Score					
Subtest	SYM	SEN	EX	Normal	At risk	Deficient
Caregiver						
Regulation				6–8	5	0–4
Attachment				7–8	6	0–5
Two-way communication				9–10	8	0–7
Behavioral organization				12–14	11	0–10
Representational elaboration				4–12	–	0–3
Total caregiver				38–52	36–37	0–35
Child						
Regulation				15–18	14	0–13
Attachment				14–18	13	0–12
Two-way communication				8–10	7	0–6
Behavioral organization				2–4	–	0–1
Representational elaboration				2–8	–	0–1
Total child				42–58	40–41	0–39
Total scale				77–110	75–76	0–74

Profile Form for 3 to 4 Year Olds

Subtest	Score SYM	Score SEN	Score EX	Normal	At risk	Deficient
Caregiver						
Regulation				4–6	–	0–3
Attachment				7–8	6	0–5
Two-way communication				9–10	8	0–7
Behavioral organization				12–14	11	0–10
Representational elaboration				6–10	5	0–4
Emotional thinking				2–6	–	0–1
Total caregiver				42–54	40–41	0–39
Child						
Regulation				12–14	11	0–10
Attachment				14–16	13	0–12
Two-way communication				8	7	0–6
Behavioral organization				2–4	–	0–1
Representational elaboration				8–14	7	0–6
Emotional thinking				2–10	–	0–1
Total child				48–66	46–47	0–45
Total scale				93–120	86–92	0–85

Sensorimotor History Questionnaire for Preschoolers

Georgia DeGangi, PhD, OTR, FAOTA
Lynn A. Balzer-Martin, PhD, OTR

Name of child: _____

Gender: __ M __ F

Date completed: _____

Birthdate: _____ Age: _____

Completed by: _____

DIRECTIONS. The questionnaire may be administered by a parent, teacher, or therapist familiar with the child's functioning in the areas measured by this questionnaire. The questionnaire has been validated on 3 and 4 year olds but may be administered to 5 year olds as well. Add the scores for each subscale, then enter the scores in the boxes at the bottom of this page. Children showing suspect performance in one or more areas involving sensory processing or motor planning should be referred to an occupational therapist for further testing of sensory integration and motor skills. Children showing suspect performance in the general behaviors and emotional areas should be referred to a clinical psychologist or early intervention professional familiar with testing and treating problems in these areas.

	SUBSCALE	NORMAL	AT RISK
A.	SELF-REGULATION Activity level and attention	0–2	3–6
B.	SENSORY PROCESSING OF TOUCH	0–2	3–9
C.	SENSORY PROCESSING OF MOVEMENT		
	Under-reactivity	0–2	3–4
	Overreactivity	0	1–7
D.	EMOTIONAL MATURITY	0–2	3–10
E.	MOTOR MATURITY Motor planning and coordination	0–3	4–15

A.   SELF-REGULATION (ACTIVITY LEVEL AND ATTENTION)

Is your child:
1. Frequently irritable?   YES (1)   NO (0)
2. Frequently clingy?   YES (1)   NO (0)
3. Overly active and hard to calm down?   YES (1)   NO (0)
4. Overly excited by sights, sounds, etc.?   YES (1)   NO (0)
5. Distracted by sights and sounds?   YES (1)   NO (0)
6. Restless and fidgety during times when quiet concentration is required?   YES (1)   NO (0)

                   TOTAL:

B.   SENSORY PROCESSING OF TOUCH

Does your child:

1.	Dislike being bathed or having his hands, face or hair washed?	YES (1)	NO (0)
2.	Complain that other people "bump" into him?	YES (1)	NO (0)
3.	Dislike textured food (chewy, crunchy) and avoid new food textures?	YES (1)	NO (0)
4.	Prefer certain clothing and complain about tags in clothing or that some clothes are too tight or itchy?	YES (1)	NO (0)
5.	Frequently bump and push other children and may play too rough?	YES (1)	NO (0)
6.	Prefer as little clothing as possible or prefer long sleeves and pants, even in warm weather?	YES (1)	NO (0)
7.	Seem excessively ticklish?	YES (1)	NO (0)
8.	Overreact or underreact to physically painful experiences? (circle one)	YES (1)	NO (0)
9.	Tend to withdraw from a group or seem irritable in close quarters?	YES (1)	NO (0)

TOTAL:

C.   SENSORY PROCESSING OF MOVEMENT

The first part of this section pertains to children who are underreactive to movement stimulation, the second part to children who are very sensitive or intolerant of movement in space.

Does your child:

1.	Prefer fast-moving carnival or playground rides, spinning equipment, not becoming dizzy or seem less dizzy than others?	YES (1)	NO (0)
2.	Frequently ride on the merry-go-round where others run around to keep the platform turning?	YES (1)	NO (0)
3.	Especially like movement experiences at home such as bouncing on furniture, using a rocking chair, or being turned in a swivel chair?	YES (1)	NO (0)
4.	Enjoy getting into an upside-down position?	YES (1)	NO (0)

TOTAL:

Does your child:

1. Tend to avoid swings or slides or use them with hesitation?   YES (1)   NO (0)
2. Seem afraid to let his feet leave the ground (getting up on a chair, jumping games) and prefer to be very close to the ground in play?   YES (1)   NO (0)
3. Fall down often and have difficulty with balance (like in stair climbing)   YES (1)   NO (0)
4. Fearful of heights or climbing?   YES (1)   NO (0)
5. Enjoy movement that she/he initiates but not like to be moved by others, particularly if the movement is unexpected?   YES (1)   NO (0)
6. Dislike trying new movement activities or has difficulty learning them?   YES (1)   NO (0)
7. Tend to get motion sick in a car, airplane, or elevator?   YES (1)   NO (0)

TOTAL:

D. EMOTIONAL MATURITY

Does your child:

1. Play pretend games with dolls, cars, etc. with sequences or plots to the game (e.g. the doll gets up, gets dressed, eats breakfast)?   YES (0)   NO (1)
2. Engage you in games that he makes up or wants to play?   YES (0)   NO (1)
3. Seek you out for affection and play pretend games where he will take care of a doll?   YES (0)   NO (1)
4. Play pretend games that involve assertiveness, exploration, or aggression (car races, soldiers fighting, or a trip to grandma's house)?   YES (0)   NO (1)
5. Understand rules such as to wait for you to say it is safe when crossing the street?   YES (0)   NO (1)
6. Understand that there are consequences to his behavior (if behaves nicely, you are pleased; if naughty, he will be punished)?   YES (0)   NO (1)
7. Have difficulty getting over a temper tantrum (takes longer than 10 minutes)?   YES (1)   NO (0)
8. Have difficulty playing with his peers?   YES (1)   NO (0)
9. Dislike changes in his routine and prefer things to stay the same everyday?   YES (1)   NO (0)
10. Seem unaware of dangers and take too many risks, often getting hurt?   YES (1)   NO (0)

TOTAL:

E.   MOTOR MATURITY (MOTOR PLANNING AND COORDINATION)

Does your child:

1. Use two hands for tasks that require two hands such as holding down the paper while drawing, holding the cup while pouring?	YES (0)	NO (1)
2. Have difficulty getting dressed?	YES (1)	NO (0)
3. Avoid trying new play activities and prefer to play games that he is confident at?	YES (1)	NO (0)
4. Have difficulty using his hands in manipulating toys and managing fasteners (stringing beads, buttons, snaps)?	YES (1)	NO (0)
5. Seem clumsy and bump into things easily?	YES (1)	NO (0)
6. Have trouble catching a ball with two hands?	YES (1)	NO (0)
7. Have difficulty with large muscle activities such as riding a tricycle, jumping on two feet?	YES (1)	NO (0)
8. Sit with a slouch or partly on and off the chair?	YES (1)	NO (0)
9. Have difficulty sitting still in a chair and seem to move very quickly (runs instead of walks)?	YES (1)	NO (0)
10. Feel "loose" or "floppy" when you lift him/her up or move child's limbs to help him get dressed?	YES (1)	NO (0)
11. Have difficulty turning knobs or handles that require some pressure?	YES (1)	NO (0)
12. Have a loose grasp on objects such as a pencil, scissors, or things that she/he is carrying?	YES (1)	NO (0)
13. Have a rather tight, tense grasp on objects?	YES (1)	NO (0)
14. Spontaneously choose to do activities involving use of "tools" such as crayons, markers, scissors?	YES (0)	NO (1)
15. Eat in a sloppy manner?	YES (1)	NO (0)

TOTAL: